THE YEAR OF THE CORNFLAKE

THE YEAR OF
THE CORNFLAKE

Faith Addis

Published by BBC Worldwide Limited,
80 Wood Lane, London W12 0TT
First published by André Deutsch Limited 1983
This edition first published 2000

ISBN 0 563 53723 X

Commissioning Editor: Emma Shackleton
Project Editor: Anthony Brennan

Set in Berling by Keystroke
Printed and bound in Great Britain by Mackays of Chatham
Cover printed by Belmont Press Limited, Northampton

To Wally

Foreword

Looking back to the 1970s which is when my books began, I realise how lucky we were to be able to do the things we did. Nowadays there are so many regulations strangling small enterprises you probably need a degree in form-filling to start a flower farm or a children's holiday home, to name just two of our ventures.

Lots of our projects could have been done more efficiently or profitably but that's easy to say now. I expect everyone feels the same with the benefit of hindsight. But when you're young and full of ideas and energy, being sensible doesn't come into it. You tend to say yes to everything. At any rate that's what we did and we enjoyed ourselves no end despite the ever-present overdraft.

One of our favourite memories is that of the anemone crop. Having back-achingly sown them, grown them and weeded them, we planned to pick the first flush in tight bud ready for sale. However the flowers had other ideas and shot into full bloom two days before they were supposed to. This meant that they were unsaleable. But the sight of a flower field vibrant with colour from end to end more than made up for a few pounds' loss.

Then came the books and the hundreds of letters I received from people who enjoyed sharing our country living vicariously. I am so pleased that with the re-issue of the books another generation can share the ups and downs of being small-holders. And to those who have written to ask 'what happened next?' Well, not a lot really. Having moved house six times in twenty years we came to the conclusion that we were getting too long in the tooth to keep doing up houses and gardens, so we have taken root in a quiet village where we have just one acre to tend. We have not 'moved with the times' and don't intend to. No computer, no digital this or electronic that. (Getting the laundry scrubbed on stones at the river's edge can get tough in winter but we Luddites have our standards.)

The children sneakily grew up when we weren't looking and are now, hard to believe, in their forties. Sara has provided two grandchildren while Marcus continues to travel the world living out of a rucksack.

Faith Addis, 2000

Give me a fat Shetland pony, two small boys and a bar of Cadbury's fruit and nut and you can keep paradise, nirvana or whatever. Throw in a warm summer evening and a river in deepest Devon. Ignore the furiously biting midges – they are a small price to pay for being here.

'Come on lads, the sun's going down. Time for bed.'

With a last look at the river where trout were beginnning to rev up for the evening meal the two boys climbed on to Rocky's back and aimed homeward.

'However did you find such a perfect place?' asked Jeremy...

Chapter One

In its way a flower shop can be as lovesome a thing as a garden but there's no getting away from the fact that it is tiring. Six days a week Brian would be at Covent Garden before dawn in order to finish his buying and be back to open the shop at nine. I used to go straight to the shop, which was in central London, after dropping the children at school, returning home in time to get their tea.

We quite enjoyed the hectic working days. We whizzed round London's one-way mazes in our distinctive little delivery vans, dispensing Interflora cheer to people who were getting married or buried or born. Sometimes, after a particularly vitriolic exchange with a traffic warden, we might fleetingly wish we were brain surgeons or Princess Anne, but not for long. We had chosen to make our bed a flower-bed and were happy to lie on it until the springs gave out.

One summer our two children, twelve-year-old Marcus, and Sara, aged eleven, asked if they might bring a friend apiece when we went away on holiday. We had booked a self-catering cottage in North Wales which slept six, so of course we said yes.

The cottage, described in the brochure as 'remote', was also rather basic. A cold-water tap in the scullery and an outside chemical lavatory were the only concessions to twentieth-century plumbing. Outside there was a View. A view of bracken, bracken and more bracken. Down in the valley we glimpsed a sparkle of river, and a brighter green than bracken indicated that there might be a deciduous tree or two.

'Fantastic!' shrieked the children 'A real *wilderness*. Let's explore!' And off they dashed.

Brian and I unpacked the wellingtons, Scrabble and books, telling each other that it was only for a week and that we could lay on lots of outings. Four days passed. Surprisingly, it didn't rain. Brian found a scythe and cleared a patch of garden, where we flopped on rugs and read twelve books each, turning as though on a spit until we were mahogany brown. In between books we walked and fished a little and felt guilty because we hadn't taken the children anywhere.

'Come to think of it,' I said, 'we've not seen much of them at all, have we? They show up at mealtimes but otherwise they're always off playing.'

'They have been good,' agreed Brian. 'Let's take them to the seaside this afternoon for a treat.

'Okay. You call them. I'll get lunch.'

Brian made a megaphone with his cupped hands and bellowed to the wilderness that lunch was ready. Instead of the familiar rush to the trough there was just the echo of 'KIDS! LU...UNCH!' then dead silence. We set off to find them. We looked in their many dens in the bracken, up trees in a neglected orchard they had adopted and finally ran them to earth at a fork in the river. There was a bendy branch overhanging the water which they loved to swing on, Tarzan fashion.

'Hello kids. Didn't you hear us calling?'

'No.'

'Aren't you hungry? It's lunchtime.'

'Please can we have sandwiches and fruit down here? Then we won't have to stop our game.'

'Oh. We thought you might like an outing. What about the seaside?'

'Seaside? Oh, *no*. Do we *have* to? It's so super here and we've only got until Saturday to finish our dam.'

The dam was magnificent and they had ambitiously started to incorporate a viaduct. Plainly we could not be such spoilsports as to take them to the seaside. So we left them alone and for the remainder of the week fed them on site as requested.

The wellingtons and Scrabble remained unused, the children's London pallor changed to walnut and their only need of adults was as suppliers of food and Elastoplast. It was a week in heaven. On the last day one of us said, 'Why don't we do this for a living?'...and the Great Idea was born.

Who said it to whom? We never knew. I think it probably occurred to us both simultaneously and was reinforced when we were looking at our holiday transparencies back in London later that same summer. The slides had come out well and zoomed us straight back to that grotto where the sun dappled through the trees and spotlighted our overgrown watersprites sploshing about in the stream. The children watched entranced.

'Wouldn't it be lovely to live there always and have a pony,' sighed Sara.

'And I could make a better raft and a proper tree-house and catch fish. I *wish* we could live there,' added Marcus.

Brian and I exchanged glances. Why *not* do it for a living? Buy a large, old house miles off the beaten track and take parties of small children for country holidays. There must be hundreds of city-bred kids who would love such a change. We could buy goats, pigs, even a cow...Our long-suffering friends listened patiently as our obsession grew. They telephoned each other:

'Have you heard their latest? Aren't they crazy? They seem quite serious this time, but they're complete *innocents* – they haven't given a *thought* to what living in the back of beyond could be like in winter.'

Our friends were wrong – both Brian and I were London born and bred and were acutely aware of our ignorance in rural matters. Over the next few months we borrowed dozens of library books relating to our proposed new lifestyle. Brian was already a fanatical gardener and could produce superb vegetables, fruit and flowers at the drop of a seed packet, but now his zeal increased and he studied every horticultural book he could lay his hands on. For light relief he read tomes about bee-keeping, and hedge-laying. When I looked at my own potential, I had a few qualms. I am a trained photographer, but had hated the commercial life and chucked it in at twenty to have babies. I get on well with children, and after having two of my own, started fostering other people's. I'd worked at London Zoo, looking after ponies in Pets' Corner, and had taken a Montessori course in nursery education. None of this seemed sufficient to equip one for life in the backwoods, and my own reservation cards at the local library raised a few eyebrows. It seemed there wasn't a lot of demand for *Elements of Goat Keeping* and *Parasites of the Pig* in central London at that time.

It was to be four long years before we realized our dream. We were incredibly busy during this period, working hard and saving hard, for the 'Boy Farm' – as our friends had nicknamed our project – would need a lot of capital. Brian and I took no holidays, but each summer we sent Marcus and Sara on holidays for unaccompanied children. By now our idea was no longer novel, and summer camps were popping up all over the place. None were offering quite the style of holiday that we envisaged, but it was enough to make us feel we might have missed the boat.

Marcus and Sara reported back faithfully from each sortie into our competitors' establishments. We learned which had the nastiest food, the nicest staff, the best beds, the boringest activities. If they managed to arrive home with their soaps and toothbrushes untouched, their opinion of their hosts was 'Super'. I distributed a detailed questionnaire among junior schools in various parts of London asking about things like favourite foods, pastimes, any particular fears, whether they liked sharing a dormitory, what pets they had. About three hundred forms came back, mostly packed with information *not* asked for. 'Best in the world I like stroking Josephine' and 'I am afraid of Richard Peters and I would like to go on holiday to get away from him.'

We evaluated all the answers and drew up a smart-looking chart to help us plan activities, meals and sleeping arrangements. Liver and 'greens' were on everyone's hate list, and 80 per cent of girls appeared to be afraid of spiders, whereas (on paper) the boys feared nothing.

As the time for farm-hunting drew near, we were both getting silly with excitement. Brian went to a farm implement sale and had a mountain of rubbish delivered to our suburban front garden. I was furious at the waste of money and phoned a junk man to take it all away. Brian insisted on keeping a horse-drawn plough, a set of harrows and a ghastly green thing that looked like an old mangle but was actually a cattle-cake crusher.

'How on earth can we sell the house with *that* lot outside the door?'

'It'll all come in useful in the country,' said Brian, eyeing the heap admiringly. 'We'll get a horse to pull the implements. You'd like a horse, wouldn't you?'

'*Me?* Push that stupid old heap around a muddy field in the middle of January?'

'Actually,' said Brian patiently, 'the horse *pulls* a plough. You don't push at all – just sort of steer.'

'Our plough hasn't any handles – or hadn't you noticed? – and I wouldn't know how to steer it anyway.'

'I'm sure you could go on a course and learn,' said Brian, whose answer to most problems is to take a course and become an overnight expert. But even his enthusiasm dimmed when we learned the cost of transporting the implements, and he reluctantly agreed to give them to a friend to put in *her* front garden, where, for all we know, they still remain. We kept the cattle-cake crusher (even one's closest friends have their tolerance levels) and are still waiting for cattle cake to come back into fashion. We sold our flower shop to Brian's brother, then put our house up for sale. Within weeks we had a buyer, a contract and a deposit, and were free to intensify the farm hunt. The plan was for me to sift through the ads in *Farmer's Weekly*, *Horse & Hound*, *Exchange & Mart*, the leading 'Sundays' and the details sent by country estate agents, while Brian quartered England in our van. He was to phone home every morning and evening to see if anything had come in for him to inspect in the immediate area.

This went on for months and we developed a loathing for that lowest form of life, the estate agent, whose flights of fantasy caused countless gallons of petrol to be wasted. Like American tourists, we 'did' Yorkshire, Wales, Herefordshire and Shropshire, eventually, as time was running out, narrowing the search to our first love – the West Country.

It was in February that Brian headed west to view a farm that was to be auctioned in three lots later in the year. He liked it, and when he arrived home later the same day, we spread out maps and drawings all over the floor. We decided to make an offer for the house and ten acres prior to auction. Next morning – a Wednesday – we phoned the agent. 'Sorry,' he said 'the farmer has withdrawn the property.' We were getting used to disappointments, but this one was exceptionally hard to bear as the farm had been the most suitable so far.

'But don't hang up,' said the agent. 'I've had a property put on our books today that sounds just the thing for you. Only thing is, it may be a bit big – twelve bedrooms – but shall I post the details?'

We weren't terribly interested in anything that day but we said yes anyway and asked him to send them first class. We always asked this, but they never did. On this occasion, the delay caused by a second-class stamp was to be responsible for a surprising adventure.

It wasn't until the following Saturday, three days later, that the details arrived. As I stood by the front door reading them, the most incredible feeling flooded over me.

I *knew*, beyond any doubt, that this was to be our Boy Farm.

Chapter Two

Hands shaking, I re-read the handout. Scarcely daring to turn the pages, I checked the details room by room. There was no mistake. A seven-bedroomed, sixteenth-century farmhouse in Devon, with a five-bedroomed cedarwood chalet in the grounds. And the price? £3000 *less* than the ceiling we had set ourselves!

I grabbed the phone and dialled the agent's number in Honiton. No reply. It was only 8 a.m. Brian had gone to help his brother Peter at the shop for the day. I phoned him and relayed the news in such a state of excitement that he couldn't hear me properly. But he got the gist and suggested I catch the next train to Honiton.

'I'll phone for an appointment to view when you're on the train,' he said, 'then they can't refuse.'

At 8.30 I phoned Waterloo to find out the train times. Oh, joy! – one left within the hour. Plenty of time to arrange for a taxi to meet me at Honiton station.

I cut sandwiches, filled the big Thermos with milky coffee, and checked the 'viewing' bag. Clip-board, five ball-points (all different colours), camera, spare film, notebook and two unread paperbacks. I left a note on the kitchen table for the children with instructions to feed the animals, adding a 50 pence piece for them to get themselves fish and chips for lunch – you could too, in 1975. The taxi was waiting for me in Honiton station yard, and soon we were on our way to Upottery. I said I had to catch the next train back to Waterloo, and the taxi driver offered to wait at the farm while I viewed it, then run me back to the station. As the car sped through the deep-set Devon lanes and the tiny village of Upottery ('Don't blink or you'll miss it,' said the driver) then up the hill to the farm, my heart began to thud with anticipation.

The house was hidden from the top of the drive. There was a breath-taking view of the Otter valley spread below us. I was speechless with wonder. The driver grinned as he watched me drinking it all in. 'They all go daft when they see the view first time,' he said.

'Who're they?'

'The holiday guests. The farm is a guest-house, these day – I often drive them out from the station. They all go daft at that view.'

Slowly we freewheeled down the steep drive and stopped in the courtyard before the house. I hoped Brian had done his stuff and they'd be expecting me. He had and they were. If Jill and Bob, the likeable couple who were the owners, were surprised at the speed with which I inspected the house, they were too polite to show it. As soon as I'd got out of the taxi I knew that 'our' house wouldn't take long to view, and I was dying to see round the grounds. I whipped through each room, rapidly checking light switches and taps, and noting the amount of woodworm damage and wet rot in beams and skirting-boards. I loved every inch of the house immediately. It was so 'right', so welcoming, and surely we could be generous enough to share the place with a few woodworms.

In a state of euphoria, I asked Jill if I could borrow a pair of wellingtons to explore outside. 'What, in this pouring rain?' she asked.

So it was raining: I'd hardly noticed. Slowly, savouring every second, I walked round the whole seven acres, noting every-thing down. There was a little yard with seven animal pens along one side and a large loose-box forming an L with the pens. There were gaping holes in all the roofs and the timber fronts were rotting. Jill had said that the yard was cobbled. It was thigh-deep in nettles and weeds, the gate embedded in mud. 'Don't you worry, farmyard,' I said out loud 'We'll soon make you good as new.' I talked to the trees, hedges, drains (very important things, drains) and barns, and promised them all that we'd take care of them. There was a smallish oak tree, completely hollow, which I climbed up to photograph the place from a different viewpoint. By now I was soaked to the skin, but in such a state of ecstasy, I hardly noticed. I floated back to the house and changed into my shoes.

'My, just look at you,' said Jill. 'let me get you a towel.'

'We'll take the house at the asking price.' Was that really my voice?

'But you've hardly seen the *house*. What about your husband?'

'Oh, I've seen him already,' I joked feebly. 'I'll write out a cheque for the deposit,' I said, opening my bag.

'Oh, no – please. The house only went on the market on Wednesday, and there's some people coming to view tomorrow. We'd like you to deal through the agents. After all, that's what they're paid for.'

It was getting close to train time, so I restrained my views on estate agents. With a quick goodbye and thanks, I dashed out to the waiting taxi and headed for the agents in Honiton. We arrived at two o'clock. The office was closed – it was Saturday in Devon as well as London, apparently. Undeterred, I phoned Brian to tell him he was about to become a Devonian, and got so carried away describing the place, I nearly missed the train.

The return journey was spent writing up my notes and drawing a plan of the farm. To my surprise – for I had no recollection of asking any sensible questions – I found that I'd noted the house was newly wired, had spring water, septic tank drainage and a sound slate roof. I suppose, after so many years of house-hunting, I was noting things unconsciously; we were both expert at recreating rooms in sketch form, even to remembering which ways the doors opened.

Brian was waiting at Waterloo and excitedly we spread out all my maps and drawings over the front seat of the van. Brian had bought an Ordnance Survey map of the area, so we were able to pinpoint the farm. He was very chuffed to find the fields were south-facing and immediately started plotting his vegetable garden. He always does this in February in any case, but *this* February Suttons Seed would see a difference in the order…Then we realized we were still in Waterloo Station and were getting colder and colder, so we drove home, told Marcus and Sara to start brushing up on Devon accents and invited our friends Tony and Belinda to celebrate.

Tony and Belinda were the best friends imaginable. From the conception of the Great Idea, they had given us nothing but encouragement and support. They had fed our kids and pets when we made trips away, had welcomed us with hot coffee at unearthly hours, and had even provided the occasional shoulder to cry on. It was Tony who had coined the name 'Boy Farm' for our project (which regrettably stuck), and the four of us had had endless fun imagining what it was going to be like.

So the celebration that Saturday evening was tinged with a lot of sentiment – we were going to miss each other terribly – and we drank far too much plonk and had hangovers deep into Sunday.

First thing on Monday, Brian phoned the Honiton agent. Very business-like, he confirmed that we'd buy the house at the asking price, then his tone suddenly changed. I could only hear his end of the conversation, but it was enough to numb me.

'What do you mean, it's sold? My wife was the first person to view it, and she told them on Saturday that we'd buy…What? I see…Oh, blast…I suppose that's that, then…Yes. Goodbye.' He replaced the receiver. Glumly. 'He says it's sold.'

'What? Who to?'

I listened with mixed despair and fury as Brian went on. 'It's the people who viewed it on Sunday. They put their offer in writing through the agent's letter-box, so technically theirs was the first.'

'Never mind *technically*! *Morally* it's our house. I saw it first and made the first offer.'

'But not in writing. It's written offers that count.'

Strangely, I wasn't defeated or disappointed – just hopping mad. I suppressed the fishwife in me, phoned our solicitor friend, Geoffrey, and poured out the whole story to him. He was comforting and practical. 'Leave it with me for a while, I'll have a think.' Geoffrey's thinks were always productive, so I rang off full of optimism, though still seething at the unfairness of it all.

Clever Geoff both thought and acted. He phoned the vendors' solicitors in Exeter and talked them into agreeing to draw up two contracts, sending both by the same post to the two prospective buyers and waiting to see who got the signed contract back first. He tried to persuade us to have a 'subject to survey' clause in the contract because although he's the most tremendous sport, he is also a solicitor, but to no avail. We'd moved house quite a few times and had soon learned that common sense and a sharp penknife are all you need when you're considering under-priced elderly houses.

On Tuesday afternoon I rang the vendors' solicitors myself. The person I spoke to (and later shouted at) wouldn't tell me if the contract had been typed out and said it was most unorthodox for me to make direct contact. By Wednesday my small store of patience was exhausted (and so was the whole family) and I phoned the vendors' solicitors again. Could they possibly, I enquired, provide their scribe with a new quill and get the blasted contract out? Politely, their spokesman said that contracts take a long time to prepare. I said that Geoffrey took under two hours. Spokesman said – coldly – weren't we lucky to have such a clever solicitor.

Brian had kept out of the hurling abuse game, attending to the vital question of how we were to get the signed contract back to Devon before our rivals. Our geriatric van couldn't possibly compete with their Mercedes. We didn't know who these rivals were but we couldn't afford to miss a trick. We'd learned that they lived in West London, so if it was going to be a road race, they already had a full hour's start. Brian thought of hiring a fast car, but then he might be gonged hurtling down the M5. He enquired about train times. We didn't know when the contract would arrive so couldn't be sure of catching a fast train in time.

A friend of Brian's suggested an air taxi, a service the friend had used house-hunting in the Outer Hebrides. Brian phoned Cab-Air at Elstree. You really could hire a small plane with pilot as easily as you could a normal taxi. The fare was a mort higher – £130 return – but it covered a party of four. This meant we could take the children (teenagers now), and when we told them, they were so excited they could hardly sleep.

Thursday and Friday passed. No contract. On Saturday, we lay in wait for the postman and, glimpsing a large buff envelope in his hand, rushed out to get it. Yes! The relief was indescribable. Brian phoned Cab-Air and booked a return flight to Exeter for that morning, then drove to our solicitor's office in Woodford. He arrived at 8.30 a.m., then had an agonizing wait till Geoffrey's partner got there at about nine-thirty (Geoff was away on holiday). The partner insisted on studiously reading the whole contract. Brian said it seemed like hours as he stood waiting to get the all-clear. Eventually the partner, with great reluctance, agreed that Brian could sign.

I stayed at home getting increasingly terrified. I'd never been in a plane before, never wanted to and firmly never intended to. But this situation was akin to pregnancy – there was no way to avoid going through with it. Perhaps I should make my will, I thought. Yes, I'd leave my puppy, Parsley, and my best camera to Belinda, who I knew would care for them both, and my share of any capital to her and some other friends. There'd be no point leaving anything to the children as they'd perish with us in the crash...Then I dispensed with morbid thoughts and made sandwiches.

At Elstree, when we got out of the van and were led across the runway to the aircraft, I was petrified with fright. When I was a child, my parents had a tiny Austin Seven car, and our air-taxi was just like that, only with wings. It didn't look big enough and certainly not *strong* enough to carry four passengers and a pilot. Weakly I leaned against the tail-bit, and it moved! I'd been frightened before but never as frightened as this; my teeth rattled, I wanted to go to the loo and my heart thumped astoundingly.

Somehow we all got in, the children letting me sit at the back, since that was supposed to be safest. The distance between front and back was so minimal I didn't think any position was 'safest', but I appreciated their thoughtfulness. Brian and Marcus were brave, and joked with the pilot. Sara was brave but sat very close to me and didn't make jokes. I was not brave. I asked the pilot where the parachutes were. My terror dissolved into hopeless apathy when he said there we no parachutes. A picture of Parsley, my cavalier King Charles spaniel, floated into my mind. Parsley was eight weeks old, a pre-birthday surprise from Brian and quite the best present I have ever had. Poor Parsley, I thought. Oh well, she's young enough to take to a new owner. I hoped Belinda would find her diet sheet.

The engine roared. I closed my eyes and clung to Sara's hand. Centuries later I opened my eyes and found we were still on the ground. The pilot had merely manoeuvred the plane to get a longer run, and the whole traumatic business had to be gone through all over again.

The others enjoyed the trip. They looked out of the windows and took photographs, and the children yelled at the traffic below. Brian told the pilot all about our race to get the contract back to Devon, and the nice man said he'd go as fast as he could. I was astonished to see him consulting a map as we flew – I'd thought all planes were guided by radar – and couldn't believe my eyes when he took both hands off the wheel...

After ninety minutes we touched down at Exeter. My stomach and heart returned to base and we rushed through the terminal building and climbed into our (pre-arranged) waiting car. We got to the solicitor's in minutes and burst into the reception area, giggly and a bit hysterical after our flight.

The elderly and hatchet-faced solicitor was Not Amused. He looked at us with distaste and asked Brian to go with him into his inner sanctum. Brian tried to rearrange his face to look like a landowner, but he hasn't got that sort of face and he followed the solicitor looking more like the Cheshire Cat.

The children and I were giggling uncontrollably now. Even the feeblest joke would have us doubled up, and the more disapproving looks we got from the receptionist the worse we became. Then I was sent for by Hatchet Face. I went in and wrote my name on the contract. I didn't dare look at Brian in case he set me off again. We each signed two bits of paper and Brian was now the proud owner of a property he hadn't even seen.

But see it he soon did, and I was happy to find that with

Brian and the children it was love at First Sight, just as it had been with me. They all found something that appealed to them – Marcus liked the nearness of the River Otter for fishing, Sara bagged for herself the biggest bedroom and started to plan which stable to put a pony in, and Brian was overwhelmed at the thought of seven whole acres to cultivate.

Brian hugged me and we hugged the kids. We couldn't stay long because we had the plane booked, so we made an appointment to pay another visit and left for the airport, looking back till the farm was out of sight.

Our farm. Our very own farm, fought for with several gallons of sweat and a £130-return plane ticket. Parsley summed it up succinctly when we got home. She wet herself with excitement.

Chapter Three

The move was fixed for September. It meant an agonizing wait, but Jill and Bob had bookings for guests throughout the summer. Still, it would give us time to organize ourselves and draw up a programme for next year's intake of holiday children.

Brian sold our small van and bought a twelve-seater Ford Transit. Jill and Bob very kindly offered to let us store things in one of the barns, so we ferried stuff down in several trips to save precious removal-van space on moving day.

As August drew to a close, we were all keyed up with excitement. Addy, Brian's mum, offered to come and help us move in, and we eagerly accepted before she changed her mind. If there's one person to have around when you move house, it's my mother-in-law. Although well into her seventies, she can get through more work in a day than most people manage in a week – *and* enjoy it.

We were joined by Addy the day before the move and she made us have a 'nice early night'. We were practised movers and the operation was hitchless. Brian led the way in the Transit, the four of us packed in with him, feeling rather like Columbus and his adventurers *en route* to the Brave New World.

We unpacked, got the furniture roughly into place and waved the pantechnicon goodbye. We were all on cloud nine and levitated about the house and fields, drinking it all in. The dogs, ten-year-old Honey and my puppy Parsley, abandoned themselves to rabbiting and the sun shone and shone. It was like a marvellous dream, only this time we didn't have to wake up and go to work. There *was* work, of course, but of such a kind that life seemed a perpetual holiday. All of us love to be physically active, and we threw ourselves into our new way of life so energetically that our flabby London muscles protested and we had to learn to pace ourselves.

The farm was called Higher Phyllishayes, which seems rather a mouthful until you learn that 'hayes' means 'dwelling', when it immediately becomes 'Phyllis's dwelling' and easier to pronounce. Our first major task was to prepare the yard and animal pens for their new occupants. The old ones had left a heritage of well-rotted manure in all the pens, which Brian lusted after. He's probably the only husband in the world who can stand knee-deep in buttercups, bathed in the glow of beautiful sunset, and say, 'What this patch needs is about twenty-five tons of organic muck.'

The manure was up to 2 feet thick in some pens, and there were seven of these, not to mention a huge loose-box equally chock-full. Once we were stuck into the work, Addy wouldn't let us into the house until we'd hosed each other down. When the pens were clean, we started on the cobbled yard, which had been buried for years; couch-grass and nettles were rooted into the earth 6 inches deep. It was incredibly hard to get a spade under each clod and prise it from its moorings and we had to force ourselves to do just a small area each day to avoid serious back-strain. We were quickly getting used to having blisters and permanently sore muscles, but there are limits.

Back in the rambling old house, Addy performed her usual miracles. She hung curtains, humped furniture and would have laid carpets if we'd let her. All eleven rooms shone with furniture polish, the windows sparkled and everywhere there were vases of leaves and flowers which she'd gathered from the garden. She organized the larder and dispatched us to the village shop to buy groceries.

Jill, the previous owner, had offered to sell us most of the things needed for a guest-house, and by the time we'd added our own stuff, it made a formidable pile: a hundred blankets, forty sheets and pillow-cases, twenty pillows, place settings for twenty and all the miscellaneous things, such as water jugs and teapots. Addy was quite undaunted by all this and shooed us outside so that she could 'get on'.

At the end of September, the cobbles were unveiled. They'd been laid so cleverly all those hundreds of years ago, that they sloped imperceptibly towards a culvert which led straight into a drain. We hosed and scrubbed the cobblestones and were immensely pleased with our beautiful pinky yard. I knew how Michelangelo must have felt when at last he'd finished those ceilings.

Now that the farmyard was habitable, we could buy animals and poultry to live in it. We'd inherited the Phyllishayes' cat, Tiggy, and some tame rabbits. We bought six hens (the Maran variety, which lay very dark brown eggs), two cocks and two goats. One goat, Toggles, had a laughing, friendly face, and we bought another, Melly, to keep her company.

The yard was coming alive. The hens hadn't started to lay yet, but we hoped that nature would soon take care of that. Farm sales were taking place and we went to most, especially the ones selling Miscellaneous. When you've got seven acres, you need a great deal of Miscellaneous, and we soon collected masses of wire-netting, fencing posts and second-hand timber.

At one sale we met Frank, a farmer neighbour. Soon after our move to Phyllishayes, Frank and his dear wife Grace had become our self-appointed agricultural advisers. 'What you want is a couple of pigs,' said Frank – and if Frank said we needed pigs, then pigs we had to have. As he pointed out, what other animals would be so useful for a guest-house? And what better use for kitchen scraps than to turn them into pork?

It was obvious from the first that our piglets would never be pork. They were as endearing as puppies, as intelligent and twice as clean. Sara christened them Phyllis and Rosie and taught Rosie to shake hands. They settled in as part of the family until they'd be ready for breeding. They became highly expert at undoing the yard gate and trotting into the kitchen, where they'd scoff the cat's food till Addy shooed them out.

Shandy the pony was the next arrival. We'd answered an advertisement from someone wanting a temporary home for a pony mare; this suited our needs as we were not yet ready to buy our own pony, and Shandy duly arrived. At first she was a perfect lady; a little slow perhaps, for she was overweight, but well-behaved and easy to catch. Sara and I hacked her quietly and even popped her over some small jumps, which she seemed to enjoy. But there were problems. For Shandy was randy, an unashamed nymphomaniac.

Mares come into season every three weeks during the summer months and normally fidget for a day or two, but it doesn't bother them. Shandy was different. At first she merely rubbed her bottom against things when she was in season, but she became increasingly ambitious and would break out of her field in search of a mate. She wasn't at all choosy and would eagerly offer herself to anything that moved – lorries, cows, swinging gates – literally *anything* that moved qualified as Shandy's spouse.

She was impossible to ride when these moods were upon her, and very difficult to catch once she'd broken out. Once Addy was doing some weeding in the rockery when Shandy suddenly appeared, nostrils flaring and ready for action. 'Shoo!' cried Addy, bravely waving her trowel, but Shandy advanced at a brisk trot, swinging her bottom invitingly, and Addy leapt for the garden shed and locked herself in. Shandy then rubbed her bottom on the posts securing the goats' tethers, the posts came out of the ground and both goats were free. Sara fetched some carrots, but as she walked towards the pony rattling the bucket temptingly, the two goats decided they should have some carrots too and came skipping over, trailing 12-foot chains with posts attached. Sara went sprawling over the chains, while Shandy, unable to believe her luck, offered herself to both goats in turn. Luckily, she caught herself in one of the chains and Sara, though limp with laughter, was able to hang on to her. Addy emerged from the shed and, with immense dignity, turned her back on the imbroglio and went indoors to do the only possible thing – put the kettle on.

The Indian summer faded and the autumn nights grew cold. Addy went home to hibernate until the spring and we prepared to face our first winter in Devon. Brian planned to use a two-acre field the following season to grow vegetables for the house and root crops for the animals; he arranged with neighbour Frank to have the field ploughed, but first we had to clear a forest of waist-high weeds. We hired a machine called an Allen scythe, a fierce-looking monster with two rows of gigantic teeth mounted laterally in front. After several yanks at the pulley cord, (like on an outboard motor), Brian engaged gear and moved forward; the scythe took off with a leap and neatly hurled him into the next county.

Brian was amazed at the strength needed to control the Allen, and after an hour or so he stopped for a break. This meant he had to start the scythe again on the pulley cord, and it was a beast to start. This, coupled with the strain of holding the machine back, put immense pressure on the joints of his shoulders and elbows, but the work had to be finished within a few days as Frank wanted to plough before the ground got too soggy. So Brian soldiered on, ignoring the pain, and got the work done. His elbows were badly swollen and his shoulders hurt so much he could hardly lift a cup of tea – which raised a problem. There were 10 tons of muck to shift for the vegetable garden. I phoned Belinda. How would she like a week in Devon, I asked enticingly, with lots of lovely fresh air?

'I'd love it, Faith. What's the catch?'

'Er, no catch, really. It's just that Brian has crocked himself up and there's some stuff to be moved urgently.'

'What stuff?'

'Well…manure, actually.'

'How much manure, actually?'

'Ten tons.'

While she was speechless, I explained that with Marcus in his first job and Sara still at school, the children couldn't help as they didn't get home till after dark. The contractor who was going to spread the muck was expensive. If Belinda and I loaded and he spread, it would work out a lot cheaper.

At last…'All right, I give in,' said Belinda. 'But I'll have to bring Josh.' Josh was eighteen months old and next day I collected them both from Honiton station. Josh had spent most of the journey playing Frisbee with British Rail paper plates and Belinda looked exhausted.

'What you need is some fresh air and exercise,' I said, encouragingly.

'What I need is an unbroken night's sleep and a gag for this young thug. Have you any spare wellies for me?'

Early next morning the contractor knocked at the back door. 'Dung spurt'n?' he enquired.

For two days Belinda and I shovelled and the contractor did the 'spurt'n'. Brian felt such a dead loss that he insisted on joining the shovellers. This set back his recovery but greatly improved his mood. He was delighted to see his beloved vegetable patch receiving this organic banquet and sent ambitious lists off to Suttons for all the things we'd never had space to grow before – pumpkins, artichokes, melons, gourds, plus commonplace vegetables, such as beans and peas, which we'd previously grown in small suburban rows.

When her visit ended, we drove Belinda and Josh to Honiton station. Belinda said it had all been very interesting and she'd send us a bill for the osteopath's fees. We waved a grateful goodbye and returned home to prepare for our next visitors – friends who were pulling up London tent-pegs and heading for a remote small-holding in North Wales. As a housewarming present they left us a tiny black and white female kitten, Small, who soon made friends with the inherited cat, Tiggy.

By the time our friends left, we'd got the farm side more or less organized and felt it was time to press-gang some co-operative children into staying at Phyllishayes and giving us much-needed practice. It would be a kind of dry run. At half-term Brian phoned around and managed to borrow all our nephews and nieces, together with any friends who might be interested. We made it clear it wouldn't be the real thing because we had only a few animals as yet; also, in late autumn the Devon weather could be pretty grim.

They all agreed to come. We went to the Cash and Carry and bought bulk supplies of groceries, soap and toilet rolls and a huge polythene sack of cornflakes. We had the freezer packed with half a lamb, half a pig and a quarter of beef; I'd never had a freezer before and kept forgetting to thaw food in time, but hoped to become more efficient with practice.

Whenever we had children staying, the playroom was to be the hub of the house. We'd put a lot of thought into making it attractive and spent more of our dwindling capital on stocking it with games, books and art materials. We even hired a colour

TV and put that there. We hoped the children wouldn't want to watch TV too much – after all, we were supposed to be providing them with outdoor holidays – but we felt we had better have it in case it rained a lot.

We also put several comfortable old armchairs in the play-room and some large floor-cushions. Later we decided to dispense with all the furniture except the floor-cushions, but for the present it looked very colourful and inviting.

On the day our guinea-pig children were expected, I really went to town on that playroom, setting the games out, pinning up large posters, sorting through some records I thought they would like and making sure all the packs of cards were complete. The children were breaking up for half-term that day and were all travelling together by train. Brian was to meet them at 9 p.m.

At eight-thirty he drove off to Honiton and I busied myself in the kitchen, making huge jugs of milky cocoa to welcome our weary little guests. I carried the cocoa into the dining room and set out some plates of home-made flapjacks. Then, feeling very Earth Mother and wishing I had a snowy white apron and a big bosom, I waited to greet them.

The van stopped and I rushed out to open the van's back doors. Before I had a chance to say, 'Welcome then, my pretty little d'yurrs,' in my new Devon accent, a procession of what looked like paratroopers rushed past me, some bending *down* to give me a quick kiss in passing. I had a confused impression that some faces looked vaguely familiar but they all went by so quickly in the dark that I couldn't be sure. There appeared to be several military-looking gentlemen among them and one was definitely carrying a dart-board. I felt I must be dreaming.

'Brian,' I gasped. 'Where are the children?'

'They *are* the children.'

'But those *men*! Who are they?'

'Guy's friends.' (Guy was a friend's son.) 'They've all joined the Cadet Corps at their school and they've come straight from practice.'

'But Guy's only thirteen. How old are they?'

'Well, they're all in the same form, so I guess they're thirteen too. They're certainly a bit big, though.'

29

'Big? They're like…like gladiators!'

'Oh, no. All-in wrestlers.'

We went in to look at them in a good light. It was evident they'd found the playroom. Incredulously we looked in. They'd manifested an instant party; the TV was on at full volume; there was a darts match in progress; four players were cutting cards for a game of poker, and the rest were taking their ease on the floor, swigging in turn at a can of Coke.

We entered. 'Hullo kids,' I had to shout above the noise. 'Made yourselves at home, then?'

Someone politely turned down the volume and one member of the poker school stood up. 'Isn't it *great* here,' he enthused. It was nephew Tim, wearing a strange hat. 'Hope you didn't mind us bringing our own dart-board – we guessed you mightn't have one.' He'd guessed right. We'd firmly decided *not* to equip the playroom with a dart-board since all small children are more optimistic than accurate with darts.

'Sod it,' said one of the dart players. 'I've left myself with double three.'

'What's your name, dear?' I asked him. 'I don't think we know you, do we?'

'I'm Collis – Tim's friend. *Great* place you've got here.'

Tim said hurridly and rather apologetically, 'Collis lives next door – he's all right, really. And this is Pete and that's David…and John…and Guy, of course, you know.'

One of the monoliths stood up and cracked his head on a beam. I'd not seen Guy for two years and made a mental note to ask his mother what she fed him on.

'Hullo, Guy. Have a good journey?'

'Great, thank you. We had a carriage to ourselves and sang all the way.'

Whatever benefits these kids were gaining from their expensive educations, it certainly didn't include a very wide range of adjectives.

The three nieces hadn't changed much, thank goodness. They'd come in nice normal sizes and were setting up a game of Monopoly. 'Isn't it a bit late for Monopoly?' I hinted.

'Oh, no. The late film hasn't started, yet.'

Brian and I withdrew to the kitchen and sat dazedly drinking the tepid cocoa. There Marcus and Sara found us when they returned from the cinema.

'All the kids in bed?' they asked, brightly.

'No. In the playroom.'

'*Playroom?* A bit late, isn't it?'

'Go and say hello.'

They came back a few minutes later convulsed with laughter. 'It's a regiment,' Marcus hooted. 'You'll have to play Last Post or Lights Out on your trumpet, Brian.'

Marcus and Sara helped themselves to cold cocoa and flap-jacks, and I wondered whether to remove the teddy bears from the visitors' bedrooms. Perhaps they'd rather have ashtrays? I'd planned to tuck in and kiss them good-night but, as Marcus pointed out, I'd need a chaperone for this lot.

Brian stuck his head round the playroom door. 'Five minutes, kids, and then bed.' Sure enough, five minutes later, the play-room was deserted and there were cries of 'Great!' from upstairs. We went into the playroom to switch off the lights and found it restored to its original tidiness; all the games had been put away and the chairs straightened – you wouldn't have known that nine children had used it except for a waste-basket full of empty Coke tins.

'There must be something in this Cadet Corps business,' Brian said.

'Perhaps tomorrow we can get them to blanco the front of the house.'

I thought they were on their best behaviour as it was their first night, but they were an unusually tidy gang and always cleared up after themselves.

Apart from Collis – he with the colourful vocabulary – we thoroughly enjoyed having the kids to practise on. I made huge quantities of the sort of food I thought they'd like and they polished it off with zest. They tidied not only the playroom but their own rooms also. Everything was acknowledged as 'great' and generally they were good to have around.

All went swimmingly. Then one day visitors called, in a huge, gleaming limousine. The kids were having lunch in the dining-room and Brian and I were in the kitchen stacking the washing-up machine. The visitors knocked and we invited them in, suitably impressed. Here was wealth, here was class; here in fact were two parents of prospective holiday children, dropping by while on a late-autumn holiday to see about booking for the following summer. Our *very* first enquirers.

Brian invited them into the sitting-room while I made tea and brought it in with our best china. We explained the set-up and emphasized how keen we were to attract the 'right type' of children to Phyllishayes. (We didn't care two hoots about social class, but for the sake of other kids we didn't want delinquents.)

The visitors sipped their tea and nodded agreeably – then from outside and with horrible clarity came Collis's familiar treble.

'Hey, have you seen their car? It's a FUCKING GREAT ROLLS-ROYCE!'

A sudden silence in the sitting-room. With a long experience of shopkeeping you learn how important it is to keep your customers, prospective or otherwise. Wildly, I began a complicated apology for Collis, inventing a broken home and a deprived background and goodness knows what else. Brian said simply, 'Collis is a horrible little boy and we can't stand him.'

Amazingly, the visitors booked their children in August.

All through the week we observed the kids at play, noting which outdoor areas attracted them and which indoor activities they most enjoyed. It was heartening to discover that our original thoughts were correct – that a small number under mild supervision in congenial surroundings would occupy themselves fully and have a good time. We asked them to feel free to criticize anything they didn't like and to give us their ideas on what was lacking. Apart from obvious things like the cold weather and too few farm animals (which would be rectified anyway when we opened formally at Easter), some of the suggestions were good. The boys wanted an assault course and permission to use the hay-barn freely, and the girls wanted more ponies and similar permission for a rave-up in the hay-barn. All the children wanted a very late bedtime and kittens and puppies to play with.

The average age of this group was eleven and a half. We were aiming to attract guests between five and twelve and hoping to get them as young as possible. We envisaged the farm as the 'nursery slopes' for children who wanted to have an unaccompanied holiday but were too young for pony-trekking, sailing and so forth. At that time – 1975 – there were virtually no other centres catering specifically for the very young, although our researches had shown there was a demand.

We heeded the advice of our 'guinea-pig' group and planned to buy ponies, several tons of hay and raw materials for a scaled-down assault course. We told Small about the kittens – Tiggy was neutered – but couldn't do much about puppies since Honey was neutered and Parsley under age.

It was raining on the last day of the children's week. They'd planned to have a bonfire and sing-song – 'You must have a bonfire on the last night' – but it came on to rain and we had to stay in. We had a party and a sing-song in the playroom but we felt they were disappointed at not having the 'bonfire' climax to their holiday, so we added 'Friday-night bonfires' to our bulging files.

It had been a thoroughly enjoyable week and we were sorry to see them go. We'd taken photographs of them for inclusion in a brochure, and the family children were coming back to spend Christmas at Phyllishayes together with their parents. They all leaned dangerously out of the train windows, yelling goodbye till the train went out of sight. It seemed awfully quiet on the empty platform.

I asked Brian how he thought the week had worked out. 'Great,' he said, still gazing down the line.

So much for the dry run. Come spring, it would be the real thing.

Chapter Four

All through the following weeks it rained without stopping. Water sheeted down the drive, drains overflowed, ditches got clogged with leaves, ponds formed all over the fields and much urgent out-of-doors work had to go by the board.

Brian spent most of the daylight hours ditching and trying to figure out a drains plan for the whole property. It surprised us that when you buy land you get no maps of the drainage system. Whenever Brian unearthed an outlet or an inlet, we were jubilant and made water-courses straight away – big, obvious courses that couldn't get hidden again.

But the main problem was around the front of the house. Phyllishayes was built on the side of a hill and stands on a platform of concrete; all the water from higher up rushed straight down to the house and in the front door. Brian tried various measures, then finally took a 15-lb sledgehammer and smashed up all the concrete fronting the house. And there was what he'd been searching for – a drain, which had lain coyly hidden for years.

The drain was out of practice and for days we poked rods down the hole, making slow progress. At last it was clear and we watched with unmitigated delight as it coped with gallons of rain-water a minute. I wish we had left it at that and not decided to look at the source of the drinking water. There was a well higher up the hill and water was gravity-fed to the house and outbuildings. Brian levered the cover off the well, and when I looked in I nearly fell down the hole. It was disgusting. There were slugs sticking to the brick sides and evidence of quite active pond life wriggling around in the water.

'We've been drinking *that?*' I said, cold with horror.

Brian shone the torch into the outlet pipe. 'Ah! There's a filter. Don't worry.'

'Don't *worry*? Don't *worry* if we all get cholera and poison the children? Don't *worry* if all the parents sue us?'

'Look, Faith, this has been here for years. Jill and Bob didn't get cholera, did they, or their guests?'

'It's not natural to drink slugs,' I shouted. 'We're supposed to *benefit* from natural spring water – you can't benefit from drinking slugs. And what about those wriggly things?'

'Scavengers, I think. They keep the water pure.'

'I am *not* drinking water-vultures in any form! I'm going to phone the plumber.'

The plumber's verdict was that the well water was perfectly safe to drink and the tenants in the well could be kept out by fitting a tighter cover. But the iron pipe carrying the water to the house was rusty and needed replacing with alkathene. If it weren't replaced, the drinking water would always be full of little bits of rust and the iron pipe would eventually fracture underground, causing a flood outside and an exploded Rayburn inside. We arranged to have the work done in the spring, before the children came; meantime, we'd make do with the rusty water.

It was at about this time that the Maran hens forsook their own chicken-house and tried to take over the hay barn. We could have overlooked this if only they had laid a few eggs, but as all they produced was dollops of muck, we confined them to their run. 'Handsome is as handsome does' seemed to apply to pedigree chickens, and we regretted the outlay of £37 on the barren birds.

In the hope of having some hens that would lay, we bought twenty ex-battery hens that we'd seen advertised for 30 pence each. Commercial egg-producers kill off their laying hens after a season as it's not economical to feed them through the winter; the poor birds are then turned into meat paste or dog meat. The twenty we bought laid eggs on the very first day, but we were shocked at the physical condition of the birds, some of which had raw patches on their bodies and blood on their combs.

We put them in a hen-house with a small run attached and left them in peace to find their land-legs. On the second day they all took turns to look out of the hen-house door, and on the third day two or three of the more intrepid birds ventured outside to explore their run. They were very timid and tottered back indoors when they saw us watching them. Everyday the poor creatures laid eggs – not very tasty eggs, and hardly surprising considering their state. We consulted the poultry book and followed its good advice regarding the moult and the subsequent build-up of body condition. Suddenly the birds stopped laying and started to moult, and once that cycle was completed they never looked back. They grew plump and healthy, established a hierarchy and settled down to enjoy the rest of their lives in the farmyard. For the next two years, they laid ten to fifteen eggs a day, except when they were moulting, and found a lot of their food in the fields.

At weekends, Sara braved the incessant rain and constructed a most ingenious outdoor run for guinea pigs. She laid a maze of earthenware drainpipes and then heaped earth over the whole thing so that only the tunnel entrances were visible. She proposed to turf the hillocks in the spring so that the guinea piggery would look established before the children arrived, but in fact, by the time we had surrounded the run with 2-foot-high ranch-style fencing (bits of wood with the bark left on) it looked marvellous – real Capability Brown stuff – and we congratulated her on a super job. The cats adopted the run as their own and spent hours peering into the tunnel entrances waving the tips of their tails expectantly. You fools, we said, and made a note to buy some cat netting before we bought the guinea pigs.

A gathering of the clans was mooted for Christmas, and Phillishayes was chosen as the venue. By Christmas Eve, fifteen assorted relatives were safely in the fold. (Heavens, how *civilized*! A handbasin in every bedroom! What the hell did they expect in Devon – a bucket?) After enthusiastically piling presents under the tree in the huge inglenook fireplace, corks popped, and Brian, luxuriating in his new role of mine host, said that perhaps there was something to be said for Christmas after all.

(A florist's lot at Christmas is not a happy one. Up at 3 a.m., home by 8 p.m. if you're lucky. Five or six consecutive days of prayer for the continued good health of your five hundred or so poinsettias and the engine of your delivery van.)

Christmas Day. Shrieks of delight from the children as they discovered the piglets with MERRY XMAS written on their backs with lipstick. One was MERRY and one was XMAS and they each had a pink paper hat which stayed on for all of five seconds. Both piglets had some mulled red wine, which they slurped up noisily, and the two goats – Toggles and Melly – had a bowl of Alpen moistened with just a hint of sherry.

After lunch, everyone toasted our first season, and Brian put his new Stephan Grappelli record on the player. The kids went outside to feed the animals and almost immediately returned, bursting through the door and shouting 'Look! Look! A brown egg!' The Maran hens. We had forgotten they were supposed to lay eggs. 'Good grief,' said Brian. 'A brown egg at last. And it only cost £37!'

With Christmas over and our visitors gone, we found ourselves still staring out at the endless rain. The start of '76 was as wet as the close of '75 – you'd never have guessed that this would be the year of the Great Drought.

The days were getting longer and we felt we'd better ignore the weather and buy the rest of the livestock. There was an ad in *Horse & Hound* for a Shetland pony for sale not too far away, and we went to have a look.

Brian said to me sternly, 'Now, look. We don't want any of the usual "ooh" and "aah" nonsense – if the pony is knock-kneed or toothless or anything, *we are not having it*. Understood?'

Later that day, Sara, returning from school, crashed in through the back door. 'Did you buy the pony? Is it here?' Trying hard to keep our faces straight, Brian and I led her to the yard.

'*Four* ponies,' she gasped. 'Four lovely little Thelwell ponies But why *four*?'

Why indeed? Why, when offered the choice of four woolly bears masquerading as ponies had we been unable to say no to three of them? From the six-month-old foal, still fluffy in her baby coat, to the sturdy black three-year-old twins, they were all irresistible, that's why. Even Brian, who was dead against having any more horses at Phyllishayes, had been a pushover when confronted with four pairs of huge brown eyes fringed with the longest lashes imaginable, and had written out a cheque on the spot.

A few weeks later, I was washing up and looking out of the window over the sink. It was a lovely day (that is, it wasn't actually raining) and the fields on the other side of the valley were looking fresh and green.

'Look Brian,' I said, 'someone the other side of the valley has got ponies too, the same colours as ours. Isn't that a coincidence?'

'Oh my God,' Brian said in a strangled voice, 'they *are* ours.'

I grabbed the binoculars and brought into sharp focus the sight of twenty tiny hooves impacting someone else's grazing. Memories of past altercations with our London neighbours – I must ask you to control your puppy/rabbits/cats, Mrs Addis – made my stomach knot with anxiety. Quickly we snatched up five halters and a bucket of oats, and set off across our neighbour's field, hoping that nobody was watching through *their* binoculars.

'We only have to catch one,' I said confidently. 'The rest will follow.' I caught the foal. The other four galloped off in the opposite direction.

'What about team spirit now?' said Brian nastily. Fortunately, Shandy spotted the bucket of oats and allowed herself to be haltered. Giving oats to an underworked moorland pony is asking for trouble – like giving neat Scotch to your teenage son – so poor Shandy had to be content with just a mouthful before being hauled back home with the Shetlands trotting in a neat procession after her.

There were no phone calls from irate farmers following this incident, so we assumed thankfully that nobody had seen the escape.

Although we hadn't intended taking any children before Easter, our advertising in *The Sunday Times* brought in some enquiries from parents who wanted to send their children for the February half-term. In fact, this suited us very well since we had our nephews and nieces coming again then, so we accepted bookings for a twelve-year-old girl and her ten-year-old brother.

Our gang arrived first and bagged the best bedrooms. A day or so later, Jill and Darren joined us. Darren was immediately accepted by the nephews and they played together as if they'd been friends for years, but his sister didn't really fit in at all. She was obsessed by boys ('fellas') and talked of nothing else. She was indifferent to the animals, bored by pony riding – thereby invoking much scorn from the nieces – and allergic to fresh air. 'What do you like to do when you're at home, Jill?' I asked, thinking I could go into Honiton and buy things for any hobby we might have overlooked.

'Well, I got this fella...'

'Yes, what do you *do* with your friend – skating, swimming?'

'No, I dress up and I do my nails and my eyes but my mum keeps telling me off.'

'Do you like reading?'

'Yes, I read a bit. I've got my books in my case.'

The 'books' turned out to be those strange little weeklies that look as though they've been printed on recycled egg boxes. I tried again.

'Jill, do you like it here?'

'Ooh, yes, it's lovely.'

'What do you like best?'

'Guy.'

'Guy?' Suddenly I am right out of my depth. 'Jill, Guy isn't part of the farm you know, he's here on holiday, the same as you. What do you like best on the farm?'

'I quite like Marcus, only he's at work all day.'

My God, I thought, it's another Shandy. What *is* it about this place? Have we got extra strong pheromones in Devon? I must make one more effort.

'Jill,' I said, 'listen. I'm very pleased you like Guy and Marcus; I expect they like you too. But it can't be very interesting for you to do nothing all day. The girls are mad about the ponies and they groom them and ride them, and the boys go fishing and play in the hay. You see it's more fun to *do* things.'

'Guy's ever so big, isn't he?'

'Yes, Guy's ever so big, Jill. How would you like to paint a picture of Guy, or make a model of him?'

'Can't draw.'

'Well, you can read, so presumably you can write. How about writing something about Guy? And Marcus too if you like.' I was getting desperate.

'All right, I will. I'd like that.'

Thank you Maria Montessori, I burbled as I scurried around getting together pens and paper before she lost interest. 'Here you are, Jill. I'll leave you to make a start. Don't worry about the spelling.'

The others came in for tea soon after this and nothing was said about Jill's literary efforts, so I guessed she was probably going to wait until we were alone together before she showed it to me. About eight o'clock, when the kids were watching TV, we heard shrieking and raucous laughter coming from the playroom. Emma, our youngest niece, ran out saying, 'You must come and see what Jill's written.'

'A sequel to *Fanny Hill* judging by that row,' said Brian.

'Oh no, it's *much* funnier than *Fanny Hill*,' said nine-year-old Emma, firmly propelling us into the kids' room. 'Show them, Jill. Go on, show them.'

Jill showed us. She lifted her jumper and rolled up her sleeves and there, painstakingly picked out in coloured felt tips were the words I LOVE GUY and I LOVE MARCUS written all over her stomach and both arms. 'She said you told her to,' said Emma. '*Did* you? Did you tell her to?'

I breathed deeply, fighting to keep a straight face. 'Well, er, yes I suppose I did, Emma...sort of...'

Jill grinned at me. 'They said I was a liar, they said you hadn't. Cor, it's ever so nice here.'

Our next booking was for a twelve-year-old American boy whose half-term holiday fell later than most. This meant that he would be the only child staying, but when I explained this to his father, he said Bobby was used to being on his own and not to worry. Bobby's parents were divorced and his father was bringing him up. This was fine in term-time but the holidays were always difficult, and especially so in England where they had no relatives. With some misgivings, we booked him for the last week in February and stocked the freezer with plastic foods, which I believed to be the staple diet of American children. When I first saw him, I wondered if he had had any sort of food at all for the past six months; he was so pale and thin and had black smudges under his eyes. He spoke quietly and politely. He came from Arkansas and sounded like a Tennessee Williams character. His father was going to be in England for a year on business and Bobby wasn't liking it much. We apologized for the weather and said we weren't liking it much either.

Breakfast on his first morning became a clash of wills.

'No thank you, ma'am. I don't eat breakfast.'

'Do you eat lunch?'

'Sometimes I have some crackers and milk, but at school I don't care for the food, so I give it to the other boys.'

'What about dinner?'

'My daddy and I eat out every night. I like salad and seafood.'

'Bobby, your father is paying to send you here to be looked after properly. You can choose your own breakfast within limits, but you must have *something*.'

'I appreciate that, thank you, but I'm not hungry. Do you have some fresh ground coffee?'

'You can have some instant coffee made with milk.' I was beginning to sound like my mother-in-law, and was determined to get a good square meal into this waif. Brian had fried bacon, fried bread and tomatoes for breakfast preceded by porridge and washed down with three cups of tea. I had a bowl of raw oats with sultanas and apple and then a boiled egg. Fascinated, Bobby watched us eat.

'Pardon me, but what are those brown things?' pointing at the sultanas.

'Dead tadpoles.'

Bobby laughed. 'You don't get tadpoles in February. What are they really?'

'Sultanas soaked in cold milk. Want to try one?'

He tasted one and his face brightened.

'Say, that's really delicious. May I please have some?'

41

For the rest of the week Bobby had oats and sultanas with milk for breakfast, lunch and tea. I tried to add raspberry flavoured vitamin powder to it on one occasion, but he caught me and refused to eat it. In the end, we compromised and I let him have the oat mixture on condition that he had a halibut liver oil capsule every day and a gram of vitamin C in a fizzy drink. Dinners were no problem and he ate whatever I gave him with no fuss. I suppose the oats had expanded his stomach by the evenings.

During the days, he accompanied us everywhere, and took a tremendous and intelligent interest in all the animals, especially the pigs. He loved Phyllis and Rosie and would ride them round the field until he fell in the mud. They were getting very big now and were due to be inseminated as soon as they were ready. We didn't know anyone with a boar and had decided to use the artificial insemination service which we had heard was reliable. We explained the whole business to Bobby, and showed him the chart that the AI centre had given us to make it easier to detect when the pigs were on heat. Bobby was enthralled and volunteered to inspect each pig four times a day. He was beginning to pong a bit, but it was worth it to see him looking so well. He got quite adept at leaping over the electric fence and 'sitting' the pigs. (To the uninitiated, the way to tell if the sow is ready for the boar is to sit very firmly on her back. If she moves she's not ready, but if she stands rooted to the ground you phone the AI centre.)

One morning Bobby came pelting down the drive. 'Rosie's ready. I can't move her.' We hurried over to look. Rosie sure enough was rivetted to the ground and no amount of coaxing or shoving would move her. 'Well done, Bobby – you can be promoted to head pig-man.' Brian went to phone the AI centre and I put the kettle on – it was difficult to know what the correct procedure was for a young pig's deflowering, but I thought some boiled water would probably come in handy.

Some time later, a car came slowly down the drive. It was our local rep from a firm of feed manufacturers but Bobby thought it was the AI man and rushed up to him as he got out of his car.

'Have you come to make our pig pregnant?' he yelled.

The astonished salesman hesitated but a second. 'Sorry son, I've got a bit of a headache today,' he said.

The boiled water did come in handy. We all had a nice cup of tea.

Chapter Five

Shandy returned to her owner in March, but before she left, we booked her in for a foot-trim with a local farrier. His name was Tony and he had been recommended by an earnest young woman I met out riding one day. Don't use Mr X she had advised, he's *always* drunk – even at ten in the morning, and the other one – Mr Y – is even worse – he gropes. Tony apparently, neither drank nor groped, and could safely be trusted to trim hooves even at ten in the morning.

''Morning.' He was short and dark, every inch an ex-jockey, cloth cap welded to his head and a rich Devon burr. 'They your Shetlands?' He nodded at the four ponies who milled round the captive Shandy like tugs round a barge.

'Yes, aren't they sweet?'

Tony grinned. 'Don't suppose old Bartlett thought they were sweet when they got into his pasture last week.'

'How on earth...? Who...?' Brian and I had no experience of village bush telegraph. Tony, paring slivers of hoof with economical movements – a joy to watch – smiled enigmatically. 'Old Bartlett's a good chap,' he said. 'You won't have trouble from Bartlett this time.'

We got the message and bid *au revoir* to our grandiose vision of post and rails. Every gap in our boundary would be secured immediately with strong wire.

Tony soon became our friend and mentor. Like Brian, he needed fuelling with tea every hour or so, which gave us the chance to pick his brains. He had twice ridden in the Grand National, then retired from racing (with a dislocated vertebra) and became a farrier. In his spare time he helped his wife run their riding school. He taught us all manner of new skills, from cementing to hedge-laying, never allowing us to get big-headed, but giving a grudging 'not bad' from time to time.

Through Tony we met Polly. 'She breeds,' Tony had said by way of introduction. Polly, an extrovert Bohemian with five wonderfully scruffy children and another seemingly due any minute, had a couple of orphan lambs for sale. They were in a cardboard box by the Aga in her crowded kitchen. Polly ploughed a furrow through a heap of snoozing Dalmatians, picked up the lambs' box and, shooing a Khaki Campbell off the kitchen table, placed the box carefully between a loaf of bread and a teddy bear. 'Four bottles a day each,' she instructed. 'Half a pint at blood heat.'

Charles, the bigger lamb, thrived and grew, but the other one – Peter – was frail and died within a week. I cried when we buried him; he was so tiny that his body went in a shoe box. Charles was lonely and trotted around the kitchen bleating for his friend.

Addy was coming to help with the Easter children and arrived at Taunton looking very smart in a new lilac-coloured coat. It was market day, and we drove there straight from the station and parked by the sheep enclosure. Addy chose the biggest, fattest lamb in the orphans' pen, named him Adam and put him in the back of the van. On the way home, he leapt into the front seat and settled down on her lap for a cuddle. He also, unfortunately, peed all down her new coat.

There were visitors in the yard when we got home, parents and their small boy, who was coming to stay later in the year.

'That Adam!' exclaimed Addy when we, the visitors and the lamb had been rapturously greeted by the dogs. She took off her coat and examined it. 'Look at this – little monkey he is.'

The small boy giggled and asked if he might hold one of the lambs.

'Of course. What's your name by the way?'

More giggles. 'Adam,' he said.

Nature abhors a vacuum. No sooner had Shandy left than Noah appeared: a strawberry roan Exmoor cross, not exactly the Darley Arabian, but with a disposition that had me writing the cheque long before his week's trial was up. He was what horse-dealers call an 'honest' pony, meaning fearless, hard-working and kind.

'He's not very tall,' Brian said. 'Are you sure he'll be able to take twelve-year-olds?'

'Of course. Exmoors aren't tall, but they're strong. He could easily carry you.'

'That's not saying much.' Brian weighed about nine stone. 'I hope for Noah's sake the Easter kids aren't as big as the last lot.'

Just before Easter, some London friends – Ernie and Christine – asked if they could stay for a night to break their journey to Cornwall. 'See you Friday lunchtime, OK?'

On Friday morning Charles – the elder lamb – was ill and refused his bottle. I left him in his pen with a hot-water bottle and hoped he would feel better for his twelve o clock feed. But he refused that too and I began to worry – having lost Peter had made me ultra-sensitive to the possibility that the same thing could happen again. I made him drink some water and rubbed his back to stimulate his bowels. He strained a bit but nothing happened. I remembered that Brian had a hydro-meter, which might make a good enema syringe, so I left Charles and went to find it. I made a soapy water solution and was waiting for it to cool when Chris and Ernie arrived. In my concern for the matter in hand, I forgot my manners – forgot that they had just had a 200-mile drive in holiday traffic and would be wanting a cup of tea. I yelled to Chris, 'I'm *so* glad you've come – can you give me a hand?'

Chris, thinking it was some culinary emergency, dashed into the kitchen and stared at the frothing apparatus in my hands. 'What on earth's that?' she asked.

'An enema.'

Chris is an actress and normally equal to any occasion, but not this one. She reeled and said faintly 'Would it be indelicate to ask, um…?'

'It's for a lamb and it's urgent. Will you hold him for me while I give it to him?'

Ernie and Brian came into the kitchen. 'What on earth's that?' said Ernie.

46

'My hydrometer,' said Brian.

'An enema,' corrected Chris. '*And* it's urgent.'

'My *hydrometer*! Why have you *boiled* my brand new hydrometer?' Brian was furious.

'It's Charles,' I explained. 'He can't go, and he's straining and...'

'Spare us the clinical details,' Brian snapped. 'And buy me a new hydrometer. I'm not touching it after this.'

'I don't know how you can be so callous,' I shouted. 'I suppose you'd be *glad* if Charles died, you and your blasted hydrometer...'

'Died?' said Ernie in alarm. 'Er, shouldn't we get him to a doctor if it's really serious?'

Even I had to laugh, and leaving Brian to explain, Chris and I hurried round to the yard. Chris held tight to Charles's front while I did what was necessary at the back. And it worked. By golly how it worked!

'Chris,' I said. 'It worked. He'll probably be better for his nine o'clock feed.'

'Good Lord,' said Chris, 'do you mean there's an evening performance as well?'

To everyone's relief Charles recovered and our friends enjoyed their quick visit, departing next morning with an Instamatic full of pictures and a new respect for hydrometers.

Spring was late, but worth waiting for. All the corny clichés about spring in Devon suddenly made sense. Limbs *did* gambol, and, what's more, gambolled in an unbelievable setting of daffodils, snowdrops and primroses. Little streams hurried towards the river as if they couldn't wait to be part of the race to Ottermouth.

'Isn't the country noisy?' Marcus commented one day when I was photographing him and Sara with some trout they had caught.

'"Doesn't the silence get on your nerves?"' Sara was quoting from a friend's letter, and we laughed as we listened to the racket. Cows, sheep, next door's free-ranging poultry and our own menagerie contributed to the chorus of creatures eager to the put the word round that the sun was shining.

Nine Easter children arrived, and Upottery's decibel level rose, as did Addy's blood pressure.

'Like gannets,' she gasped, surveying the heap of washing-up. The plates had been scraped so clean they hardly needed washing. 'That pie was meant to be for two days.'

'It's a tribute to your pies, Mum,' said Brian. 'We did warn you they'd have hearty appetites.'

'You said that little American boy – Bobby is it? – only picked at his food last time.'

Bobby, on this his second visit, had changed from pick to shovel.

'It's the competition,' said Brian. 'Old Honey was just the same when we had Parsley. She used to bolt down her food to stop Parsley having it.'

'I'd give him Parrishes if he was mine,' said Addy firmly. 'He's still very pale.'

Ozone seemed a better idea than Parrishes, so we took the children sea-fishing at Lyme Regis and caught twenty mackerel, which the pigs ate, swallowing them whole like seals. The kids loved hand-feeding Phyll and Rosie and said it made them feel brave. They also loved bottle-feeding the lambs, taking furtive swigs from the bottle first – 'Of course I'm not *drinking* it, just *testing* it' – and emerging milky mouthed from the stable for a refill.

There was so much for them to do that by suppertime they were worn out and by eight-thirty in bed. This was a mixed blessing, since no matter how early we got up, or how quietly we made tea, a small person would appear before the first life-reviving sip had been taken. If there's one thing we can't stand at six a.m., it's bright-eyed, happy children. Cockerels are bad enough, but at least you don't have to make conversation.

'My bum's sore.'

'Oh.' Did one prescribe arrowroot or a surgical rub? 'Where is it sore?'

'Here. Down my thighs and all *over* my bum.'

'Oh, good.' Not arrowroot. 'They're your riding muscles.'

'What shall I do?'

'Have another ride on Noah today. The stiffness will wear off.'

Small feet pound up the stairs. 'Hey, you lot – do your bums ache? Bags I ride first today.'

We liked our Easter guests and, what was more important, they liked each other. Some of their activities needed strict supervision – we made it a rule that nobody was to go to the river alone – but within our own boundaries they played or worked as the fancy took them.

Brian spent every available moment gardening, and welcomed volunteers to help with the half-acre vegetable plot. The kids helped to level the soil and construct bean and pea supports. They pegged string lines across the earth and Brian sowed enough seed to provide vegetables for the year. Nobody predicted the drought and Brian was content.

Toggles, the elder goat, came into season one day and had to be driven to a stud some 3 miles away. The billy was an experienced old thing and took only a few seconds to earn his fee. But, surprisingly, the awful billy-goat stench clung to Toggles, the car and us for days.

The animals were my department, and Sara's too during school holidays. We showed the children that there was more to looking after animals than just feeding. If anyone elected to feed say, the pigs, they had to complete the operation by changing the drinking water and cleaning the pen. Then back to the house to report proudly to Addy – 'I hosed and swept the pigs' bedroom all by myself.'

Addy saw to the house, dispensed Elastoplast and made sure nobody died of starvation.

'I've done 10 lb of potatoes, Faith, do you think that'll do?'

'10 lb? Crikey, that's a lot.'

'Well, we can always – get your mucky fingers *out* of my mixing bowl, young man – we can always fry them up for breakfast.'

We shared the children's excitement over some of their 'finds'. A patch of four-leaved clover had us hurrying to the garden to pick one for luck. And there were the newts.

'In the garden pond, please come and look. Please.'

'Newts?'

'*Yes*. They've got yellow spotted waistcoats and freckly faces.'

'They're beautiful.'

They were indeed, and their tadpoles were huge. Frogs and water-boatmen lived in the pond too, and everyone enjoyed lying on the concrete surround, peering at the teeming life below.

We had some parents visiting one day with their nine-year-old son, Rupert. I gave Rupert a conducted tour round the farm while Brian chatted to his parents. He was a fey-looking child with large blue eyes and very fair hair. He didn't say much, so I prattled away in my best Joyce Grenfell trying to entertain him. Then I remembered the tadpoles.

'I must show you the pond, Rupert, you'd like to see all the newts and tadpoles, wouldn't you?'

He poked around with a stick, stirring up the mud so that we couldn't see anything.

'Shall I get you a little net? Then you might be able to catch a tadpole and put it in a jamjar.'

'Yes, I like fishing,' said Rupert.

'Oh good, I thought you would. What do you catch, sticklebacks?'

'No, not really,' said Rupert. 'Last year I won the West of England Junior Fishing Championship.'

'What do you fish for?' I asked faintly.

'Sharks. We live at Falmouth you know. Very good shark fishing at Falmouth.'

The rabbits' run was the children's favourite meeting-place. From a bedroom vantage point we could see them squashing together in the 8-ft-square run, scooping the patient rabbits on to laps to make more room. Sometimes Parsley and the two lambs were invited to the pow-wow. Addy urged me to take a photograph. 'You'd never think they had 7 acres to play in,' she said. 'I wonder what they do it for.'

'They're having a vote today.' I had heard the Secret Plan proclaimed.

'A vote?'

'Yes. The new baby guinea-pig needs a name.'

The pair of guinea-pigs we had introduced into Sara's labyrinth had produced on Easter Day, a single male baby, the sweetest creature imaginable. He was about the size of a ping-pong ball, with tufts of fur sprouting in all directions. The outcome of the vote was a foregone conclusion, and Jesus was duly christened.

Unhappily, one of the cats ate him when he was only a few days old. The younger children grieved noisily. 'If only we'd called him Hercules,' they sobbed, 'this would never have happened.'

'Why have you bought *Horse & Hound*?' Brian, in a permanent state of apoplexy over hoofmarks in his garden, glared at the offending publication. 'Nothing but trouble, those blasted horses. How can we get a hay crop if they keep treading all over the place?'

'What do you expect them to do – levitate? And what about all the lovely manure you're getting?'

'*I'm* not getting it – it's spread all over the field. Can't you train them to go in one place?'

'Of course you can't, they're not dogs. And you know they're the main reason why we're getting so many bookings.'

'Humph,' said Brian, unconvinced. He wasn't happy at the way the emphasis was going as regards the ponies. Instead of a farm holiday with a pony ride or two thrown in, it was becoming a riding holiday from a farm-based background.

'I think we'll have to sell three of the Shetlands, Brian,' I said sadly. 'We need a bigger pony for the summer children, Noah won't be able to cope with all these.' I waved a fistful of booking forms.

We had stressed to enquiring parents that this was a holiday geared to the needs of *small* children, but they still booked in their eleven-, twelve- and even thirteen-year-olds. We were in no position to be choosy the first year, having spent nearly all our savings on the plumbing.

'Let's keep Rocky.' Rocky, one of the black geldings, had endeared himself to everyone. He could be as mischievous as the next Shetland when he was in the mood for a frolic, but he knew where to draw the line, and in the company of small children, he was as placid as an old sofa.

Good homes were found for the other three Shetlands and local papers scanned for a largish pony. Then fate took a hand, and sent us two ponies, or to be precise, a pony and a cob.

Some friends – Sue and Keith – who had helped transform our wilderness into a thing of beauty and who still carry the scars, asked if they might buy a couple of ponies and keep them at Phyllishayes. The long, irregular hours they worked made it impractical for them to keep horses at home.

So keen were they that directly we had agreed to the scheme, they cancelled their proposed holiday tour of the USA and arranged to come to Phyllishayes instead. Brian was flabbergasted.

'Cancelled *America*?' he kept saying. 'For a couple of *horses*?'

Tony offered to vet prospective ponies, and to transport them home for a week's trial. He scoffed at the idea that we would find ponies capable of carrying adults *and* temperamentally suited to children on the leading rein. To his chagrin, I found them both within three weeks.

'Beginner's bloody luck,' he grumbled as we drove home with pony number one. Wellington, a grey Welsh gelding 13.2 hands high, had been, in Tony's parlance, 'a bugger to box'. For nearly an hour his owner had coaxed and pleaded – be a good boy for Mummy, poppet – while Wellington clowned about on the ramp. Then Tony ran out of cigarettes and Wellington's game was up. Tony took him firmly by one ear, hissed something menacing in the other, and Wellington walked in.

I was dying to know what magic phrase had done the trick, but Tony was maddeningly secretive and threaded the horse-box through the narrow lanes without speaking. Only after re-equipping himself with tobacco did he relent, and even then, all he grudgingly divulged was an ancient recipe for hair-restoring and a cure for pneumonia.

'Thanks very much,' I said sarcastically, and then giggled as I pictured bald bronchial horses queuing for Tony's nostrums.

Before long Wellington's partner joined us. Monty, a handsome 14.2 cob, had a shining black coat and an air of quiet dignity.

Sara and I sat on the gate watching the ponies grazing.

'Aren't Monty and Wellie like Sue and Keith?' Sara said.

'Like Sue and Keith? Keith's not black.'

'Not physically, silly – their personalities. Wellington's like Keith – always on the go – and Monty's quiet and calm, like Sue.'

'Oh, *Sara*. That's stretching it a bit. Wellie's an awful fidget.'

'Yes, that's what I mean. He's kind and quick-thinking too. How would you describe Keith?'

'Well, dynamic for a start. Impetuous, quick-witted, kind – I see what you're getting at.'

'Go on. What about Sue?'

'I don't know, Sara. It's difficult to pin labels on friends.'

'Try.'

'All right. Serene, I think, and imperturbable – the sort to keep cool in a crisis. And kind, of course, and subtle too.'

'Exactly. You've proved my point. I think you unconsciously chose Wellie and Monty because they reminded you of Keith and Sue.'

'Freud's got a lot to answer for, my girl. Have you done your homework?'

'No, it's beastly *Macbeth* again. Can I go hitch-hiking in the summer holidays?'

I sighed. This was a well-worn battleground. 'Only if you're in a group and only if there are older boys.'

'It's impossible. None of the other girls' parents will let them go if there *are* boys and you won't let me go if there *aren't*.'

'I can't understand the other parents. Someone must have a brother surely? What about Lindsay or Robert?'

'*Drips* both. Wouldn't be any fun with them acting like policemen. Besides we'd be in moral danger with boys.'

'I doubt it.' I had met Lindsay and Robert. Definitely no moral danger.

The phone rang. 'I'll get it, Sara, you get back to *Macbeth*.'

'Unto the breach and all that?'

'English Literature failed and all that. Buzz off.'

It was Polly on the phone with exciting news. She had found us a cow!

Chapter Six

'Who was that you were talking to on the phone?' said Brian,
   'Polly. She's got a cow for sale.'
'A cow?'
'A Jersey house-cow. The owner has died and Polly's trying
to find a good home for her.'
   'Why don't they bury her?'
I ignored this and thought about the problems of hand-
milking a cow.
   'I wonder if they're like dogs,' I said.
'Definitely a bit bigger,' Brian said.
'You're in a very good mood today – are you ill or something?
I suppose you're thinking about manure as usual?'
   'Well,' said Brian, 'you must admit a cow has more in its
favour than a ruddy horse. Milk *and* manure.'
'But if they're like dogs,' I said, 'they might take to a new
owner. I think house-cows are one-man animals.'
'Let's go and have a look – you never know, she might take
to us.'
   As we drove over to Polly's farm, we discussed the problem
of what to look for in a cow. We decided to treat it as though
it were a horse.
   'It's not a horse, you know,' said Polly's husband, Reg, as I
tried to lift one of Bambi's hooves.
   Bambi was beautiful: large, liquid eyes, mealy mouth like
an Exmoor pony, kind disposition and a large udder.
   'The owner used to brush her every day,' said Polly. 'She
was very fond of her.'
   'Good cow that,' said Reg. 'Good milker.'
'Er, we don't know how to milk.'
'Doesn't matter, she's dry anyway.'
'Dry?'

'Calf's due mid-May,' Reg said, as if that explained everything. 'To a North Devon,' he added.

Polly translated. Bambi had been to a bull on 6 August in the previous year. The bull was a North Devon and the resulting calf was scheduled for 16 May this year. Bambi's milk had therefore been dried up for the past two months in order to rest the cow's system.

'But 16 May is only two weeks away. We don't know anything about cows' calving. Perhaps we'd better wait until she's had it.'

Polly said, 'Oh, Bambi's had quite a lot...er, one or two calves with no trouble, hasn't she, Reg?'

'Fifth calver,' said Reg firmly. 'Seven-year-old cow, no trouble calving at all.'

'How much do you want for her?' Brian asked.

'Well,' said Reg, 'seeing as Faith's a new friend of Polly, I'll let you have her for £110 and I'll get her delivered.'

We hesitated. It seemed an awful lot of money for such a small cow; until now we hadn't realized that cows came in so many different sizes and Bambi was much smaller than we had imagined. Reg's Friesians were gigantic by comparison. Polly watched me looking at the Friesians.

'They bully poor little Bambi because she's a newcomer and she's too sweet-tempered to fight back.'

Brian and I both weakened; he because he was thinking how manageable Bambi looked, and I because I wanted to stop the bullies.

We had a final inspection to convince ourselves. Everything seemed to be in order, and she *was* exceptionally docile.

'Why does her udder hang so low?'

Reg said hastily, 'She's near her time, poor lass, and she's a bit engorged. 'Twill tighten up when the calf comes.'

We believed him.

We paid for Bambi and arranged to have her delivered at the weekend. As we were leaving the farmyard, a duck and ten ducklings came out of the house and waddled in single file towards the field. The ducklings were enchanting and even stony-hearted spouse couldn't resist them.

'Brian, I *must* have some ducklings – aren't they gorgeous?'

'Absolutely. Let's buy some for the first batch of summer children.'

Polly pointed out that these particular day-old ducklings would be gangling teenagers by July: why not wait until the children came and then buy new ducklings? Even I could the sense in that, so we placed an order for six ducklings to be collected later. Then we drove home and were just in time to hear the tail-end of the weather forecast on our radio.

The weather was playing us up again. Having experienced one of the wettest winters since records began, we now began to suffer a prolonged dry spell. Brian had planted enough vegetable seeds to supply the needs of the house for the entire year and was getting seriously concerned about the poor germination rate. He fixed up a makeshift hosepipe from the tap in the yard and ran it down to the vegetable field, which was area of about half an acre. The pressure from the tap wasn't strong enough to get a good flow going and only a small trickle of water actually reached the seedlings; a lot of them died and Brian got rather depressed. He had worked so hard to set up the garden and it was heart-breaking to see how much would have to be re-done when the rain came.

Our brochure said that whenever possible, the children's food would be home-produced. It would not only be horribly expensive to have to buy vegetables, it would also be somewhat dishonest. Every day we carted dozens of buckets of water and concentrated it on selected rows – peas, sweet corn, beans, sunflowers, potatoes, tomatoes and cucumbers. All the salad garden had to be abandoned for the time being – you can plant radishes, lettuces and so on at any time – and also the root crops, which we were hoping to use for animal winter feed. Brian had worked himself to a standstill, so I persuaded him to have a weekend in London with some friends who were giving a party on the Saturday. Then Sara decided that she would like to visit some of *her* friends if there were a free lift going. Marcus gallantly offered to stay and cart water with me, and we stood in the road waving goodbye to the van, feeling rather smug at being the family Cinderellas.

After we had finished the animal feeds for the evening, we thought we had better go and move the hosepipe along the rows. Suddenly Marcus said, 'Can you feel anything?'

'No,' I said flicking drops of water around the tomatoes. (I'm not allowed to do this when Brian is around: he says give them a good drink or nothing.)

'Stop a minute,' said Marcus, 'and look up.'

I looked up. It seemed to be getting dark early and...what on earth was that?

'It's raining,' said Marcus. 'You know – wet stuff drops out of sky – makes things grow.'

'Oh, what a shame,' I said.

'A *shame*? You've done nothing but moan for weeks now about the dry weather.'

'But Brian and Sara are missing it. The one day that they go away it has to rain.'

'Perhaps they'd better go away more often then,' said Marcus. 'I'm going to put my bike under cover.'

He had a Honda 50 motorbike, which he cherished, and he hurried to the garage to make sure it hadn't dissolved.'

'Hey, look at this.'

'What's "this", a speck of rust?'

'No, a cow.'

'Bambi! I'd forgotten she was coming today.'

There, being unloaded from Tony's horse-box, was our very first cow. She looked quite unperturbed after her ride, and ambled towards the field.

'Open the gate,' Tony said.

'What, just let her loose?' I said. 'I've a stable ready for her.'

'What does she want with a stable? Just turn her loose and be quick about it or she'll go back up the drive.'

Marcus opened the gate to the field and Bambi plodded forward.

'She looks as though she knows where she's going, doesn't she, Tony?' I said.

'Ar,' said Tony. 'She'll go straight to the water first, cows always know how to look after themselves. More than some humans you might say.'

The bait was irresistible. 'Which particular humans, Tony?'

'You and Brian.'

'What have we done now?'

'How much did you pay for that cow?'

'£110 including delivery. He did pay you, didn't he?'

Tony's sphinx-like face flickered briefly into a smile. 'Aye, he paid me.'

'Then what's the problem?'

Silently, Tony handed me the Movement Order form that the Ministry demands whenever a farm animal moves to different premises. I read it through.

'It all seems perfectly legitimate to me,' I said.

'It is legitimate. It's perfectly *legitimate* to describe a seventeen-year-old cow as a seven-year-old cow, but it's not right, is it?'

'Seventeen? But Reg said...'

'Reg saw you coming did Reg. 'Tisn't every day a farmer gets a chance to sell a pup. Couldn't resist it, could he?'

'How do you *know* Bambi is seventeen?'

Tony looked at me pityingly. 'Quite *apart* from the fact that Bambi wears her udder round her ankles' – he paused to let this shaft sink in – 'and quite *apart* from the fact that she's no flesh on her, I happen to have seen her around for at least twelve years, and the old lady that owned her bred her herself in 1959 or thereabouts.'

'1959?' said Marcus, who had been quietly listening. 'I was born in 1959.'

'And he's sixteen,' I said triumphantly.

'Seventeen actually,' said Marcus. 'Next week – 9 May.'

'How long do cows live for?' I was humbled now and apprehensive that Bambi might suddenly drop dead.

'Fifteen to twenty years.'

'So she's all right then?'

'She's a fine little cow,' said Tony. 'I'd give you £40 for her anytime you want to sell. Knacker's price you know.'

'She's not going to the knacker's,' I snapped. 'She's got a good home here.'

'I grant you that,' said Tony. ''Tisn't every farm where the pigs get a bottle of wine apiece as part of their rations.'

'A bottle *between* them and anyway it was Christmas Day,'
I said defensively.

'What did the goats get – caviar?'

'They're herbivorous, you ignorant peasant.'

Marcus, the traitor, told Tony what the goats had had for
their Christmas treat. I resolved to come out after dark and let
down the tyres of his motorbike.

'Have you got a shallow dish – like a baking tray?' asked
Tony as he bolted the back of his lorry.

'Yes, I've got plenty of baking trays. What do you want it
for?'

'You're going to need one for Bambi when you start milking
her.'

'Milking her – I thought you meant to cook her in – why
should we need a baking tray for milking?'

'Can't see you getting a bucket under her unless you dig a
hole in the ground. Never mind, she's a good beginners' cow.'

And with this mystifying intelligence, he drove away.

Marcus and I watched Bambi for a while. She seemed
perfectly happy pulling at the grass, so we assumed she must
have some serviceable teeth left. We went indoors to have
supper and to phone Brian.

I had to shout down the phone so that he could hear me
above the noise of the music and voices. It sounded a very
crowded party.

'Good news, Brian – it's raining.'

'That is good news.'

'And the cow has been delivered.'

'Good ole Bambi.'

I estimated that this would be the right moment to reveal
the age of good ole Bambi.

'She's a bit older than Reg said,' I shouted.

'Good *older* Bambi – is it still raining?'

'She's seventeen and it's still raining. Are you having a
lovely party?'

'Lovely lovely party. Everyone's lovely. Don't turn the hose
off, will you? Rain might stop.'

'Brian will you forget the blasted garden for one evening

59

and get some more drink down you? You're supposed to be relaxing and you don't have to drive anywhere. You can get paralytic for once – it'll do you good.'

'Right you are, I'll tell the others. We've all got to be done good to, we'll *force* ourselves to take our gins and tonics...'

He replaced the receiver and I turned to find Marcus scribbling on a notepad.

'What are you doing?'

'Getting it all down to be used in evidence against you. Brian'll never believe you said he could get paralytic.'

'Yoohoo – anyone in?' a voice called from the back door.

'Oh good, it's Ursula.'

(Ursula was our nearest and dearest neighbour. She had introduced herself a week after we had moved in by diving head first under a bramble patch in our field shrieking 'Sin!' Quite mystifying. Then she had emerged, elderly and rather upper crusty, with a mischievous Cairn terrier on a lead. 'I'm frightfully sorry about Cinnamon, we were just coming to call on you when he saw a rabbit. I'm Ursula Villar. I live in the white house next to your field.'

Over coffee we learned that Ursula and her late husband had settled in Upottery after her husband's retirement from the army. He had been an officer in the King's Own Troop – a mounted regiment. Brian had beat a hasty retreat. Ursula and I had sat for an hour or more, engrossed in horse talk and sowing the seeds of what was to become a firm friendship.)

'Hullo Ursula, come in.'

Ursula came in carrying a squirming Cinnamon. 'Can't stay. Hello, Marcus dear, how's the job going?'

'Fine, thank you, Mrs. V. Would you like some tea?'

'No, thanks. I just popped in to see if you knew there's an ancient Jersey in your paddock. Heavily in pod,' she added.

'She's ours, Ursula,' I said. 'Isn't she pretty? She's due to calve on the 16th.'

'I say, you *are* going the whole hog, aren't you? Goats, pigs, lambs, ponies and now cattle. How are the bookings coming along?'

'Sixty so far.'

'Jolly good. Is Brian's mother coming to help again?'

'No, not in the summer holidays. She says she feels her age in the hot weather. We shall advertise for a couple of students later on.'

Bambi didn't have her calf 16 May. All the morning she grazed contentedly, knee deep in buttercups. She didn't seem to mind our following her around all day – we even ate our lunchtime sandwiches in her field in case we missed anything – and didn't seem restless at all. According to our cattle book, the cow's pin bones drop just before calving, the vulva expands and there is much restlessness. Bambi's ancient pin bones were permanently dropped, and as for her vulva, the less said about that the better.

By the evening, we were getting anxious about the delay and kept referring to the textbook which assured us that cows can be as much as three weeks late calving. We inspected Bambi at 1 a.m. and set the alarm for 5 a.m. It was lovely getting up at five and walking round the field in the dew. We watched the sun rise and took some photographs of the valley in the early morning mist. Bambi, needless to say, was all in one piece, but she was a bit more restless – probably due to the fact that she was getting sick of us peering up her backside every half hour.

After breakfast we inspected her again. She was fast asleep under the oak tree, so we thought we would nip into Honiton for a couple of hours to get some shopping.

When we got home, we went over to the oak tree to see how she was getting on. She had finished her nap and was standing in the middle of a huge bramble patch looking at us rather anxiously. We pushed through the brambles, and there on the ground was her tiny son, his beautiful red coat still steaming in the sunlight. Bambi was so proud of him and kept licking him until he got up and tottered round to find his breakfast. She obviously knew far more about calves than we did, so we simply checked that the afterbirth was all in order – messy but necessary – made sure that he had a good bellyful of colostrum, and went away to leave her in peace.

Two days after the calf was born we had our first experience of hand-milking. We positioned the calf, whom we called John, on Bambi's right-hand teats and let him suck for a moment to get the milk going, then Brian milked the two left teats into a gallon container. Tony had been quite right about the udder; it reached nearly to the ground and Brian had to position the container very carefully to prevent the pendulous teats knocking it over. He tugged away for a while and managed to get a few ounces of milk before he got cramp in his fingers, so I had a go. I was equally unsuccessful, and my fingers ached after a few minutes. Then the calf poked his face under the teats and had a pull at our side at which point Bambi became bored with our company and walked away. In dismay we looked at the milk in the container. It barely covered the bottom.

It took over a week to get the hang of milking. Bambi's conviction that young John would turn into a veal chop if she lost sight of him for a second didn't help. We had to immobilize cow and calf to ensure peace in the parlour – we even tried a few snatches of 'Greensleeves' and 'Cherry Ripe' to put her in the picture – but it was ages before she trusted us enough to give more than half a gallon.

Sara was the best milker, but one day was unlucky enough to get her head in the direct line of fire when Bambi was dunging. Brian and I made matters worse by laughing and Sara, her waist length fair hair looking like green seaweed, flounced to the bathroom praying loudly for the return of the good old days of milkmen and milk bottles.

All through May, the hot, dry weather continued. Local councils imposed hosepipe bans, farmers started to take an early cut of hay and everyone avidly listened to the daily bulletins of the Met men.

Brian looked grey and drawn. One evening, after a particularly windless day, he keeled over in the garden and said he couldn't breathe. 'I think it's the pollen,' he wheezed. I realized it was pretty serious when he made no objection to having his temperature taken – he didn't even ask which animal had used the thermometer last – and my fears were confirmed by the reading.

'A hundred and five. I think I'd better phone the doctor.'

In rural areas you don't have to give a doctor two weeks notice before you fall ill. Within the hour a competent-looking GP was trying to raise a vein in Brian's arm in order to get a blood sample.

'There's a lot of farmers' lung about,' he explained. 'I shall have to get your husband's blood tested. When did he last see a doctor?'

'About 1948, for his National Service,' I said. 'He hasn't had time to be ill since.'

The doctor nodded. 'Self-employed?' he hazarded. He called twice after that to give Brian injections to ease the breathing. These were given between the ribs and were very painful. On the eighth day he said the lab tests had shown no farmers' lung.

'The antihistamines should do the trick, but he's delaying his recovery by worrying about the weather.'

I explained about the vegetables and the sixty children. 'When can he get up, Doctor?'

'When he stops worrying, the asthmatic symptoms will ease, then he can get up.'

The vicious circle was broken by Phyll and Rosie, who had been plotting a Pigs' Liberation Movement for some time. They were still electrically fenced in an area with very little shade and no running water; they had eaten every blade of grass inside the fence and were dying to explore the next patch. We had intended to move them some time ago, but Brian's illness intervened and they had to stay put for a while.

One day their need for fresh grass overcame their fear of the fence; they broke the wire and headed down the field towards the potato patch. Both pigs were fairly pregnant but not enough to stop them galloping about joyfully in the long grass. Fortunately, they forgot their original objective – the potatoes – and stayed rooting in the grass long enough for me to rush indoors and turf Brian out of his sickbed.

'The pigs are out!'

'Which way?' Brian groped for a dressing-gown.

'South.'

'God – the potatoes! We'll have to extend their run straight away and get them back in.'

Now I was in the soup. I had concealed from Brian that I too had become a casualty. The strain of doing all the water-carrying on my own – 40 gallons for the animals alone – had made my shoulders seize up exactly as his had done last year and I was managing as best I could on thrice-daily pethidine tablets.

'Why didn't you *tell* me?' It sounded as though Brian was feeling better.

In order to extend the pigs' paddock, we had to drive fencing posts into the hard ground with a sledgehammer. It was agony for me and virtually impossible for Brian.

'Yoohoo, anyone at home?'

Ursula.

'In the pigs' field, Ursula.'

She dodged under the fence. '*Heel*, I said, Cinnamon, and heel I meant. I say, Brian, you look ghastly – like a stick of spaghetti. What at you doing out of bed?'

'Pigs are out.'

Ursula cast an experienced eye over the scene, tied Cinnamon to the hedge and picked up the sledgehammer.

'You hold the crowbar in position,' she commanded, 'and Brian and I will knock in the holes for the posts.'

Somehow, agonizingly slowly, two invalids and an old-age pensioner constructed a new fence. The pigs smirked as they trotted obediently into their fresh enclosure. How they loved to get their own way.

Back in the house, sipping a well-earned cup of tea, Ursula said to Brian. 'You know what your trouble is, don't you? You're too breedy for this farm work.'

'Breedy?' said Brian.

'Blood, don't y'know. Look at you – sinewy, small feet, highly strung – built like a Derby winner. What you need,' she said turning to me, 'is a Clydesdale or a Suffolk Punch type – bone not blood.'

'He did use to win races when he was younger,' I agreed, regarding Brian's fetlocks in a new light.

'There you are then,' said Ursula, as if that settled it. 'I must be going now. Hope you both feel better soon.' And hauling the reluctant Cinnamon from under the table where he had been making dishonourable proposals to Parsley, she strode off.

'What would Hyperion like in his nosebag today? Truffles? Pâté de foie gras?'

'Well, I must admit I do feel a bit better,' said Brian. 'How about bacon and tomatoes and fried bread?'

'You certainly *think* like a carthorse. Why do you have to have the body of a weak and feeble Arabian?'

Brian spluttered into his tea. 'Wait till I tell my mother what Ursula said. I mean – you just don't get highly bred in Hackney.'

Chapter Seven

Brian's illness, caused by the extraordinarily high pollen count, set us thinking about what we should do if any of the children succumbed to hay fever. We asked all visiting parents (quite a few came to vet us before booking) if their children were prone to hay fever, and a small number were. In the event, these kids saw to their own medication quite casually, even to the extent of informing us *before* their antihistamines ran out that they were getting low.

We had been having a lot of correspondence with two sets of foreign parents who had had details about our holidays from the British Tourist Board. Both wanted to send their children to stay during June, and this suited us as we would have more time to devote to the language problem if they were the only guests.

The first to arrive was eight-year-old Jocelyn from Spain, the only child of a Spanish mother and a Swiss father. They wanted Jos to spend fourteen weeks with us in order to improve her English, and they also wanted us to find a tutor for her. It so happened that Ursula had, among other things, been a teacher before her retirement and she agreed to take Jos for regular lessons in the three Rs and general knowledge.

Jos and her father arrived in early June. From the start Jos was what Addy would describe as a handful. She was highly intelligent and spoke English fluently. Her father told us that at home Mama spoke to her in Spanish and he in English. His own command of our language was confident and endearingly ambitious.

'We wish for her to learn the idioms of English. During three months she shall have native. Yes?'

'Yes, fine. No trouble at all, Mr D. There-will-be-many-children-here-to-talk to.' I found I was speaking to him as though he was both deaf and retarded and I was ashamed. 'Er, about her clothes...'

'You wish for me to bring the baggage?'

'Mr D, does Jos have some *suitable* clothes to wear? Her dress is very pretty of course, but she needs casual clothes like jeans and shirts.'

'Jeans?'

'Trousers. Like a boy.'

'Her mama will not like.'

'But Mr D, her mama is not here. I will be doing Jocelyn's laundry and I must insist that she wears different clothes. She will look more like the English children.'

'So. I agree. You will buy for Jocelyn the English clothes. You will send to me the bill.'

Jos was radiant. She was dressed in an elaborate outfit comprising many layers of smocked stuff – presumably this was what upper-class Spanish children wore – and she looked hot and uncomfortable. She clapped her hands with pleasure at the thought of wearing trousers.

'Oh Papa, may I have an anorak too?'

She spoke like a Dalek, all on one level.

'You may have the clothing which is proper. Mrs Addis will choose you.'

After an informal meal, during which Jos ate nothing (Mama force-fed her every dinner, we were horrified to learn) Mr D drove off to catch his plane back to Madrid. Jocelyn watched his departure with indifference.

'I will milk a cow now,' she announced, tottering down the drive on 3-inch wedge-heel sandals.

I followed her and we found Tony in the yard shoeing Noah.

'Hello, Tony. I didn't hear you come down.'

'No, I didn't come in – saw you had company. Hello, little girl – you going to a party?'

'This is Jos – she's Spanish. Jos this is Tony. He puts shoes on the ponies for us.'

'I am to have an anorak,' said Jos.

Tony carried on shoeing. He put seven nails in his mouth and picked up his hammer. Jos patted Noah on the rump and

Noah moved a few steps sideways, which sent the paring knife flying across the floor.

'Bugger off,' Tony roared, glaring at Jos. He hates shoeing in the heat at the best of times. Hastily I removed Jos back the house.

'What was that row?' Brian asked.

'Jos met a native.'

'He said bugger off,' said Jos.

Brian laughed. 'Her mama will not like,' he said.

Next morning I took Jos to Marks and Spencer in Taunton and bought her two complete outfits – jeans, T-shirts and sweaters; also wellingtons, sandals and gym shoes. She was so excited she didn't know which to wear first.

'Why not choose your anorak now and decide later,' I said. She chose a bright red anorak and insisted on buying a red umbrella to match.

It was marvellous to see what a difference proper clothes made. She was a flabby child and badly co-ordinated – they don't go in for much sporting activity in Spanish girls' schools – but directly she wore comfortable things, she was at least able to run about freely.

On the baking hot June day that we bought the clothes, Jos left the shop wearing jeans, T-shirt, anorak and wellingtons.

'When will it rain?' she pestered.

'Don't *you* start about rain. Use your umbrella as a sunshade.'

We got a few odd looks from the sweltering shoppers in Taunton, but Jos didn't mind. As soon as we got home, she changed her wellingtons for gym shoes and ran around on the grass revelling in the new sensation.

Her father had warned us that mealtimes were a battle with Jos, and Jos told us that her parents had sometimes forced her to eat by holding her nose and shovelling food down her throat. We decided to treat the problem a bit more casually.

Every mealtime for the first few days I put a doll-sized portion on Jos's plate and made no comment at all if she left it. Since she received no snacks between meals, she very quickly cottoned on and was soon asking for second helpings. By the end of the first week, she was eating three large meals a day and in addition would often join us for tea and biscuits in between meals.

But she was a difficult child to have around; she had apparently spent so much time bossing the servants at home that she had a very arrogant attitude. She told us that at home they had a different servant for all the chores – laundry, cooking, sewing, etc; they even had a woman whose sole task it was to wash down the walls!

We showed her how the other half lives – she was amazed that I did my own washing-up – and after a while she began to use the vacuum cleaner, make her own bed and even sweep the floor.

Ursula found her difficult to teach at first. She was above average in academic subjects, but didn't respond to the usual motivation that one uses with eight-year-olds – praise, high marks and suchlike. Jos wanted to control the lesson, so Ursula made her some peg dolls and let her teach the dolls. It worked very well, except that we got tired of hearing about how stupid those dolls were; Jos could go on for hours in her sharp staccato voice, and woe betide any peg doll who got a long division sum wrong. They usually ended up in a shoe box with the lid on. She badly wanted to learn to ride, but was not prepared to go through the necessary elementary stages.

'I will not be led like a baby – I will gallop,' she insisted. So I bridled Rocky, led him to a flat grassy part of the field and lifted Jos on to his bare back. I checked that her safety hat was firmly secured then I stood back.

'Squeeze Rocky's sides with your leg, Jos.'

Rocky broke straight into a trot; Jos managed to stay aboard for a few seconds before sliding sideways on to the ground. As Rocky is only 36 inches high, she wasn't in the least bit hurt but from the fuss she made, you'd have thought she had broken both legs.

'The horrible horse has tossed me to the ground!' she cried.

After this, her riding lessons progressed normally, and in fact she turned out to be very competent indeed. By the end of her fourteen-week stay, she was as good a rider as any eight-year-old I've seen, and was even capable of controlling the 14.2 cob, Monty. He thinks it's undignified to take orders from kids, but Jos used her servant-bossing voice on him and he behaved like a lamb for her.

The Italian children were the next arrivals – two brothers from Florence, who spoke not a word of English. Their parents brought them by car, and we liked them so much (the parents) that we invited them to stay the night with us. We all had a delightful evening and after the children had gone to bed we sat up into the small hours discussing the current Italian political dramas. It was refreshing to leave our world of orphan lambs and muck-heaps for a few hours and make our atrophied brains do a bit of work for once.

The children – Cosimo and Michelli – were adorable. They were probably sending us up the whole time, but since none of us could understand them, it didn't matter. They seemed to find our whole way of life a joke and were always giggling together. They managed to find some sort of linguistic common ground with Jos, and, she was sometimes able to translate for us; this made mealtimes quite a bit easier.

The weather was boiling hot and all three children took a siesta every afternoon, leaving a lovely child-free hour or two. Unfortunately, they were so refreshed by their naps that we couldn't expect them to go to bed at eight o'clock, so instead we used to take them riding in the cool of the evening.

Cosimo and Michelli had much the same views as Jos about riding.

'Gallopo?' they enquired, sitting deep in their saddles like cowboys. Here we go again. I thought.

With the aid of Cosimo's phrase book, Sara and I got both boys mounted on Noah and Wellie and nicely positioned in their saddles; we struggled to make them understand that they were to hang on to the ponies' neck straps and *not* the rein if they felt insecure. After a few minutes they both grew impatient with walking around in a circle and demanded 'gallopo'. They were jealous that Jos was trotting Monty round the field on her own.

We released the ponies, who immediately started grazing,

much to the boys' irritation. They clicked and flapped their reins, and the ponies started to trot up the field towards Monty. To our annoyance, the boys were not frightened at all, and with much panache persuaded Noah and Wellie to canter. This was not going according to plan at all and we stood helplessly watching our two complete novices careering round the field as though they were glued to their saddles. Noah and Wellie thoroughly enjoyed playing cowboys and took good care of their small riders: they took the neck rein aids and the Italian commands in their stride and we realized then how lucky we were to have such marvellous ponies.

The boys were exhilarated when they eventually managed to guide the ponies back to us. They dismounted stylishly and flung their arms round the ponies' necks.

'I loave you No-ah,' Michelli said carefully. Cosimo addressed Wellington in Italian but the message was obvious – he 'loaved' his pony too. Jos was furious; she pointedly untacked Monty in a very correct fashion and kept muttering about stupid boys who couldn't do a rising trot.

The long June days fell into a leisurely pattern: every morning after the chores were done Sara and I would take the children and dogs to swim in the river (Sara was just finishing her O-Levels and had plenty of free time), leaving Brian to get on with the gardening in peace. Sometimes we took a picnic and after lunch, if it wasn't too hot, the children could sleep in the shade; mostly, though, it was far too hot to stay out and we lunched at home. Then, after the children's sleep, we would all see to the animals before having our own tea. Three times a week Jos had to go to Ursula's for her lessons and she resented this so much that we wrote to her parents to ask if she could be excused lessons once the other holiday children arrived. It seemed so unfair that she should have to study when nobody else had to. Luckily her parents were sympathetic and agreed to her stopping at the end of July.

Cosimo and Michelli's fortnight flew by and their parents were due to collect them on 8 July. Rosie's piglets were due on the 7th and we all hoped they would be born before the boys left. We hadn't been able to get the boys to understand why we kept inspecting Rosie, all they knew – via Jos – was that Rosie would have a bambino some time. Some of the things we showed them baffled them completely. For instance, I had some fertile eggs incubating in the linen cupboard, but when I showed the boys the eggs, they hooted with laughter and tapped their foreheads meaningly. I expect they told their parents that English families keep their eggs with the blankets as a matter of course.

Rosie failed to produce piglets on the allotted day, so Sara and I decided to take sleeping bags out to her field and spend the night there. Rosie loved having us to keep her company, and kept trying to lie down between us on the sleeping bags. She was so clumsy and we found it wasn't at all conducive to sleep to have half a ton of affectionate pig snuggling up to you. We had a candle in a jam jar by our heads, but Rosie soon discovered this and ate it. In the end we got so irritated through lack of sleep that we took ourselves outside the electric fence and spent the rest of the night there. Rosie stayed as near to us as she could and snored loudly all night, but she didn't feel like having babies. A farm worker looked over the hedge about 6.30 a.m.

'What are you doing?'

'Waiting for our pig to farrow.'

'Pigs like a bit of peace.'

'Peace?' we queried. After all, what could be more peaceful than a beautiful summer morning in company with one's favourite human friends?

'Peace and quiet.' The head disappeared.

'Do you want us to leave you alone, Rosie?' we asked. Rosie said she felt a bit peckish and did we have any more of those tasty candles. Sara went off to get her some pig nuts and I went indoors to prepare breakfast.

The boys' parents arrived at eight-thirty and sat down to breakfast with us. Michelli finished his meal and asked if he could leave the table. He wandered off to say goodbye to all the animals in turn. He was back in minutes babbling excitedly in Italian – Rosie, it seemed, had had her bambino!

We all poured out to look. It was just as well that Rosie

was a gregarious pig – suddenly she found herself surrounded by the League of Nations all talking at once about her piglet. She grunted contentedly as the piglet settled down to feed and rolled on to her side. The she gave a little heave and pushed out a placenta.

'The afterbirth,' I wailed, 'She *can't* have only one measly piglet after all these months.'

I soaped my arm in a bucket and gave Rosie an internal examination to see if I could find any more piglets. Actually this was the first time I had done an internal on a large animal and I was rather nervous about having an audience. Rosie was most obliging; she just shut her eyes and thought of England in a very relaxed fashion. The visitors stared in horror at all the muck and gore and Brian tactfully suggested that they should all go back to the house and leave me to it.

I continued my piglet hunt, but it was no use; Rosie was sticking at one and there was nothing I could do about it. The piglet weighed 6 lb and was the fittest-looking baby imaginable. Miserably, I gave Rosie a drink and put the afterbirth in the bucket to stop the dogs getting at it.

The Italians were now in the ponies' field taking pictures of the children cantering bare-back round in circles.

'Michelli wants you to name the pig after him,' said their mother.

'It's a girl – shall we call her Michelle?'

Michelli was pleased. He said to Cosimo – 'English pig Michelli,' and they both laughed.

Brian gave them a last ride in the link box of the tractor, and their parents took still more pictures: then, with much hugging and kissing, we all said goodbye and they drove away.

Rosie's sole piglet, Michelle, was a problem. It cost £110 a year to keep a sow, excluding the cost of piglet food, and unless the sow rears reasonably large litters, it is economic madness to keep her. Most pig-keepers have more than two sows and can foster surplus piglets from an overproductive sow on to the one with a small litter. Unfortunately, Phyll wasn't due to farrow for another week and Rosie needed piglets straight away.

So Brian spent the rest of the morning telephoning round

large pig units in Devon to see if we could buy some orphaned or surplus day-old piglets. Eventually he was recommended to try a small pig-breeder from the next village, who was reputed to have a sow famed for her large litters.

For once we were lucky. The breeder, Miss Kerr, did indeed have some piglets that needed a foster mum, so we jumped into the van and tore along to see her.

'This is Bella,' said Miss Kerr, elderly and benevolent, leading us to a huge sow who was lying asleep in the shade of a tree. Bella had plenty of company, as Miss Kerr believed in letting all her animals roam around freely, and the paddock contained no fewer than three pigs, two cows, two goats and countless ducks. They all looked wonderfully content and strolled across to say hello to us.

'Aren't they friendly?' we exclaimed, as various snouts an muzzles explored our legs.

'Why shouldn't they be?' said Miss Kerr. 'They have lovely life here, don't you, my darlings?'

The animals and ducks thronged round their mistress, hoping for titbits. It was an idyllic scene which only a Thomas Hardy or an H. E. Bates could do justice to. We were loath to get down to business and could have stayed watching for ever in the hot sunshine.

'Off you go girls, it's not teatime yet – go on, shoo.' Miss Kerr firmly ushered them all out of the way and knelt down to talk to Bella, who felt too hot to get up.

'Poor Bella suffers in this heat,' said Miss Kerr. 'She had seventeen piglets a few days ago and hasn't enough milk for even one or two.'

'Seventeen?' we gasped. 'Our pig had just the one.'

'I'm not surprised. It's this heat you know, lots of people are only getting ones and twos lately.'

'But why?'

'Various reasons. The boars' fertility is affected for a start, and even if they hold their first service, the sows can reabsorb their litters if the conditions are wrong.'

'I'll never be able to watch Wimbledon again,' I giggled. 'Can you imagine the commentator: "Billie Jean has held her first service." It just won't be the same.' Brian glared at me but Miss Kerr laughed. 'It hasn't done poor Bella much good to hold her service. Look, no milk at all,' and she squeezed one of Bella's empty teats.

'Where are the piglets?' I asked.

'Indoors. I've been feeding them on goats milk, but they've all died except six. They had no colostrum you see,' and she led us back to the house.

In the kitchen, a long-haired guinea pig and a rabbit were mounting guard over a large box containing the six piglets. Two cats sat on the table surveying the scene through slitted eyes.

'Aren't you afraid the cats will kill the guinea pig?' I said.

'Do you go around killing your friends?' said Miss Kerr gently. 'I must confess they kill the odd duckling now and then, but they know they shouldn't. Animals do try to please us you know, but you have to explain the rules clearly.'

Here's someone who can teach me a thing or two, I thought, and resolved to pay another visit to Miss Kerr as soon as possible. We got down to pig business. 'You can take all six piglets,' said Miss Kerr, 'and I will charge you £4 each for any that you manage to rear. If they all die, of course, there will be no charge. I think that one,' pointing to a pathetic little pig with diarrhoea, 'will die today, but the others will have a good chance once they have some colostrum.'

'Why have they got black spots?'

'They're Gloucester Old Spot pigs. Rare breed you know. Used to be very popular because they're so hardy and have big litters. Bella always has at least fifteen and rears the lot. This wretched drought has broken her record – up till now she's never lost a piglet.'

We were thrilled with our new spotty babies and pleased that they were a rare breed. We thought Miss Kerr was rather a rare breed herself as we watched her bustling round the homely kitchen looking for a couple of clean cups for us to have some tea. She told us that she farmed 20 acres single-handed and that the animals we had seen in the paddock were only part of her stock. She had several more pigs and eleven beef animals in another field; also some more poultry in a walled garden round the back. We told her all about our seven acres and the children's holiday idea. She was horrified at the thought of all those children.

'My dears, they will disturb the animals you know. Small children can cause havoc.'

'What about if we explain the rules – like you do with your cats?'

She sniffed cynically. 'Cats are much easier to train than small children. Now hurry up and finish your tea; the piglets are due for a feed soon.'

Very carefully we carried the box of piglets out to the van and Brian drove home as though we had a cargo of Dresden china.

Rosie was lying in the shade feeding Michelle. Miss Kerr had told us to engage Rosie's attention while she was lying down and then put the piglets on to the milk-bar without her seeing them. I squatted down on Rosie's shoulder and scratched her under the chin while Brian lifted the piglets out of the box by their hind legs (they don't squeal if you lift them like this) and placed them carefully in a row next to Michelle. All went well and Rosie found herself feeding seven piglets without realizing it. The one with diarrhoea seemed very weak, but all the others sucked vigorously for some minutes before suddenly falling asleep like puppies. Rosie got up gingerly and stared in amazement at her new family. Michelle stood out like a sore thumb, being twice as big as the others and pink into the bargain, but Rosie didn't seem to mind. She sniffed them, then ambled off to see what was in her trough. She grunted with pleasure when she found her favourite snack – bread soaked in chocolate-flavoured milk – tastefully arranged on top of her pig nuts. I had long discovered that the way to a pig's heart is flavour everything with chocolate.

Next morning the weakest piglet was dead, but the other five thrived and grew into beautiful pigs. We intended to give them all names connected with roses, and got as far as Fragrance, Petal, and Rose Hip for the girls, but then some visiting children christened the two boys Fart-face and Blue Bum, and the names stuck.

After Michelle was born, some of the chicks that had been incubating in the airing cupboard hatched out. We had put ten eggs on top of the hot tank, but only three of them were fertile. I suppose Marlon the cockerel was affected by the heat the same as everyone else. They were so sweet, and rushed around the kitchen cheeping loudly for their mother. Small made it plain that she had no intention of becoming a vegetarian and her hips quivered as she practised her panther leaps under the kitchen table.

'This place is getting to be like a zoo.' Brian was in a bad mood. 'Will you stop trying to train the cat not to eat the chickens? How on earth is she supposed to know the difference between mice and chicks?'

'Miss Kerr said you can train them.'

'And how many cats and guinea-pigs do you imagine Miss Kerr got through before she had a compatible pair? You really are so *gullible*. Put the chicks outside.'

'You can't put three chicks loose in seven acres. How would you like to be loose in a strange country with nobody to look after you?'

'I'd love it. I'd rather be anywhere than stuck in this house with lambs in the lavatory and chickens in the kitchen.'

'Lambs in the lavatory? What are they doing there?'

'I didn't stop to ask. I should imagine they're peeing all over the floor – that's all they ever seem to do.'

I went to investigate. It was much worse than Brian had described. Charles and Adam had not only wet and messed on the floor, they had also unravelled half a toilet roll and the loo was festooned with soggy bits of paper. The lambs were very pleased to see me and waggled their tails in anticipation of their bottles.

'You little horrors, how did you get shut in there?' I scooped them up and took them back to the yard. Assuming Jos must have left the gate open, I shut it and went back to the kitchen to prepare their bottles. No sooner had I put the milk on to heat, than the lambs appeared again.

'Get out,' Brian shouted, but they came in.

'There must be a hole in the fence,' I said.

Brian stomped out wearing his martyr's face. I fed the lambs quickly, then locked them into their sleeping quarters before going to help with the fence.

'There isn't a hole at all, they're climbing up the manure heap and jumping down the other side,' said Brian.

'Could you build them a run in the field with wire netting all round?' I suggested.

'I could if you would do a couple of days' hoeing for me.'

I considered. I quite liked hoeing in soft soil, with a cool breeze blowing, but the drought was causing huge cracks to appear in the rock hard earth and any form of weeding was torture.

'No, I can't do the animals and hoeing. I'll think of some way to control the lambs. Will you build me a coop for the chicks?'

'For *three* chicks?'

'No, a big one. If we buy some more day-old chicks, we could rear them all together.'

'*More* chicks?' Brian had visions of the kitchen becoming a deep litter house. 'What on earth do you want with more chicks?'

'Table birds. You know – like Mrs Edwards has. She buys day-olds from the hatchery and rears them in coops, then when they're big enough, she free ranges them in her orchard.'

'How do you know all this?'

'I asked her. She said they can get to 10 lb in twenty weeks if you buy good stock from the hatchery.'

So Brian agreed to build a run for day-old chicks and another one for the ducklings we had ordered from Polly. When the chick pen was ready, I went to the hatchery in Honiton and collected seventeen fluffy yellow chicks. I had ordered only twelve, but the man in the hatchery had some oddments left over and gave me the five extra ones for nothing.

When I got them home, I rigged up a warm nest for them on the old-fashioned hay-box principle. The hay nest was warmed by a hot-water bottle at night, and by morning it had conserved enough heat to maintain itself at an even temperature throughout the day. (I have since discovered that this only works efficiently if the outside temperature stays about 70°F.

In 1976 there was no problem of chilly summer days.) The seventeen hatchery chicks accepted our three linen cupboard ones and they all had a marvellous time charging round their little playpen, taking dust baths and basking in the sunshine. Every night I shut them in the heated box and they would snuggle up to their hot-water bottle mother and sleep from 8 p.m. to 6.30 a.m. Apart from having to fill the bottle once a day, they really were no trouble to rear, and they provided hours of interest for Jos and the cats.

Now I tried to think of a way to stop the lambs being quite so free ranging, but none of my experiments worked and for the next few months they had the run of the grounds while we all tried to remember to keep the kitchen door shut.

There were only a few weeks left before the holiday guests *en masse* were due, and we were busier than ever. We had advertised for three girl students to help with the children and had quite a few applicants to interview. They were all agreeable youngsters but we were looking for one particular quality in addition – a sense of responsibility.

How lucky we were. The three we chose – Liz, Sue and Vicky – fitted the bill perfectly. Liz, a mature student doing law at Exeter University was sensible, practical and had a driving licence: Sue and Vicky, sixth formers at a local school, were experienced in handling children and ponies respectively, and had a lively air about them that we liked. Liz told us that during her previous summer vacation, she had worked in the kitchens at a well-known progressive school. I showed her my recipes, which I had copied from a book written by the school cook, and Liz hooted with laughter. She told us that the children had hated their school meals and were always sneaking off to buy fish and chips and doughnuts in the nearby town. I was rather disappointed at this revelation but Brian was jubilant. He had been dreading an endless diet of raw grated vegetables and jacket potatoes, whereas I was looking forward to it. We have never seen eye to eye over food, and this was to have been my chance to indulge my own preferences.

'What they definitely will *not* eat,' Liz said, 'is raw grated beetroot.'

'Hooray!' said Brian. 'Will they like bacon and tomatoes with white bread?'

'Brown bread,' I insisted. 'I may concede raw vegetables but I am *not* giving them white bread.'

Liz said she thought they wouldn't mind what colour the bread was provided they had plenty of jam to go on it.

'Faith's going to buy chocolate spread by the bucketful,' said Brian. I scowled at him as I don't like my image spoiled. Although by nature a health food crank, I do have a great weakness for all things chocolatey and am always delighted to find others similarly inclined. Hence my affinity with pigs and young children.

Having chosen our three helpers, we made arrangements for them to move in just before the children arrived. This left us only one free weekend before kick-off and we invited Sue and Keith to stay as it would be their last chance until September to ride their ponies.

We had hoped for a quiet weekend, but at the last minute some parents phoned to ask if they could bring their small son to visit us on the Saturday, and since they had already booked him in for a two-week stay later in August, we felt we could hardly refuse.

Unfortunately, Phyll chose to give birth on that Saturday. Brian went off to Honiton to collect the visiting parents from the station, and in his absence Sue and I acted as midwives to Phyll, leaving Keith to amuse Jos and keep her out of our way. Sara had gone ferreting with a friend from school and Marcus was out fishing. Phyll gave birth to five lovely big piglets with no trouble at all, but then she seemed to be having difficulty with the sixth. We decided to be on the safe side and phoned the vet, who was, fortunately, on a case in our area. He arrived in about ten minutes and gave Phyll an injection of pituitrin. She responded quite quickly to this and produced another piglet and then, to our disappointment, the afterbirth. The vet tried to be comforting.

'Never mind, you've got five good piglets. Some pigs are losing whole litters in this heat.'

'Five piglets? She's got six.'

'I'm afraid number six is going to die – he's been stuck too long inside,' and he swung number six backwards and forwards by its back legs. It did look very limp.

'Is there nothing you can give it?'

'No, I'm sorry There's no chemical stimulant to revive a newborn piglet. All you can do is try resuscitation, but in this case you'll be wasting your time.'

He packed up his things and drove off, leaving us to regard the piglet miserably.

'Let's not give up,' said Sue, 'let's take him indoors and try resuscitation.'

She picked him up and carried him back to the house. I filled a hot-water bottle while she rubbed his icy little trotters and massaged his back.

'He's still breathing,' she said optimistically.

Keith and Jos came in as we were enveloping the piglet in hot towels. Keith is much nicer than Brian about animals in the kitchen and immediately started to help rub some warmth into the limp creature.

'That pig is dead,' stated Jos flatly.

'Not quite, Jos. Do you want to help to rub him?'

'No. I will take Parsley for a walk on a lead.'

Poor Parsley rolled her eyes at us appealingly. She didn't like walks on the lead, but it seemed a good opportunity to get them both out of the kitchen, so we made her go. The piglet stopped breathing.

'Quick,' said Keith. 'Give it the kiss of life.'

Sue began mouth-to-mouth resuscitation, and number six started to breathe again. Frantically, we rubbed his body and feet and he held on to life for a few more minutes. Then he stopped breathing again and Sue redoubled her efforts to get some air into his lungs. At this moment Brian appeared.

'Christ Almighty, what's going on now?'

'Ssssh! Where are the visitors?' I hissed.

'Just coming in, and don't shush me. The whole family is ghastly. I've had an awful time fetching them and I want some tea. What's that in the towel?'

'Don't let them in here, *please*. It's Phyll's piglet and the vet said he's going to die.'

'That's all I need, that is. A dead pig in the kitchen and some stupid parents all in one day. Why is it going to die anyway?'

'Phyll had uterine inertia and this one was stuck for over half an hour. She had six altogether. *Get rid of those parents.*' I could hear them coming.

'They want to meet you – they may as well see how we really live.'

He started to quote from our brochure: '"A holiday for the child who loves the outdoor life." That's rich. All the outdoor life ends up in the kitchen.'

The visitors tapped on the door as they entered. 'Good morning, we are the parents of Rudi. Are you Mrs Addis?'

Brian hadn't said anything about them being foreign. I threw him a look of loathing as I shook hands and made welcoming noises. I tried to shepherd them straight out again, but they wanted to know what Sue was doing on the floor. She was red in the face from blowing life into the piglet but she managed to gasp 'How do you do' to their feet.

'My wife and our friends are resurrecting a dead pig,' Brian said, unnecessarily loudly I thought.

'So? You are joking, yes?'

'I am not joking. They do it all the time. In a minute they will give it some brandy.'

Brandy! Sue and I hadn't thought of that. I got the brandy from the larder and while Sue held open the piglet's mouth, I trickled a teaspoonful of brandy down his throat. He gasped and took several good breaths. Poor little number six; after just a few more minutes his heart stopped beating and his soul was transported to the land where the mud is always cool and the troughs are never empty.

Keith tactfully put the kettle on and Jos came in leading Parsley.

'Ah, Jos, would you like to show this little boy all the animals? His name is Rudi and he will be coming to stay with us soon.'

This appealed to Jos's bossy nature and she grabbed Rudi by the hand and dragged him outside. If she could have used a collar and lead for him too, she would have done. We could hear her telling him to shut the gate even before they had got as far as the yard.

Somehow Sue and I cleared part of the disaster area that was our kitchen and invited the visitors to sit down and have some tea. Brian had had the foresight to buy some Cornish pasties when he was in Honiton, so all I had to do was quarter some tomatoes and we had Instant Lunch. Conversation was distinctly strained – the presence of the piglet, though decently shrouded, was inhibiting – and we burbled on about the excellence of Brian's early tomatoes until we couldn't thing of anything else to say about them.

Since it was obvious that Rudi's parents would cancel their booking and demand their deposit back, none of us made any effort to be anything other than civil towards them. We didn't like them – they were starchy and grim-looking, and their child seemed too quiet for a seven-year-old. So when Sara and her friend came in for lunch carrying a pungent-smelling ferret in a box and three dead rabbits, nobody commented; indeed, it was a welcome break to get off the subject of tomatoes and discuss the best way to cure rabbit skins.

'You have many animals here?' Rudi's father asked Sara.

'Er, yes, lots.'

'Is good. Rudi likes animals. We haff no pets.'

I bet you don't, you miserable old thing, I thought. Brian looked envious.

'We have many pets,' he sighed.

'Is good. Rudi will learn much here.'

Like how to turn your kitchen into a mortuary, I thought. Perhaps he wasn't too bad after all. But the kid *was* strange as later events were to prove. We gave the family a quick guided tour, then Brian took them to Honiton to catch their train.

When he got back, we had all cheered up. Marcus had caught five trout; Sara and her friend had skinned their rabbits and were pegging out the pelts, and Keith had buried number six. Brian and I gave Phyll her chocolate drink and admired her family. It was lovely being back to normal again.

That evening we all went down to the village pub on the ponies. Jos, over the moon at this unaccustomed treat, supervised the ponies while we fetched the drinks outside and then shared her Coke with Wellington, who curled his lip in disgust.

'Try him on a pint of bitter,' suggested a wag on the next table.

'I wish we did not have other children next week,' Jos said.

'I'll drink to that,' said Brian.

'Well, I won't,' I said. 'Kids are what the farm is all about.' 'Fair enough,' said Brian. He looked dolefully at the cloudless sky. 'Let's drink to rain.'

'To rain,' we echoed, but the gods misconstrued the toast and sent a further ten weeks of drought instead.

Chapter Eight

Sara was still pestering to be allowed to hitch-hike to the Gower coast, where three of her London friends were planning to camp during the holidays, and any hopes we had that Marcus would give up a weekend to accompany her to Wales vanished when our three student helpers moved in. Saturated in Brut and wearing a fatuous expression, he took to doing press-ups on the lawn in the hope that his manly physique would be noticed by the girls. We pointed out that half his body beautiful was invisible under his long hair and that he would stand a better chance if he looked less like a thatched cottage.

The girls, while not finding him physically repulsive, treated him with no more than sisterly affection. Marcus, however, lived in hope for the rest of the summer and bought himself slogan-infested T-shirts which ran in the wash.

Sara's friends were being driven to Wales by 'someone's cousin', an old crock who had sportingly offered to take both girls and tents in his estate car. Correspondence with one of the mothers revealed that the old crock would be thirty next birthday and for all his declining years was prepared to make a detour round Bristol and pick up Sara *en route* for Wales. And with that she had to be satisfied – no hitch-hiking, just a pre-arranged lift.

Liz, Sue and Vicky settled in quickly and had soon organized duty rotas, riding programmes and days off. One of their better suggestions was to get some more ponies to spread the work load. As Polly was prepared to lend some of her children's ponies, we made our peace over the Bambi swindle and arranged to collect a couple of ponies when we got the ducklings.

'They're Muscovies,' explained Polly, capturing six in a cardboard box, 'I think these are females, but if not, I'll swap them when they grow up, then you'll have six the same. I can let you have an unrelated drake later in the year.'

The yellow and black ducklings were even more enchanting than the chicks and splashed in and out of a shallow dish of water we had given them to play in. They soon became very tame and used to follow Jos around whenever we let them out. Small didn't show any interest in them, and this surprised us as she had been a fanatical chick-watcher. The reason for her lack of interest only became apparent on the day before the children came, when she astounded everyone by producing two lovely kittens right in the middle of the dining-room. We had noticed that she had been getting less active than usual but had put it down to the heat. As she had been given to us as a stray, we had no idea how old she was and had assumed she was still a kitten. Now she had made her own contribution to the children's holidays, and was so proud of herself that she purred continuously for two days. One kitten was pure white and the other black and white, like Small.

Twelve children were booked in for the first week, some we had already met during pre-holiday visits, others were recommended by our own friends and one or two were unknown quantities.

Scott fell into the last category; he was an American boy of ten, who arrived with one leg in plaster. His mother explained that he was inclined to be accident-prone. We looked at him dubiously: he was fat and pasty and had a petulant mouth. He didn't look you in the eye when he spoke and both Brian and I had forebodings about him.

Apart from Scott, the other kids were delightful; there were nine boys and three girls, one of whom was called Jos. Spanish Jos didn't want to share her name with anyone, and insisted on being called Jocelyn all the time the other girl was there. The children's ages ranged from six to thirteen years and they all got along very well together once they had sorted out their own hierarchy.

After supper on the first evening, Brian rapped on the table for silence. 'Attention please, inmates.' The children stared at him apprehensively. 'I just want to explain a few things now that we're all here. First, we're very pleased to see you and hope you all have a lot of fun here and enjoy yourselves. You do look a remarkably healthy bunch – I feared you might all be cross-eyed and incontinent.'

Some of the older ones, who knew what incontinent meant, laughed, and one boy said: 'Wait until tomorrow, sir, we might surprise you yet.'

'You're Stephen, aren't you?' said Brian. 'Please don't call me sir – you're on holiday, remember? I'm Brian and this is Faith and the girls are Vicky, Sue and Liz. That Old English sheepdog over there is Marcus. Our daughter is called Sara, but she's going away on holiday tomorrow, so you don't have to remember her name. Where was I?'

'Fearing that we could wet the bed,' prompted Stephen.

'Second,' continued Brian, 'some rules.'

All the kids groaned and made exaggerated gestures of agony.

'Rule number one. If you feel hungry between meals, you must go and see Faith and she will give you a bar of chocolate.'

You could have heard a pin drop. Olivier himself can seldom have had such rapt attention.

'Rule two. *Nobody* is to go down to the river alone. You must always ask one of the grown-ups to take you. That's all.'

'Only two rules?' asked nine-year-old Adam. 'I thought there would be millions.' Brian sat down and a minute tot of six climbed on to his lap.

'I like your rules,' he said. 'They're sensible.'

I wondered if, in fact, he had absorbed rule two. He was so young and it was his first time away from home. I tested him with an old but effective infant-school teacher technique.

'Tell me the rules, Rory,' I said. 'I didn't hear them properly.'

'You should *lissun* then. He said I mustn't go to the river and I must eat lots of chocolate.'

'Thank you. Now shall we all go outside for a bit before bedtime? It's much too nice to stay indoors.'

Visiting all the animals to say goodnight took an hour. Everyone wanted to stroke Bambi's calf, John Bull, who had become the friendliest little soul imaginable. Bambi was friendly too, but most of the kids were scared of her horns and kept their distance. By the time every goat, pig, pony, cat and dog had been wished goodnight, the smaller children were yawning and made no protest as we aimed them towards bed. The older ones watched TV for a while, then they too went to bed co-operatively.

Brian and I felt elated at the successful start and put the kettle on to have a staff meeting round the kitchen table.

'What do you think of them, girls?'

'A nice bunch of kids – all except Scott,' Liz said.

'That Stephen,' giggled Vicky, 'wanted me to kiss him goodnight. I had to tell him that only boys under ten got goodnight kisses.'

'Bet you wouldn't have said that to Steve McQueen.'

'Isn't it a coincidence that three of the children are Welsh? Perhaps they'll get some good songs going for bonfire night.'

'Mary's mother told me that Mary is nervous of boys,' I said.

'Mary's mother is deluding herself, then. Mary's already asked Mark if he'll be her lamb-feeding partner.' We had suggested to the children that they paired up for bottle-feeding the lambs so that everyone had the same number of turns.

'What shall we do tomorrow?' Sue asked.

'I want to stay here all day tomorrow,' I said. 'Toggles' kid is due any day now and I mustn't be away for too long at a time. How about riding in the morning and river in the afternoon? I'll give a hand with the rides, then you three can take them to the river on your own after lunch.'

'That little fair-haired boy is very quiet, isn't he?'

'Oh, that's Rupert. Did I tell you that he won the West of England junior fishing championship last year?' And I told them about Rupert and the tadpoles.

'He looks very frail,' said Sue. 'I can't imagine him catching a shark.'

Next morning I was awakened at 5.30 by a thumping noise on the landing outside our bedroom.

'Brian, are you awake?'

'No.'

'What's that noise?'

'Go to sleep.'

'It sounds like a log being rolled along the landing.'

'Mm.'

The noise stopped and I tried to go back to sleep, but it was too light outside. Then I heard the back door open and a rhythmic tapping started. I got out of bed and looked out of the window. Scott was manoeuvring himself down the terrace steps and the tapping noise was coming from his plastered leg. I watched him progress as far as the rose bed, then he stopped and picked up a stick. Before I could do anything about it, he swung the stick at the rose bushes and decapitated several blooms with one swipe.

'Scott!' I leaned out of the window. 'Stop that at once.' He looked up to see where my voice was coming from and raised his stick in salute. I hurriedly pulled on some clothes and went downstairs to sort him out.

'What the hell do you think you're doing?'

'I couldn't sleep. It's too hot.'

'Do you know what the time is? It's half past five and you've woken us up. Go back to bed.'

'But I can't sleep.'

'Then you can read in the playroom until getting up time. I won't have you bashing the flowers just because you're bored.'

I propelled him indoors, left him in the playroom and firmly closed the door. I made some tea and carried two mugs upstairs.

'Brian, are you awake?' I knew he wasn't but I felt peeved that I had been woken up and he hadn't. Actually it was quite pleasant to be up and about before the day became unbearably hot, and we went downstairs to enjoy the quiet before the children came down to breakfast.

We hadn't been there long when Sara came down carrying a small hold-all. She was getting the 8 a.m. train to Bristol.

'Is that all the luggage you're taking?'

'I knew you'd say that. I don't want to lumber myself with a lot of luggage in this heatwave.'

I rummaged through the hold-all. There was only a pair of jeans, a bikini, two T-shirts and some underwear.

'Sara you must take something warmer as well. Look, you haven't even packed a sweater or a coat.'

'In this heat?'

'Well, it might rain soon. Tell you what, you can borrow my thin anorak – the one that rolls up – it's not a bit heavy and at least it'll keep the rain off.'

Sara sighed patronizingly. 'Okay, if it'll make you stop worrying, I'll take it.'

'You're too kind,' I said sarcastically. 'And don't lose it. It cost £6.'

'Shall I take my warm woolly vest as well?'

I chucked a teaspoon at her and missed. Brian said. 'That's enough you two. Go on, Sara, hop it if you're going before the kids come down.'

Sara hopped it and I was glad to have my mind occupied with seventeen breakfasts. I always worried when our own kids went away.

The children came down and demolished vast quantities of cornflakes, eggs and toast.

'They're eating that brown muck,' Brian observed as he cut himself a slice from his white loaf. 'They must be starving, it tastes like sawdust.'

'And yours tastes like reconstituted Harpic.'

'Good. I'll have a nice clean stomach.'

It was too hot to go through our brown versus white routine today, so we called a truce until we had more energy. Brian took off for the garden and the girls and I went out to catch the ponies, ready for the children's rides.

'Hands up anyone who can ride,' I called, as we finished tacking up the ponies. Six hands were raised and the girls and I looked at each other happily. If six of the children could already ride, then we could put three riders in each batch of non-riders, lead these on a one-to-one basis and still have one of us free to supervise overall. This happy state of affairs lasted about a minute. Once we had the first six children mounted, it was apparent that none had ever been on a pony before.

'I thought you said you could ride,' said Vicky to one of the Welsh boys.

'I can. My grandad had a pony for the bread round.'

'Did you ride your grandad's pony?'

'No, but he used to give us rides in the cart.'

We groaned and made three of the children dismount. Then we tried another three who had claimed riding experience. This time the success rate was higher – two of them had manifestly ridden before and gathered up their reins before adjusting their own stirrup leathers. The third child was the tiny Rory, who sat like an unset jelly.

'Have you been on a pony before, Rory?'

'N...no. I've seen it on the telly.'

In the weeks to come we found that a large proportion of our riders had learned their skills solely from the comfort of an armchair. They weren't deliberately telling lies, they really thought that they could ride because they'd watched it on TV. We led the ponies out of the yard and up to a flat part of the field. Some of the boys made Red Indian noises at first, but soon stopped when they realized that they needed to concentrate on the job in hand. We got the ponies going in a largish circle and Vicky stood in the middle to give some elementary instruction.

'Relax your shoulders, Mark, and lower your hands. Stephen, you're sitting very well but you don't need to kick him on all the time – yes, I can see you've ridden before but we don't want trotting at the moment. Mary, your pony is grazing, so use your legs to move him forward. No, he can't feel that, no you won't hurt him. What's the matter, Rory?'

'I feel sick.'

'Look straight ahead instead of down at the ground and you won't feel sick.'

The girls and I took it in turns to stand in the middle while the others led the ponies round. After a while all six children were able to stop and start their ponies quite well and were enjoying their rides. We did half an hour in a circle, then led them round the perimeter of the field so that they could practise steering.

'Alan, don't steer with the reins – Wellington isn't a car you know – just support his head gently and steer with your legs. Imagine the propeller is at the back, that's much better. Remember to keep your heels down, it gives you a better grip.'

After an hour of this, we took a much-needed breather; the sun was so hot that you could see the grass shimmering, and the ponies were sweating heavily. The six children who had been waiting for their rides grew impatient as we swigged mugs of orange squash. Clouds of flies buzzed round the ponies, who swished their tails and hoped we would forget the second hour.

'I'm jolly glad we have the extra ponies,' I said. 'Imagine doing three shifts.'

'Next week we'll have to do more than three,' reminded Sue. 'There are twenty children coming, remember?'

'Perhaps it'll rain.'

How many times did I say 'perhaps it'll rain' in that terrible drought of '76? A million?

The second hour dragged. Apart from the heat, Scott tried to spoil everyone's fun by drawing attention to himself all the time. He had insisted on riding, despite having his leg in plaster, so we had removed both stirrups from Noah's saddle and lifted him into it. His first action was to yank so hard on the reins that Noah barged backwards into Monty, who naturally resented this and bit Noah on the bottom. After we had soothed both ponies, we made Scott hold only on to the neck strap and knotted the reins up out of his reach. Sue led him round and tried to shut him up as lesson two commenced.

'OK, kids. You saw the others stopping and starting, so you know what to do. Squeeze your legs against your pony's sides – *behind* the saddle, Graham – and if you feel wobbly, hold onto your neck strap. Watch how Jos does it.'

Jos glowed with pleasure as she demonstrated, and couldn't resist gilding the lily. She pushed Monty into a collected trot and executed a passable figure of eight.

'Thank you, Jos, get back into line now. All you others copy the way Jos is sitting – head up, nice straight back, heels and hands down. Simon, hollow your back.'

'What does hollow your back mean?' asked Simon, crouched over his pony's back like a jockey.

'It means sit up and push your chest out.'

Simon sat up and pushed his chest out. The pony lengthened

its stride and Simon grinned delightedly. 'It's super!' he cried. 'It feels *much* easier this way.'

Tiny triumphs like this were the reward for all our work, and we treasure memories of children like Simon who, by instantly obeying an instruction, were themselves rewarded by the immediate result.

'Heels down, hands down,' we panted monotonously as the end of the second hour approached. We felt like zombies and our clothes clung to us messily.

'Right. That's it then, kids. Stop your ponies but don't get off. DON'T get off.' Too late. Graham had tried to dismount with both feet still in the stirrups and was sitting under his pony wondering what had happened. The others were laughing – glad it hadn't happened to them.

'You see,' I said, pleased to hammer home two important points before an accident occurred. 'That's what happens if you don't pay attention. The way to get off – dismount – is to take both your feet *out* of your stirrups first, then lean forward and swing your right leg across the saddle before you jump down. Jos will show you.'

Jos showed them. They all copied her with varying degrees of success, and stood, getting back their land legs. I went over to each child in turn and showed how the safety catches on each saddle worked.

'You see how the leather just slides off if you leave the safety catch in the "open" position? Now if you snap it shut – like this – the leather is trapped. If you fall off and the catch is locked shut, you might be dragged along because the stirrup leather doesn't fall off with you. Do you all understand?'

'Graham's safety catches were left open then?' asked Alan, flipping the catch up and down with his thumb.

'Yes. All the safety catches are always left open. You can check them yourself every time you ride just to make doubly sure.'

'Why do they make the catches to lock shut at all?' asked Jos.

'Experienced readers sometimes prefer them locked for jumping and fast cross-country riding. The lock *will* open with a hard jerk, which is what would happen if you fell off when the horse was going really fast. But for you lot, just walking and maybe trotting, I prefer to have the catches open.'

We untacked the hot ponies and stayed for a while to watch them rolling. Each selected his favourite patch of grass before having a luxurious roll – Rocky looked like a little bear and was too fat to be able to roll over completely, so he had to do one side at a time – then they all got up and shook themselves. The children loved the show and tried to make Rocky do it again, but he was too keen to get back to the serious business of the day – grazing. We were beginning to feel a bit peckish ourselves, so we put away the saddles and bridles and went indoors to see about some lunch.

The 3-foot-thick walls of the house had the advantage of keeping it cool, even on the hottest day, and we thankfully took the rolls and fruit through to the dining-room, where the children were helping themselves to mugs of squash. I leaned out of the window and shouted to Brian that lunch was ready. He had stopped weeding and was bending over Toggles, who was tethered under a hedge next to the vegetable patch. He looked up and gestured towards Toggles.

'I do believe Toggles is having her kid,' I said. Immediately the dining-room was in an uproar.

'Can we watch?'

'Does she want some lettuce?'

'My mum says it hurts.'

'Can we call him Butter? Because he butts?'

'You're supposed to boil some water.'

'You have to cut her open with a knife.'

'There'll be lots of blood.'

'Is there a daddy goat?'

'SHUT UP the lot of you. If you want to see the baby goat being born, you can bring your rolls and come and sit quietly and watch. But nobody is to talk at all and it might take quite a long time.'

We shepherded them down the terrace steps and seated them in a semi-circle some little way from Toggles. Leaving the girls to keep order, I walked over to Toggles, who was obviously in the second stage of labour.

'Quick,' Brian whispered. 'Get the camera and we can photograph the birth.'

Hoping Toggles would hold out for a few more minutes, I got the camera and sat in the long grass to watch. Toggles strained and the water bag slowly descended. She rested. Another strain and two tiny hooves were just visible. Brian started shooting frame after frame of the children, who were entranced by their first experience of birth and were amazingly silent. Then Toggles pushed again and the hooves were accompanied by a nose and forehead.

'Good girl,' I murmured, thankful for a normal presentation in view of the attentive audience. One last heave from Toggles produced the whole kid, neatly parcelled in a wet membrane. The children squeaked with excitement and Liz shushed them sternly. I pulled the membrane from the kid and wiped its mouth and nose. 'It's a boy,' I called to the children, and aside to Brian – 'Pity about that.'

The kid staggered to his feet and tottered around his mother. Toggles ignored him, so I rubbed his back with some grass and waited for the afterbirth to appear.

'She'll probably mother him when she's finished,' Brian said. Toggles strained again and this time it was I who was nearly squeaking with excitement.

'*Another* kid – look it's coming.'

It came. Another boy! He joined his brother and they both wobbled up to Toggles.

'Hope the film doesn't run out,' muttered Brian. 'I've taken thirty shots already. Just look at those kids' faces.' He meant human kids: they were all sitting like statues, every atom of attention on the drama before them. Brian managed to get shots of the goats in the foreground framed by the semi-circle of children. 'Should be a good brochure next year,' he grinned.

The afterbirth came away neatly, and we moved Toggles and her sons to a cleaner patch of grass. So far she hadn't taken any interest in them at all. Brian held her collar, while I encouraged the kids to suckle, but as soon as they had got the idea, Toggles kicked them hard. I had to restrain her back legs in order to allow the babies to feed; this was not in the goat book and we hoped she would develop a maternal instinct quickly.

Alas for our optimism. Toggles made up her mind that she wanted no part of being a mum; she hated her twins and lost no opportunity to butt them and kick them.

'I think we'd better get her into her own pen to rest. She might change her mind once she's had a drink and a sleep.'

The girls ushered the children back to the house and sent them upstairs to get their swimming things. Brian carried the little goats and I led Toggles to the yard. We made her a deep bed of soft straw and filled her water bowl to the brim with fresh water. We left her to get acquainted with the babies in peace.

The girls counted heads and towels, pointed the children towards the river and stepped smartly aside as the mob raced down the hill.

The River Otter could have been tailor-made for the pleasure of small children. It is very clean – rumour has it that the river water is the purest in England – and fast flowing, but nowhere is it deep enough for a child to get into danger. Every half mile or so there are sturdy little wooden bridges – 'Pooh Sticks' bridges – where the children could play an endless variety of games. The bridge nearest to our house has 3-foot concrete pipes set in the water and the braver children enjoyed the challenge of wading upstream bent double inside them. The water is always icy cold, since it rises not more than a few miles away, and here and there are tiny natural waterfalls. For people who don't want to build dams or swing from the bridge there are small backwaters full of young trout and other freshwater inhabitants. It would be a strange child indeed who didn't enjoy the river, and our current gang were only driven home by hunger and a wish to see the new baby goats again. They streamed into the kitchen all talking at once.

'We had a super time. Alan nearly caught a fish.'

'Jos wouldn't take her clothes off.'

'Scott threw my boat in the brambles and Liz clouted him.'

'My feet turned blue.'

'What's for tea?'

'I left my flip-flops in the rushes.'

'Parsley swam and her ears floated.'

'I took a photograph.'

'Can we see the baby kids?'

'What's for tea?'

Liz, Sue and Vicky skilfully blocked the doorway to the dining-room.

'We told you to hang your wet swimming things on the line before you came in. No tea until you've done it.'

'I can't reach the line.'

'Mary will help you.'

They all went out again.

'Phew,' said Vicky, 'I could do with a cup of tea. Do you know, they never stop talking?'

'How did they get on at the river?' I asked, dispensing mugs of tea and biscuits.

'They loved it. Scott was a pain in the neck and kept pushing people in, but Liz smacked him and he sulked for quite a while.'

'Not long enough though. He chucked Simon's boat into the bushes and we couldn't make him get it because of his blasted leg.'

'Jos was so funny. She hadn't seen boys naked before and was very Spanish about it.'

'What did she do?'

'Well, she insisted on changing behind a tree so that the boys couldn't see *her*, but she was intrigued to watch *them* changing.'

'I wonder if she'll tell Mama about it when she writes home.'

We finished our tea and started to get the supper things wheeled in to the dining-room. The children poured in and fought amicably over who was sitting where, then sat expectantly, cutlery poised. When the food appeared, a cheer went up and they all set to ravenously. I had made two huge steak pies with home-grown potatoes and peas, followed by raspberry crumble and cream. They couldn't have been more appreciative if they'd had fillet steak and zabaglione.

'That was super,' said Alan, scraping out the cream jug. 'I couldn't eat another crumb.' Alan was a tall ten-year-old with hollow legs, so his mother had warned us. 'I feel sick it was so lovely.'

Egon Ronay couldn't have paid a greater compliment, and I patted heads benignly as I helped clear the tables.

Supper over, we went out to the yard to see how Toggles and the kids were getting on. The kids bleated joyfully and ran across the straw to be petted. Now that they'd dried off, their coats had fluffed up a snowy white, while their tiny hooves were a highly polished black. They were quite perfect and the children were ecstatic.

'We must name them – can I choose their names?'

'It's not fair, we must all choose.'

'Let's have a vote.'

'I choose Snowy.'

'Chalky.'

'Billy.'

'Butter.'

'William.'

'Tippy- toes.'

This open-ended debate would have continued all night, but Liz suggested a secret ballot. This stopped them in their tracks, since half didn't know what it meant, but liked the idea of something secret, while the other half approved the fairness of a vote.

'Everyone will write down a name on a piece of paper,' Liz explained. 'Then we fold the papers in half, put them in a box and shake it up. Then someone who hasn't chosen a name will pick two pieces of paper out of the box and read out the names.' Considering the way the children had been shrieking out the names of their choice, it seemed a bit illogical for them to surround themselves with so much secrecy when it came to the committal of these same names to paper. With much arm shielding and protruding of tongues they solemnly recorded their choices.

In later weeks we, the staff, were to become criminally proficient at ballot rigging, but at this stage we were just bungling amateurs and the little goats got lumbered with the names Bill and Billy. It didn't really matter which was which since, short of cloning, you couldn't have had two more identical twins.

They didn't mind what they were called as long as they had their junior fan club to look after them. Toggles disliked them so intensely and so permanently that it seemed pointless to force her to suckle them five times a day, so shortly after their birth, they were switched to bottle-feeding. The children were delighted and organized themselves into a complicated rota of kid- and lamb-feeding. Actually, the lambs were practically sheep and didn't really need bottles at all, but as it provided such satisfaction for the children, we left them to it.

The thorny question of the ultimate fate of the kids and lambs had not occurred to our first-week children, and we were happy to leave them in their innocence. After much discussion, Brian and I had decided to answer the children's questions truthfully (none of our guests were vegetarian), but not to volunteer information.

This wasn't a problem for the time being, but Scott's behaviour was. Towards the end of the first week it got so bad that we had to consider sending him home. While having the highest regard for the teachings of Reich and A. S. Neill, we felt that our first responsibility was towards the children as a group and that it was not our job to humour a determined troublemaker.

The crunch came when, after a glorious afternoon's mackerel fishing, the children returned home with their catch and started to feed the fish to Phyll and Rosie. Scott was in a particularly spiteful mood since he had been prevented from spoiling the boat trip. He stomped around aiming kicks at the little piglets, knocked over all the buckets of fish and, by way of an encore, pushed one of the small children straight on to the electric fence.

Brian hauled him indoors, leaving the girls and me to redistribute the mackerel – not such an easy task as it sounds, since each child claimed to be able to identify his own fish!

Scott was lectured at length about the evils of bullying,

then sent to his room to think about things. Brian told him that he could have one more chance, but that if he caused any more trouble, he would be sent home.

After the other kids had washed the worst of the fish from their persons and assembled for supper, I went upstairs to fetch Scott. The room, which he was sharing with two other boys, was in chaos. He had thrown most of the clothing out of the window – his own and the others' – then he had turned the room inside-out. All the bedding was strewn around, drawers pulled out and pictures torn. I shut the door on him, went downstairs and telephoned the number that his mother had left with us in case of emergencies. His parents had gone away for their own holiday somewhere in America and were not expected back in England for another week. His grandmother was English and lived in London. She didn't sound at all surprised to hear that we were fed up with Scott and said that she would take him tomorrow if we could put him on a train to London.

Scott showed no remorse for his behaviour and calmly packed his suitcase as though he'd experienced being expelled before. Perhaps he had. At any rate, we were all so relieved to be getting rid of him that nobody could be bothered to ask.

Chapter Nine

Some of the children were staying for two weeks and were envied by the ones who were going home on Saturday. The Welsh children had fulfilled our expectations as regards singing, and the Friday night bonfire was quite a lump in the throat affair once the bawdy songs were over. Even Jocelyn was in tears, and she was staying until September.

The bonfire died down to a red glow and the children lay on their backs and watched the stars appear. They were all rather maudlin from too much singing and the heady night air; hoarsely they exchanged addresses and promises of undying friendships. It was all very sentimental. I liked it when they got to the stage of promising to return to Phyllishayes 'every year until I'm really old' (thirteen!).

As it turned out, the first Saturday change-over was utterly chaotic. We had planned that the day should be programmed with military precision: trains would be met on time, parents would be presented with their own offspring to take home, and new arrivals would be welcomed calmly and sincerely.

I suppose military precision only works if you have trained personnel, faultless machinery and a field-marshal to put it all together. A field-marshal, that is, who doesn't get side-tracked into chatting up the mothers of the aforementioned personnel. We turfed all the kids out of bed at 6.30 a.m., and while they groped for their clothes, we callously stripped all the beds. There was the most amazing amount of straw and earth between the sheets, and by the time the bedding was piled up along the top landing, the place looked and smelt just like the farmyard.

Vicky then went downstairs to start cooking the breakfasts, Sue supervised the children's last-minute packing, Brian went out to feed the animals and Liz and I carried all the laundry downstairs and dumped it in the utility room.

My twenty-year-old Hoovermatic took one look at the laundry and fainted clean away. No amount of wheedling and coaxing and promises of new hoses would wake it up, so I set to and washed the lot by hand. It was nine o'clock before I finally staggered out to the line, thankful for once that it looked like being another scorcher.

It said on our booking form that the holidays ended Saturday a.m. and started Saturday p.m. Obviously it didn't say it clearly enough because shortly after 9.30 a steady trickle of new arrivals appeared in the drive. We were so green in those early days that instead of sending them away until after lunch, we tried to welcome them in. I say tried to because it is quite impossible to give your attention to new people when you know there is hoovering to be done, lunch to cook, departing trains to catch and sobbing children to comfort. (A lot of departing children cried, and we started off by being very kind to them until we discovered that it set the others off.)

Brian was always dreadful on Saturdays, but never more so than on that first one. He enjoyed meeting the parents and had to be dragged into the van and pointed towards Honiton to put some children on the 10.40 a.m. train.

'*Don't* linger in Honiton. You've got to be at Taunton station to meet the 12.50 and back in Honiton for the 1.50.'

'Let me just say goodbye to Alan's mother. I've got plenty of time.'

'I'll say goodbye for you. *Please go*.'

Alan's mother had slim brown legs reaching to her armpits and wore a pretty dress that only just succeeded in containing her bust, which was also suntanned.

'Just off then Mrs…er? Lovely to have had Alan. Hope to see you next year,' (Without your blinking beautiful mother I thought. Anyway, I bet *she* can't milk a cow or deliver a piglet.)

'Thank you for coming. Goodbye.' I flash her a plastic smile and pray she's not going back via Honiton or Brian will never make it to Taunton.

There was a brief lull in activities and the girls and I met in the kitchen for a quick cup of tea.

'How's it going, girls?' I poured five cups of tea.

'Whose is the fifth cup?'

'The TV repair man. Didn't you see the van outside?'

Vicky and Sue burst out laughing. 'We thought he was a father. We asked him which one he wanted. No wonder looked surprised.'

Jos stomped in carrying some shreds of paper. She looked cross. 'What's up Jos?'

'The remaining children and I,' she began pedantically, 'have had the secret ballet to give the names to the children of Small.'

'Ballot, not ballet. What have you chosen for Small's kittens?'

'My choice was not chosen. It's not fair. I chose Pinky and Perky.'

'What were the other names?'

'The white one is to be called Humphrey and the smallest one Smallest.' She spat out the last name scornfully. 'I tell them Smallest is an *adjective* not a proper noun, but still it wins the ballet – ballot I mean. It's not fair.'

'Never mind, you might be lucky with the next animal. There's a puppy coming next week, only it's a secret.'

'A secret!'

Jos danced off in seventh heaven, her disappointment forgotten. There was nothing she liked better than a secret, and we knew that nothing short of thumbscrews would make her reveal it.

We finished our tea and consulted the wall chart to see who was still to go and at what time. There were some parents in the playroom, but until Brian had removed some more departures, we thought we'd better leave everyone in the playroom until there was time to identify them.

Then Liz had a good idea. 'I'll write the new kids' names on labels and pin them on as they arrive.'

'Marvellous. Next Saturday we must be firm about afternoon arrivals only.'

Just then Brian rushed in with a woman in tow.

'Sorry I'm a bit late. This is Mrs Weaver. I've just been showing her around. Any chance of a cup of tea?'

Plastic smile on again. Where the hell does he *find* them?

'How do you do, Mrs Weaver? Do you take sugar? And *Mr* Weaver, is he with you?'

'How do you do. No sugar thank you. What a glorious view.'

'Mr Weaver is bringing Helen's suitcase in,' said Brian blithely.

I glared at him and went to dig out his Taunton departures from the playroom. It was hell in there. Two newcomers were having a pillow-fight and the repaired TV was on full blast. No sign of a parent. The day was taking on a dreamlike quality: I removed the two next victims and ushered them into the van.

'Goodbye kids, hope to see you next year.' I collided with a father.

'Hullo, you must be Mr Weaver.'

'I'm Mr Thompson actually. I seem to have lost my wife. Are you Mrs Addis?'

'Yes, how do you do? I expect your wife is in the kitchen.' She was. Together with Mrs Anderson and Mrs Elliott. Brian was doling out mugs of tea and regaling them with anecdotes about our previous existence in the flower trade; they were loving it, and one of them kept touching his arm as she laughed. I hate people doing this but Brian didn't seem to mind in the least.

'Sorry to break up your tête à tête, ladies, but Brian has to be in Taunton by 12.50.'

I dragged him out of the kitchen door, digging my fingernails into his arm until it hurt.

'You irresponsible oaf,' I snarled, as soon as we were alone. 'Those poor kids must be *roasting* in the van while you sit around like a drone.'

Actually the kids were not roasting in the van: having found it too unbearably hot in there, they had got out again and were nowhere to be seen. I badly wanted a cold drink and a divorce, in that order.

Liz was unpegging the sheets from the line and chucking them into laundry baskets.

'Shall we make the beds before lunch? Sue's finished hoovering upstairs, so we only have to clean the handbasins.'

'Who's looking after the children?'

'Vicky.'

'Who's making the lunch?'

'You are.'

The prospect of making lunch for this mob was daunting. I am innumerate at the best of times, but trying to work out how many lunches were needed for fifteen new arrivals, minus seven departures, plus five staying on, plus ourselves, plus an unknown quantity of parents was too much for the few remaining grey cells. So I cut a foot or so off a long slab of cheese and carried it through to the dining-room together with some fresh loaves, tomatoes and a bowl of apples. The butter in the sideboard was somewhat liquid from the heat, but I didn't care. I found a thick felt-trip pen and wrote 'Please help yourselves to buffet lunch' on a piece of cardboard. Then I banged the dining-room gong and fled to the sanctuary of the kitchen.

Brian's tea party had broken up and only Mrs Thompson remained. She was admiring Small's kittens and Small was purring loudly.

'Ah, Mrs Addis. I wanted to have a word with you about Ian – he gets bitten you see.'

Wearily I filled some large jugs with orange squash and loaded them on to a tray. The noise of the running water and an interruption from Jos, who wanted to know what 'buffet' meant, effectively muffled Mrs Thompson's injunctions about her son's bites. I thought she was going on a bit and merely made appropriate responses like 'Savlon' and 'Anti-histamine cream'. After all, we all got bitten, didn't we? After the bonfire last night (was it only last night?) everyone was covered in midge bites; one of the children called them midget bites.

'But Ruth's all right,' concluded Mrs Thompson. 'You don't need to worry about Ruth.'

'Good. *Thank* you for telling me.' Somewhere from the depths of my inertia, I dredged up the plastic smile – a bit limp by now, but weren't we all in this heat?

'Excuse me.' A small, handsome boy stood in the doorway, patently bewildered by the notice on the door that said 'Private Parts'. It should have read just 'Private' (not that anyone paid any attention to it) but someone had added 'Parts' in black felt-tip and I had forgotten to clean it off.

'Hello dear, come in.'

'Well, actually my parents asked me to find you or Mr

Addis. There's a bedroom with my name on the door, so we took my suitcase in – a girl showed us upstairs.

'Jolly good,' I said in hearty tones. 'Do you like your bedroom? What's your name, by the way?'

'Lee. It says on the door Lee and Johnathan.'

'Yes, I know. Jonathan will be arriving later if Brian hasn't used the train list to clean the windscreen.'

'What?'

'Sorry, I was thinking aloud. Do your parents want to see me now?'

'Well, actually there are two lambs in one of the beds and Mummy thought someone should know. I don't mind,' he said hurriedly, as he saw me getting up a head of steam.

'Actually my cat sleeps on my bed at home, but Mummy thought lambs might, er well...you know?'

I did know. I tore up the stairs and along the landing to Lee's bedroom.

'Mr and Mrs Willett? I'm so sorry about the lambs; they're getting beyond a joke now they're so big.'

Fortunately, the parents were more amused than annoyed, and the blankets looked dry. I called along the landing for one of the girls to remove Charles and Adam.

'Charles,' mused Mr Willett. 'I can see Charles is an obvious choice, but why Adam?'

'Oh, just a whim of my mother-in-law.'

'Would you mind if we had a look round while we're here?' asked Mrs Willett.

'I'd love to have a closer look at these dear little piglets we saw in the field.'

'Of course. I'll show you round.'

The Willett family were so pleasant that it was fun showing them all the animals. Lee ran around excitedly; patted Rocky, found some eggs in the hen-house, wondered at the spotty pigs and enthused over Bill and Billy. Bambi had taken little John away and hidden him in some shady spot, but I promised Lee that he would see all the animals in due course.

'This will do Lee so much good,' said his mother. 'He loves animals and as we live in London, he can only have a cat.'

I wondered if cat singular would like a little friend. I was due to collect two ginger kittens on Monday, as well as the secret puppy, and it was high time I started to distribute some of these surplus babies to good homes. Lee and I waved goodbye to his parents and I asked some of the previous week's children to look after him while I attended to household matters.

Liz, Sue and Vicky looked quite worn out. They had been so busy with work and new arrivals that they hadn't had time to stop for lunch. I shooed them into the kitchen and we had a quick snack and a cup of tea. The breeze from the open window reduced our crimson faces to a fairly unpleasant pink – the outside temperature was in the nineties – and we hurriedly compared notes on the new arrivals. It was thus that Brian found us on his return from Honiton with new boy Jonathan.

Nine-year-old Jonathan was one of those tiring children who ask lots of questions and don't wait for an answer. Brian had tried to shut him up with a Mars bar, but the chocolate slurry all down Jonathan's T-shirt seemed to show that he was a boy who could talk and chew at the same time. Wearily Sue stood up. 'Come on, Jonathan, I'll take you to your room. Have you brought a flannel?'

'I've been stuck in traffic jams a mile long while you lot sit around in the cool,' Brian complained. 'You should see holiday traffic – caravans and caravans – I can't think where they'll all find room to camp.'

The very nicest thing about Phyllishayes is its isolation. Although only 7 miles from Honiton and 12 miles from Taunton, you seldom see evidence of the West Country tourist industry. Visitors are so busy pelting down the A30 that our valley is left for the sole enjoyment of us peasants – a very agreeable state of affairs.

'How many kids have arrived so far?' asked Brian, pouring himself a cup of tea.

Liz looked at her list, so neatly ticked it seemed as though her part of Operation Saturday had gone very smoothly.

'I make it nineteen arrivals and seven departures. There's just Mark Elliott still to come.

'Elliott? I'm sure I met a Mrs Elliott this morning,' said Brian.

'You didn't appear to be on surname terms with any of the mothers this morning,' I said acidly. I was still peeved that he had avoided the irksome parts of greeting the newcomers – getting parent's temporary holiday addresses and emergency phone numbers, prising the children's pocket money from them before it got lost, listing any specific allergies and noting medical treatments. All necessary but tedious.

'I can't help my charisma, can I? Some of us have it and some of us haven't.'

'You don't have to have it in the middle of the kitchen. Why can't you be furtive like other husbands? Entertain them in the hay-barn for instance.'

'What, and miss out on all the cups of tea?'

'I've never heard of a charisma that has to be propped up on PG tips.'

'Mrs Elliott,' said Liz doggedly, 'was the mother of Sharon this morning.'

We all roared with laughter but Liz stuck to her guns. 'And this afternoon's Mrs Elliott will be bringing Mark. Two Elliotts, see?'

'Isn't that the boy who's bringing his ferret?' asked Sue innocently.

'No,' said Brian.

'Yes,' said I simultaneously.

The girls hastily took themselves off.

'No use mate,' I said cheerfully, 'the ferret's a *fait accompli*.'

'Fate worse than death you mean. Ferrets stink *and* bite.'

Mark's ferret did stink, but it didn't bite, as Mark was very sensible about it and kept it in its cage for the first few days, by which time it had made friends with the children who wanted to handle it.

Actually, it proved to be quite an ice-breaker. When Mark arrived and unloaded the ferret cage from the car, he was immediately surrounded by all the other kids, none of whom had seen a ferret at such close quarters before. In no time they were all deep in ferret talk – what doesn't it eat, cor don't it pong, isn't it ugly, isn't it sweet, what's its name and so on.

Mark installed it in a cool corner of the big barn and presented me with several pounds of liver to put in the freezer. I thought this was meant as a contribution to the common food supply and was rather touched until he explained it was ferret food.

'I'm afraid I shall have to ask you for bread and milk though,' Mark said.

'Brown or white bread?'

'Oh, brown of course. My book says white bread is very bad for animals.'

Lovely Mark, lovely ferret.

Thankfully, we waved goodbye to the last parent and settled to take stock of our new brood. Twenty seemed an awful lot more than twelve. For a start they had more feet. I thought it was an optical illusion when I glanced at the row of wellingtons neatly lined up beneath the coat hooks – surely twenty children should have forty wellingtons? I counted them and made it fifty-four. Light dawned and I went in search of my lord and master.

'Did you check the children's luggage when you put them in the van?'

'Naturally.'

'Well, there are fourteen spare wellingtons in the porch.'

'Damn. I'm afraid my mind isn't on wellies in this drought.'

We started a lost property box there and then, but despite our diligence, could have set up our own Oxfam shop by the end of the summer.

Brian and the girls took the children off to start the animal feeding and I set about preparing the human supper. Then, annoyingly, the phone rang. At first I thought it was a hoax call. The person said he was from the BBC and was making a film about unaccompanied children's holidays. Would we be prepared to let ourselves be filmed by the BBC team?

'Hang on a minute.'

Pausing only to chuck a tea towel over a dish of raw meat, I rushed out to the yard and asked Brian and the girls if they wanted to be film stars. They weren't over-enthusiastic.

'I don't want to be gawped at by hordes of cameramen,' said bikini-clad Vicky.

'They'd over-excite the children.'

'The lights would frighten the piglets and ponies.'

'I'd have to shave and wear a tie.'

'We'd have to clean the house all over again.'

'They'd drink beer all the time and tell dirty jokes.' (This was Vicky again.)

I went back to the phone.

'I'm sorry, but the general consensus seems to be that we don't want our week disrupted.'

'But think of the publicity, Mrs Addis. Your farm would be seen in millions of homes. You'd get fully booked for next season.'

'Hm, that's a point. When would you like to come?'

'Well now, let me see. We should like to send an eight-year-old boy to stay with you for a few days prior to filming.'

'A sort of spy do you mean?'

He laughed politely. 'Something like that. One of our team – Diane – has a small boy and we plan to send him ahead of us as we film and ask him to compare the places he stays in.'

'He must be a pretty precocious eight-year-old.'

'Oh, Jeremy is a very debonair young man.'

Jeremy sounded ghastly to me. I should hate to have my eight-year-old son described as debonair. I consulted the diary.

'We have a vacancy on Saturday the 14th.'

'Oh no, I'm sorry. We're working to a very tight schedule. Could you take him on Monday?'

'*This* Monday? No, we're fully booked.'

'He could sleep on the floor. Surely you could squeeze in one more for a day or so?'

He would have to sleep on the floor, the boys' bedrooms only take two beds. 'When do you want to film?'

'Tomorrow week, Sunday the 8th that is. I'll come down on Friday or Saturday and camp – with your permission of course – and the film crew will start work on Sunday and finish on Monday.'

Supper over, we sent the little ones upstairs to get ready for bed and the older ones into the playroom to watch TV. We loaded the washing-up machine and collapsed round the kitchen table for a reviving cup of coffee before the next round – bedtimes.

'This has been the longest day of my life,' I groaned. 'I feel *senile*.'

'It wouldn't be too bad if only it was cooler,' Liz said. 'I don't know how we'll get them to bed in this heat.'

'I should think they're pretty tired tonight, they usually are on a Saturday.'

'Aren't they getting on well? The new kids settled in immediately. Of course, the old kids helped a lot.'

'Rupert didn't grieve for long after Mary went home, did he?'

'About twenty minutes. Directly he saw Amanda he forgot Mary.'

'Little swine.'

'What's the programme for tomorrow?'

'The odious Jeremy has to be met on Monday, so I think I'll collect the puppy and two kittens tomorrow instead of Monday. How about a whole day at the river tomorrow with a picnic? Then they can ride in the evening.'

'What *twenty* rides?' said Vicky in horror. 'We'll die, we'll just die.'

'Oh yes, I was forgetting it being twenty. How about a rota for riding and doing ten a day while this heatwave lasts?'

Liz volunteered to draw up a riding rota and we agreed to arrange for five children to ride each morning and each evening on alternate days. The ponies were not going to collapse on just two hours work a day each, although they did their best to impersonate broken-down Victorian cab horses whenever we prepared them for work. Wellington was the expert at this and always sank his head right down to his knees as though his last gasp had come.

The phone rang. It was BBC David again. The girls and Marcus crowded round the phone to eavesdrop in case it was David Attenborough or even Dimbleby.

'Mrs Addis? We've been having a word with the English Tourist Board. You seem to have a remarkably high staff/child ratio – one to five, is that correct?'

'There are five of us and twenty of them,' I said carefully, sensing a mathematical trap. I wished Brian had answered the phone, he never has to use his fingers for adding up. 'And each girl has a day a week off.'

'Why do you need so many helpers?'

I put my hand over the mouthpiece and giggled hysterically at the girls. 'He thinks we're overstaffed!'

How do you explain to some stuffed shirt who has probably never left his office that twenty high-spirited children need constant supervision? And that while they are being supervised, someone else has to shop and wash and cook for them. And while that someone is doing *that*, yet another is seeing to the care of the pigs, goats, cows, sheep, poultry, ponies and house pets. Not to mention old greenfinger himself, busy trying to grow enough to feed everyone in the worst drought in memory.

I said weakly, 'Would you send your six-year-old anywhere he wasn't properly looked after?'

'Oh, please don't get me wrong, I'm not criticizing, I think it's very good, and so does the Tourist Board. They recommend you very highly, you know.'

'And well they might. Do you know it costs relatively more to board a dog than to send a child here? *And* you have to have a licence.'

'Well, I don't know about dogs. I look forward to meeting you all in a few days' time.

He rang off. A small girl wandered into the kitchen.

'You know you said we could swap beds? Well, we got stuck on the landing. Can you help us please?'

'*Stuck?* -What do you mean stuck, Alison?'

'Sharon. The bed's stuck on the landing.'

We all followed Sharon up the stairs. There was half a bunk bed plus mattress wedged firmly across the landing. Under Jos's guidance, the children had interpreted literally the permission to swap beds.

'Oh, my God.' Brian sat on the top stair holding his head in his hands. 'I wonder if David Thingy would like to swap jobs.'

Vicky leaned helplessly against the wall. 'It's too funny for words,' she spluttered. 'There was Faith going on about them all being properly supervised and all the time this was going on while we sat and drank coffee!'

Chapter Ten

On Sunday, while the children were taken to the river, I collected the puppy and two kittens and hid them in the chalet. The puppy was a cross-bred spaniel, pathetically grateful to be out of the dark shed where I had come across him when looking at some second-hand saddles a dealer had advertised earlier in the week.

With uncharacteristic diplomacy I had stifled the urge to phone the RSPCA and had offered to try to sell the puppy. The dealer hummed and hawed, then said I couldn't take it before Sunday as he had a man coming.

'Didn't the man turn up?' I asked, wincing as the dealer lifted the puppy by its scruff.

'Said he wanted something with more bone.' A lump welled up in my throat as I took the lightweight puppy, weaned on barleymeal and water. 'I'll phone you in a week's time Mr C.'

'Bring it back next Sunday if it's not sold, there's a lady coming dinnertime wants a pup for the kids.'

Next stop the kittens. Two fine, sturdy animals just six weeks old and scheduled for drowning that very day.

'Too many cats on this place,' said the farmer, who looked a kind man.

'But why *drowning*? And why so late?'

'The mothers hide them; we don't see them until they're running around. We give them to six weeks and if nobody wants them they go in the bucket.'

The lump in my throat trebled in size.

'Neutering?' I wheezed.

The farmer tied up the kittens' box with baler twine. 'No sense in that,' he said. 'No money in cats.'

The three refugees took a dim view of car rides and yowled all the way home. The kittens took an even dimmer view of their worming and de-fleaing ceremony and resisted tooth and claw, unlike the puppy who passively accepted his medication. I gave him a small feed laced with vitamins and calcium, which he gulped quickly, then wagging his stumpy tail he clambered into the kittens' box and flopped down to sleep. They batted him on the nose just to show who was boss, then all three curled up and slept.

On Monday morning there was a collective 'Ah' of delight from the children when they saw the new animals. The puppy ventured a yard or so out of the chalet but shot back indoors when he saw the size of the world. The kittens stalked ahead of him, their tiny tails held high like flagpoles. This put the pup in a quandary: should he stay and defend the chalet single-handed or go with his new mates into the crocodile-infested beyond? Friendship won, and he waddled after them up the rockery steps.

Lee swooped on one of the kittens – ginger-coloured – and cradled it in his arms.

'Orlando. You're just like Orlando. I wonder if Mummy…?'

I wondered about Mummy too, and kept my fingers crossed. A ten-year-old girl called Jo took charge of the puppy. She was so sensible and knowledgeable I was surprised to learn that she hadn't had a dog of her own.

'But we're moving house soon and the new house has got a garden. Mummy said I can have a dog then.'

'When are you moving?'

'This week. That's partly why I'm here.'

'Would you like to look after the puppy while you're here, Jo? I'll mix his food and tell you when to feed him, but you could see that he has a regular routine and plenty of sleep.'

Jo sighed happily. 'I'd really love that, thank you. I know how to look after a puppy – I've read lots of books about dogs – and I'll see he doesn't get too much fussing. Precious Pup,' she added.

'Precious Pup?'

'That's what I'll call him.'

Oh crikey, I thought, poor old Jos. But if there was even

half a chance of finding a home for PP, Jos's choice of name could wait.

The children were so occupied with the baby animals that day that they refused the offer of an outing to the seaside and voted to stay at home all day. Small's kittens were getting more attractive now. Bill and Billy were always ready for a game, and even the guinea-pig had obligingly had another litter. It surprised the children that baby guinea-pigs were so immediately interesting compared to baby rabbits, who were nest-bound for three weeks and child-shy for another three.

Brian went off to Taunton to buy some peat and to collect Jeremy from the station. It was Liz's day off, so Vicky and Sue child-minded and I settled down indoors to catch up with the post. Then the peace of the afternoon was shattered by a blood-curdling yell followed by sobbing. I rushed outside.

'What happened?'

Ruth had her arm round her brother Ian who was crying buckets.

'Ruth, what happened?'

'Ian got bitten.'

'Who by?'

'Wellington.'

'*Wellington*? But Ruth, *none* of the ponies bite. Was Ian teasing him?'

'No, he wasn't, I promise you. Didn't Mummy tell you about Ian? He gets bitten.'

'Ruth, listen. People don't "get bitten" just like that. There must be a reason.

Ruth said resignedly, 'Everyone says that, but ever since Ian was a baby, animals have bitten him. He loves animals and never teases them, do you Ian?' Ian shook his head. 'I'm sorry I got bitten again. I've never had a horse bite me before.'

'Tell me exactly what happened.'

I took Ian and Ruth into the kitchen and got out the first-aid box. While I cleaned the wound on his back Ian explained. He had been standing in the ponies' field watching them, when Wellington had wandered over to him, sniffed him and then bitten him. Just like that. I was amazed and disinclined at that stage to believe him. I dabbed witch-hazel over the rapidly appearing bruise and gave him a drink and a biscuit. 'Why didn't you get bitten yesterday?' Even as I said it, I realized how ridiculous it sounded, but Ian thought it a reasonable question.

'We were at the river all day yesterday and I only played with Bill and Billy after tea.'

'And Bill and Billy haven't got any teeth yet,' concluded Ruth.

'Words fail me. You'd better go and fish for newts or something until teatime.'

I went upstairs to Lee's room to make up another bed. Jonathan's mattress was in Mark's room, so I assumed he was making his own sleeping arrangements; it was very convenient if he was, since now I could use his bed for Jeremy. All the bedrooms looked as though a tornado had been through them. We had told the children to treat the place like home. Obviously they all had valets there...

Brian appeared some time later. 'Come and meet Jeremy – he's lovely and you'll love him.'

He was and I did, at first sight. Brian is so spot on sometimes. After all, there are lots of small boys with freckles and no front teeth, so how did he know that this particular one would captivate me so thoroughly?

'Hello, Jeremy. I'm Faith.'

'Hello. Would they be wee goats I saw outside?'

'You're Irish! How gorgeous; they didn't say you were Irish.'

'Did they not?' Jeremy said politely. He was obviously dying to go outside to meet the wee goats instead of standing being inspected. He had fair hair and was on the small side for an eight-year-old, but sturdy and robust-looking. I had imagined him being pale and thin and critical, so his appearance alone was a nice surprise; the bonus was his enchanting personality and soft Irish accent. Brian stood there beaming at us – you'd have thought from his proud expression that he had been personally responsible for manufacturing Jeremy instead of merely collecting him from Taunton station.

'Come on Jeremy, I'll show you round,' he said.

116

'I'll show Jeremy round.'

Jeremy grinned to himself. 'Can you not both show me?'

We went outside and spotted Lee, the boy with the nice parents.

'Lee, this is Jeremy – Jeremy, meet Lee. You two are sharing a room for a few days.' Lee said, 'Hello Jeremy. Will you come and help me collect the eggs? I can't carry them all at once.'

'Surely,' said Jeremy.

'You foreign?' said Lee.

'No, are you?'

'No.'

The two little boys eyed each other for a moment.

'Can you run?' asked Lee.

'A bit.'

'I like races. I'm good at races. You look a bit fat for running.'

'I am too,' agreed Jeremy.

'Oh, by the way, Lee,' I interrupted. 'Why has Jonathan taken his things into Mark's room?'

'He talked all night,' said Lee shortly. 'I told him to shut up.'

'I talk a bit myself,' Jeremy volunteered.

'I think I like talking to you,' said Lee. 'Shall we go and get those eggs?'

For the rest of the week the two boys were inseparable and I used half a colour film trying to record them at play: the golden boy with his sweet smile, and Lee with his huge brown eyes and long legs built for winning races.

Quite apart from the pleasure of having Jeremy that week, we also enjoyed the fact that the group as a whole preferred to stay on the premises rather than go on outings. Brian and I are not all that keen on the seaside, even out of season, and dislike it even more when we have to sit on a scorchingly hot beach and count heads every few minutes.

But Jos loved the seaside and wasn't too pleased that this week's group only wanted to go once. She liked Lyme Regis best because she could spend her pocket money in the kiosks that abound there in high summer. Mostly she bought dreadful plastic jewellery, which she would wrap round her neck and wrists and then rattle up and down in front of us for admiration. She had never had pocket money before, but she made up for lost time and soon mastered the art of getting value for money: value for her, of course, meant quantity, as it does for most eight-year-olds. It was quite staggering what you could buy for 50 pence in 1976: most of the kids would usually manage to get something to wear, something to eat, and something to play with *and* have change from 50 pence.

One outing that the children did enjoy was to Widecombe Bird Gardens, about ten minutes' drive from Phillishayes and therefore no challenge even to the most determined car-sickness sufferer. The Bird Gardens are more like a small zoo and have llamas, rare sheep and miniature ponies, in addition to a huge collection of birds of all descriptions. We used to take the children plus two of the girls up to Widecombe and leave them there for a couple of hours each week, and they would return home bearing trophies and souvenirs bought from the gift shop. I only wish we had been more commercially minded in those early days; it never occurred to us to *sell* souvenirs to the children, they just took them. To this very day poor Noah has a very uneven growth of mane and tail where the children used to cut bits off to remember him by – perhaps they'd have been more careful if we had charged 2 pence a strand!

I packed them all off to Widecombe in the middle of the week so that I could have a few hours free to do a bit of muck-ing out in the house. Normally, we avoided any housework at all except on Saturdays, but I thought if David from the BBC came to do some pre-filming research, he would be so put off by the state of the place that he would call the whole thing off. So I hoovered, and prised bits of yuck from the dining-room carpet, waved a duster at the worst of the cobwebs on the ceiling and decided to ignore the handbasins in the bedrooms. Since we had stopped the water supply to the bedrooms, the children were using the basins to house their collections of pond life, and very nasty they looked. I wondered about a *whole* hard-boiled egg for newts; it looked vaguely obscene bobbing about in the muddy water. I fished it out and gave it to Small, who appreciated it far more than the newts had.

Brian came in to take a breather from weeding and looked round in wonder.

'What day is it?'

'Wednesday.'

'Who's coming?'

'BBC.'

'I wish they'd come every week. Look, you've even done the cobwebs.'

'Don't worry, it won't become a habit.'

'How are you going to stop the kids messing it all up again? The Beeb aren't filming until Sunday.'

'Tomorrow we'll take them to Honiton Show and keep them out as long as possible. Friday they can go mackerel fishing and Saturday it all gets cleaned again anyway.'

'Oh God, Saturday,' Brian groaned.

We both dreaded the coming of Saturday. The drought was now so severe that we were unable to use any tap water at all except for drinking. That meant getting the sheets to the launderette in Honiton early enough to be sure of finding three vacant machines. Also, there was a mind-spinning number of trains to be met both at Honiton and Taunton.

The animals were the ones that suffered most from the water shortage, especially the pigs. Their feet were sore from walking on hot, brick-hard soil and their backs got sunburned very quickly if we didn't rub oil into them regularly. They had enough to drink but were so desperate for water to cool themselves that they would often tip their water trough over and lie in the puddle. The piglets were small enough to squeeze under the pig houses or into the hedges where it was relatively cool: they were about the only creatures who didn't seem to be affected by the heat.

We sat and thought about Saturday for a while.

'How about washing the sheets in the river like real peasants?'

'How about not washing them at all like real peasants?'

'Perhaps it'll rain.'

'Enough of this scintillating exchange,' Brian said getting up creakily. 'I'll go and fetch the kids from the Bird Gardens.'

119

'Will you refill those 5-gallon drums while you're out? There's a standpipe in the village now, so that'll save having to go to the river in the van.'

'You got through that water quickly today.'

'I know. The ponies drink masses.'

'We'll get camels for next year. See you later,' and off he went.

I set the tables for supper and sorted out forty large potatoes for baking. The children had shelled a huge mound of peas for me, so all I had to do was cut some cold meat and boil the peas – a nice easy supper for once. Marcus chugged down the drive on his motorbike, then joined me in the kitchen. His face was all dusty, apart from a clean ring where his helmet fitted. He looked like a miner.

'Spare a drop of water, lidy?'

A few minutes later the children disgorged from the van and rushed into the kitchen.

'Ian's been bitten again.'

'His hand is half missing!'

'Look at all that blood – he'll die, won't he? He'll *bleed* to death.'

Brian brought Ian in. The hand wasn't half missing but the handkerchief round it was crimson.

'What happened, Ian?' I had a distinct feeling of *déjà vu*.

'A peacock bit me – I'm sorry.'

'Peacocks peck.'

'Never mind the alliteration,' said Brian crossly. 'Do something about that hand.' He is not over-fond of bleeding children.

I filled a bowl with water and immersed Ian's hand. Once I had removed the handkerchief, the situation didn't look so dramatic, but the water turned bright red and Ian began to cry.

'Don't worry, Ian. Look, it's only a surface wound.' Ian looked unconvinced, so I poured away the bloodstained water and showed him the peck marks. Three of his knuckles were skinned but the bleeding had stopped.

'Watch this,' Marcus said to Vicky. 'You haven't seen old Mother Culpeper in action, have you?'

'What do you mean?'

'Shut up, Marcus,' I said, 'and make me a bowl of salt water.'

'Saline solution,' said Marcus, pouring water from the kettle, 'is one of her more innocuous cures.' He stirred in a large handful of salt and handed it to me.

'What are the others?' asked Vicky.

'Don't you *know*?' said Marcus delightedly. 'When we were kids, we didn't get cough mixture and antibiotics like everyone else. Ho no, we had herbal concoctions and cobwebs gathered on a full moon. You wouldn't *believe* some of the things she gave us.'

'Marcus,' I said warningly, 'you're frightening Ian.'

'Don't mind me, Ian,' said Marcus. 'Just thank your lucky stars you didn't have a nosebleed.' He and Vicky fished the baked potatoes out of the oven and carried them through to the dining-room.

'Daisies up your *nostrils*?' we could hear Vicky's incredulous voice. 'Did it work?'

Pointedly I applied a liberal sprinkling of antibiotic powder to Ian's washed hand. I didn't know how much of Marcus's remarks he had taken in, but I wasn't taking any chances. And anyway, I was fresh out of cobwebs...

Although they'd enjoyed the Widecombe outing, none of the children wanted to go to the Honiton Show on Thursday; they wanted to build a tree house in the hollow oak tree and train the new kittens to climb up into it. But Brian and I love agricultural shows, so we over-rode their objections and bundled them all into the bus.

Actually, once we were there, the children had a very interesting day. Some of the bigger boys got themselves employed as stall-holders and sold tickets for sideshows. Two or three small ones ended up as lost property and we had to be summoned over the PA system to collect them – this led to some of the others getting jealous, so they pretended to be lost just to hear their names announced in public. Ian got himself bitten by a foxhound, who was tired of being paraded round the ring, but there was a St John Ambulance Brigade in attendance so

I left them to cope. Mark and Jonathan stole a bale of straw from behind one of the tents and put it in the back of the van as a nice surprise for us when it was time to go home; they were surprised and aggrieved that we were cross and made them put it back.

Jo collected lots of free samples of dog biscuits for Precious Pup, and Jos spent the day advising some of England's leading showjumpers how to ride. It was a really fabulous day out and the kids sang all their bonfire songs in the van on the way home; this made them nice and tired, so we dispensed with river washes that night and got them bedded down quickly, before they revived. I gave the smaller ones a cursory wipe over with a damp flannel, but felt this was but a token gesture since their beds were full of half-eaten hamburgers and furry bars of chocolate. Jo generously handed round her free samples of dog biscuits, and as I bade the little girls goodnight, I was glad their mothers weren't there to see their daughters solemnly munching Bonios in bed.

Chapter Eleven

BBC David wasn't Attenborough or Dimbleby. He arrived the next afternoon when the children were busy with animal feeds, and directly he had prised himself out of his car – it was one of those you put on rather than sit in – he seemed spell-bound by the children and animals. Mind you, any art director would find it hard to invent a backcloth like the incredibly peaceful Otter valley, so I suppose he must have thought it a bonus to have it tailor-made, so to speak.

At any rate, he kept saying things like 'sensational' and 'amazing' and 'we must get a shot from here'. He wandered around chatting to the children, who tolerated his questions good-naturedly and carried on with their activities. Rupert and Amanda sat in the shade under the hollow oak tree and fed Bill and Billy. Jo pinioned Precious Pup between her knees and gave him a good grooming with a baby's hairbrush. Mark lay on his back in the grass and let his ferret walk all over him, while Jeremy and Lee supervised the ducklings, who were learning to swim in an upturned dustbin lid. Some of the small girls had made a den out of hay bales and were having a kitten party with dolls' crockery. The kittens didn't like orange juice or penguin biscuits, so the girls kindly consumed the party food and watched the kittens playing Tarzan on the hay bales.

David took all this in and made notes. He saw the eggs collected, the piglets fed, the cow milked and little John Bull given his medicine. (John had picked up a tummy bug from somewhere and was on thrice-daily penicillin.) He asked us if any of the children were homesick or didn't fit in, so we told him about Scott and how we had to send him home.

Soon it was time for the Friday night bonfire – a very small and controllable one in view of the drought – and as before most of the kids cried after they had sung songs such as 'We

Shall Overcome', 'We Are Sailing' and that ghastly Coca Cola song whose refrain I have thankfully forgotten.

After we had tucked them into their evil-smelling beds and confiscated their souvenir mackerels, we repaired to the kitchen for a TV conference.

David explained the set-up. He was part of a team doing a feature for the programme *Nationwide* on unaccompanied holidays for children, and we were next on the list to be filmed. The finished programme would be transmitted in five- or ten-minute sections later in the year.

Jeremy would be briefed by his mother, who was part of the *Nationwide* team, on the morning that filming was to start. Since he was to play a sort of starring role we were asked to wash him thoroughly before filming commenced. David was nice, apart from the irritating affectation of wearing sunglasses in the house, but plainly he didn't know much about eight-year-olds if he thought a thorough wash would last through a day's filming.

Having made quite sure that we understood his requirements for the filming, David took himself off to camp on the grass behind the house. His tent, like his car, was minuscule. It was one of those special ones made for Arctic explorers and Everest climbers, and David had to inch his way through a kind of funnel at one end.

We sat at the open window and watched him until his feet disappeared down the funnel.

'He'll be safe now from the blizzard.'

'Wonder if he wears those sunglasses in bed?'

'Why is he camping anyway – weren't there enough bedrooms for him to choose from?'

'They all smell like Billingsgate. I suppose even that overgrown polythene bag was preferable.'

'Mmm,' we all nodded in agreement.

'Can't we make a new rule – no more souvenir mackerel for the kids?' Brian said.

'They're supposed to put them in the freezer,' I said.

'Then why the hell don't they?'

'They say they can't recognize their own fish once it gets all frosty,' Liz said.

'Can't they write their names on the bags?'

'They've lost the freezer pen. Someone left it up in the tree house. It really would be much simpler to feed all the mackerel straight to the pigs.'

'That's settled then.'

We sat for a while in companionable silence watching the moths bombing in through the window. The night air was lovely; the honeysuckle had got together with the stocks and they made a combined effort to overthrow the mackerel. Nature can be very kind sometimes, but still it didn't rain.

Saturday started deceptively well. Since there was no water to spare for the washing-machine, we just chucked all the sheets and pillowcases into bin bags and put them in the van ready for the first trip to Honiton. Brian would smile sweetly at the lady in charge of the launderette, cross her palm with silver and we should have clean bedding coming back with the 2.23 train arrivals.

There were fourteen new children expected, and six staying on for a further week. I didn't know what to do about Jeremy, so I assumed he would be going on Sunday evening after the filming had finished. Meanwhile, we put him in a small double room with Rudi, son of the European parents who had witnessed the sad demise of Phyll's piglet on their pre-holiday visit.

Brian threaded string through fourteen pairs of wellingtons and looped each pair round the appropriate neck with the injunction to stay like that until it was time to go. Naturally, this led to all sorts of new games; chucking wellies up the stairs, putting wellies on hands *and* feet (the lost property box was raided for this one), yodelling into a wellie and so forth.

We tried to persuade all the kids to watch Swap Shop on TV until it was time to go, but the TV was on the blink again and was showing the picture through a haze of snowflakes; this failed to hold their attention, so we gave up and I went to phone the TV rental firm yet again. They were extremely courteous as usual and promised to try to get a repair man round later that day.

By ten o'clock everything was running well. The girls were

125

hoovering upstairs and bravely emptying all the handbasins, I had washed up the breakfast things and started to prepare lunch, Brian had loaded all the suitcases into the van and all the children were present if not correct.

Most of the children who were staying on wanted to go to the station to wave goodbye to their friends. Brian looked at me imploringly, but I hardened my heart.

'Do take them, Brian, it'll get them out of our way for part of the morning.'

'But how can I cope with them at the station? They'll get on the train and fall on the line.'

'They can't do both. You could leave them in the launderette while you go to the station. They won't come to any harm in the launderette for ten minutes.'

'Oh, all right, but don't blame me if I lose a few.'

The van lurched up the drive looking a bit like a centipede with all the kids waving their wellington-clad hands out of the windows. Someone had written FAREWELL FILISSHAY in the dust on the back doors. David thought this was 'amazing' and made a note of it.

I finished making three dozen cheese and tomato rolls and put them away in the larder with tea towels over them. We had decided to be firm with any new parents who arrived in the morning and send them away again until after lunch; this meant far less food to prepare and less chaos in the morning.

'Faith.' A forlorn Jeremy stood at the door fighting back tears. I scooped him indoors and sat him on my lap.

'What's up, Jeremy?'

'Lee's mummy and daddy are here. Oh, Faith, I wish Lee didn't have to go home. I wish I didn't have to go tomorrow too. Bill and Billy will miss me and they'll feel sad inside of them.'

'We'll all miss you, Jeremy, you're the nicest eight-year-old Irish boy called Jeremy that I've ever met.'

He pondered on this for a moment and then chuckled. 'Sure and there's not many of those here.'

I wiped his damp face and stood up. 'Shall we go and see if Lee's parents will let him keep the ginger kitten?'

126

Jeremy held tightly to my hand as we went to look for Lee and his family. We caught up with them at the chicken house, where Lee was demonstrating how he collected the eggs from the nesting boxes.

'Mummy, this is my friend Jeremy. We shared a room all the week and he's not foreign – they all talk like that where he comes from and Faith says we can have Orlando if you say yes.'

'Lee, one thing at a time!' Mrs Willett looked at me enquiringly.

'Who is Orlando?'

'He's a ki – good God,' I said. Lee had lowered the flap of the nesting boxes and revealed Orlando curled up in the hay.

'This is Orlando, Mummy. I put him here so as not to lose him before you came.'

'He's very pretty,' said Mrs Willett, lifting Orlando off three eggs. Both little boys moved in swiftly for the *coup de grâce*.

'He's house-trained,' said Lee.

'And wormed.'

'And friendly.'

'And an orphan without a mummy *or* a daddy to look after him.'

Jeremy's Irish background was very evident sometimes, and I silently applauded his professionalism as he concluded with a guileless: 'The poor wee thing.'

We found a nice roomy cardboard box for Orlando and poked some air holes in it with a potato peeler. Jeremy and I stood in the drive and waved to the Willett family until the car was round the corner.

'I'm glad that Lee got his wish,' said Jeremy, looking his old cheerful self again. 'It means I shall get my wish too.'

'What's your wish, Jeremy?' I hoped it was another kitten.

'It's unlucky to tell your wish. I'll tell you tomorrow when my mummy comes. Will I go and get you some fresh grass for the guinea-pigs?'

'Where from? The whole place looks like the Sahara.'

'There's some long grass growing where the stream comes into the ponies' field. And some dandelions.' He collected an empty bucket and wandered off on his errand.

He was hardly out of sight when Sue called out of the window, 'Faith – a parent on the phone.'

'Hello, Mrs Addis speaking.'

'Hello, I'm Mrs Baker – Garry's mum. We've put Garry and on the train, so I thought I'd let you know.'

'Thank you, Mrs Baker.' I consulted the list pinned on the wall by the telephone. 'That's Garry and Craig, isn't it? Arriving Honiton 2.23?'

'Yes. I hope they're good boys, they're a right pair of bleeders at home, but you just give them a good clout if they give you any lip. Garry's got the return tickets and the pocket money in an envelope but I've told him to give it to you straight away or he'll spend it.'

'That's fine, Mrs Baker, don't worry about the boys, we'll look after them.'

'I'm not worried about the boys. Craig's mum'll phone tonight when she gets a minute from the bar.'

'The bar?' Was Craig's mum an alcoholic? Or a barrister?

'You know – the pub. His mum and dad run a pub. Anyway, there's the pips. All the best, sooner you than me, cheerio.'

'Cheerio.'

'Who was that?' Sue asked.

'The mother of one of a pair of right bleeders.'

'Did she *say* so? His own mother?'

'Yep. Never mind, forewarned is forearmed I believe. What time is it?'

'Gone eleven.'

'Brian should be back soon, then. He's got to get Ruth and Ian to Taunton by twelve.'

Liz had skilfully vetted all the cars inching down the drive and had admitted only those parents who were collecting their offspring. There were an awful lot of them and they all congregated in the dining-room, eagerly accepting my half-hearted offer to make them some tea.

Soon there was a nice air of conviviality and the fathers exchanged horror stories of traffic hazards, miles per gallon and other motoring news, while the mothers heard all the children's news at high speed and full volume. From what I could hear in the hubbub, it appeared that the highlights of the holiday had been the calf's gastro-enteritis and the freedom from hot baths. It sounded more like Cold Comfort Farm than the Boy Farm of our dreams. Where, I wondered, were the lyrical descriptions of riding ponies at twilight, finding new-laid eggs in the hedges, exploring the river, seeing a kingfisher and a heron? Where indeed?

'John's diarrhoea went all up the wall, Mummy, it really did.'

'Oh dear, poor child.' (Screams of laughter.)

'John's a calf, silly. John Bull – he's a *bull* calf you see.'

'Rupert ate a tadpole for a dare.'

'You should see where Ian got bitten.'

'...and his feet didn't half stink.'

'So that's why my hair's dirty – didn't you see it on the news – the worst drought in history?'

'Sometimes we don't even pull the chain.'

'Please, Mummy, *please*.'

I pricked up my ears at that one. Helen, daughter of one of Brian's tea-party ladies, was manipulating her mother into a kitten acceptance. She was not as good as Lee, but then she didn't have Jeremy as an ally: even so, she was nearly home and dry. Her mother had agreed to go and look at it – 'Only *look* mind, I'm not promising...'

Jeremy, handing round the biscuits, gave me a cheeky wink and a thumbs up sign.

'Sure is a good day for kittens,' he whispered. 'Will we get some more for next week?'

The significance of his question was lost on me at the time because Brian rushed in with the six children in his wake.

Thanks to the presence of the collecting parents and the din that the children were making, I couldn't quite make out what was causing Brian to be in such a lather. He gulped down a mug of tea and between exchanging pleasantries with the parents managed to disclose something about that bloody ferret in the launderette being the last straw. David, who had come indoors to cool off, whipped out his notebook. 'Amazing,' he murmured scribbling away busily.

'What last straw? What are you talking about?'

'The *numnahs*, idiot. She wouldn't accept the numnahs. And then that bloody boy's bloody ferret...

The parents had gone quiet and were listening with interest to Brian gibbering. It must have sounded like some sort of quaint Devon bartering system – I give you twenty numnahs for your ferret and two goes in your washing-machine – and they waited for the climax.

'And then she said people had even tried it with New Zealand rugs in September, so I just grabbed the kids and got out.'

'Oh, dear.' Light was beginning to dawn. I checked Ruth and Ian for wellies and train tickets and ushered them out to the van. 'Goodbye kids, don't get bitten by the train, Ian.'

'Goodbye, thank you for having us.'

I handed Brian the next list of train times and waved to the van as it pulled off again. Then I went in search of Jos.

I was waylaid by Jonathan's mother. 'Excuse me, Mrs Addis, but what is a numnah?'

'A saddle cloth.'

'And what is New Zealand rug?'

'A thick horse blanket with a canvas outer cover.'

'I see. Thank you.'

I don't think she did see. Not what I saw, which was poor Brian accompanied by six gypsy-like children and a loose ferret trying to pacify an irate launderette lady. I was rather surprised that she had accepted the forty fishy sheets. I would much rather have horse sweat in my washing-machine than fish scales.

Jos was in the tack room replacing the unwashed numnahs on the saddle-racks.

'Jos, did you take the numnahs to the launderette this morning?'

'Of course. They are very dirty. At home we have our laundry done every day, not just once a week.'

'Yes, I know you do, but you've got servants, so don't start that old flannel again.'

'Flannel?'

'Never mind. Look, I know you meant well but please don't

have any more bright ideas on a Saturday. Would you like to wash these things yourself?'

'Me? Wash with soap powder? Ooh, yes *please*. I would like to do so very much.'

'All right then you can. You'll have to fill a plastic bowl with warm soapy water and wash them one at a time. Then you can rinse them tonight in the river when we go down for our wash.'

Jos occupied herself for the rest of the morning with her washing and I wondered if she would mention it in her weekly letter to her mother. 'Dear Mama, today I did the ponies' laundry. It was very hot kneeling on the cobblestones in the sunshine and my hands went all crinkly after two hours...' Jos always wrote to her mother in Spanish, so we never knew what she said. Her father had written to us several times saying that he was pleased that Jos was happy with us and hoped that her English was fluent. Some of her more fluent phrases would have been more appropriate on a building site, but hopefully she would forget them when she was restored to her genteel family in September.

I was still day-dreaming when Helen skipped into the yard. 'Can I have a box for the kitten, please? We're ready to go now.'

Kitten number two was safely stowed away in a box and Helen put it on the back seat of their car. A tiny paw appeared at one of the air holes, to all intents waving goodbye.

Parents, children, wellingtons and souvenirs were seen safely into cars and waved off. It was blisteringly hot and I didn't envy anyone driving in holiday traffic. We flopped down in the dining-room and ate our rolls and fruit, thankful for the relative cool of the house. It did seem strange to have only seven children: we were all able to sit round one table and chat.

'A parcel came this morning addressed to Wellington and Monty, did you see it?' said Jo.

'No where is it?'

'I put it by the phone with the rest of the post. Shall I get it?'

'Thanks. I'm too hot to move.'

Jo handed me the parcel. The children watched excitedly as I unwrapped it, then looked utterly mystified as I laid out four fly-fringes on the table.

'What are they?'

I read them the accompanying letter. It was from Sue and Keith. 'We were at a horse show last week and noticed lots of horses wearing these fly protectors. Thought the ponies might appreciate them in this heat. See you in September, love Sue and Keith.'

'Great,' said Vicky. 'We can put them on after lunch.'

'How do you put them on?'

'Like a brow-band. The ponies can wear them on their head collars all the time and we can slip them on to their bridles when they're working.'

We quickly finished our snack and carried our plates through to the kitchen. Tony was there brewing himself a huge pot of tea.

'Hello Faith, hello girls.'

'Are you going to drink *all* that tea?'

'Course not. I met Sid on the way down and he wants a cup.'

'Sid?'

'TV repair. He's gone in the front door.'

'Sid? We had George last week.'

'I don't know about George. This one's called Sid. Be a good girl, Vicky, and ask him if he wants sugar, will you?'

Vicky went through to the playroom and came back grinning. 'He says no sugar thank you, but could he have the pleasure of murdering the last child who touched the TV.'

Tony poured two mugs of tea and I took one into the playroom.'

'I'm so sorry to have to get you to mend it again,' I apologized. 'It's the children – they can never agree about which programme to watch.'

Sid sat back on his heels and said sternly: 'You'll have to put Sellotape over the push buttons. Television sets just can't cope with being fiddled with all the time.'

'I know just how they feel,' I sympathized. 'And we really

will make an effort this week, I promise. It's a good idea to put Sellotape over the switches. I should have thought of it myself.'

'Are they maladjusted kids?' asked Sid curiously. 'George said it was a sort of Borstal.'

'No, they're not, they're just high spirited because they're on holiday I think,' I said rather lamely. I really couldn't think of any possible excuse for having to have a brand new rented TV repaired four times in the last two weeks.

Leaving Sid to wrestle with the mysteries of the television set, I went back to the kitchen to show Tony the ponies' new presents.

'Lovely,' said Tony, dutifully admiring the fly-fringes, 'how about a dab of eau de Cologne on their foreheads too? Spoilt buggers only doing two hours' a day!'

'Come off it, Tony,' I protested. 'It was *your* idea to put them on a two-hour day in this heat. You remember? You said you'd seen a pony die of heatstroke at a gymkhana the other week.'

'Did I? That was kind of me. Wish I could work a two-hour day; this heatwave's getting me down. Do you want to see young Rocky's new shoes? I made them this morning.'

He laid the set of shoes out neatly on the table next to the fly-fringes. They were exquisitely made; the back pair measured 2¼ inches across and the front pair 3 inches.

'They're super, aren't you clever to make them so tiny,' said Vicky.

'Yes, I am. I'll put them on when I've had some more tea. Where's Brian today?'

'Fetching new kids from Taunton and Honiton.'

'Poor old Brian – the holiday traffic's murder,' said Tony.

We went outside and were practically cremated by the sunshine. It bounced back off the concrete and seared into our rubber-soled shoes. Looking up the drive, everything was viewed through a shimmering haze and it looked as though even quite large bushes and trees would die of thirst; their leaves drooped pathetically and were already turning brown.

I wondered how the filming would go tomorrow. Perhaps

they would opt for a sort of Impressionist tableau of the place, with the children and animals melting into the horizon...

To my disappointment, the ponies did not leap about with delight when they were fitted with their new fringes later that day. In fact, I don't think they even noticed them since they just continue grazing after we had fastened them on. They looked very amusing, though, peering through the leather thongs. Up until then we had been soaking pieces of cotton wool in fly-repellent oil and securing them to the ponies' head collars, so now, what with their fringes and cotton wool, they looked somewhat overdressed at the head end. Their tails should have been down to the ground, but overcropping by the souvenir-hunting kids had shortened all their tails by at least 12 inches.

It was very pleasant idling in the shade and admiring the ponies, but all too soon we heard the familiar crashing of the Transit's first gear as it came slowly down the drive.

'I wonder what would happen if the brakes failed coming down the drive,' observed Mark.

'It would go through the larder window.'

'And have to turn left at the sink!'

Convulsed at their own wit, the seven children ran back to the house to meet the newcomers. The girls and I followed slowly, knowing that in addition to the new children to see to, there would be forty sheets to wrestle on to twenty bunk beds.

Chapter Twelve

It was unfortunate that the week the BBC had chosen to film us was the one week in the whole of the holiday season that we found ourselves playing host to no fewer than four 'dumped' children; children, that is, who had not chosen to come but who were sent by parents who wanted to get rid of them.

Not that dumping in itself is a crime. I can't think of many mothers who have not occasionally longed to see the back of their offspring for a while, and more often than not, the dumpees will bite on the bullet and find, to their surprise, that they can enjoy themselves away from home.

We should have realized that the holidays we were offering in 1976 would be open to this kind of abuse because (a) we were in our first season and glad of any bookings and (b) we were very, very good value for money.

We charged £28 per week, and for this the children received full board and lodging, riding, seaside outings, mackerel fishing and visits to places of interest. There were no extras at all; we paid for all the treats. The children brought pocket money with them, but this was for spending on presents for their families or on novelties at the seaside.

Brian unloaded the eight children he had collected from the stations and we introduced them to the six (seven, counting Jeremy) who were staying on. Jos and Sharon were very pleased to be asked to show the new girls where everything was, and once again Mark's ferret proved a big hit with the boys.

While they sorted themselves out, under Sue's tactful observation, Liz and Vicky went upstairs to make the beds and Brian and I received the last of the arrivals who were coming by car.

Gavin's parents were the first to finish their tea; they had rushed through our little chat – it was too informal to be termed an interview – and were eager to be on their way. They told us they'd booked themselves into the Cornish hotel where they'd spent their honeymoon.

'It's only for a week, old man,' said Gavin's father, pressing a £10 note into the boy's hand. 'You be a good boy, mind. All this fresh air will do you good.'

Gavin's mother had the grace to look a little guilty. 'We'll ring you every day and I'll bring you a nice present,' she promised.

He might have had the present, but they didn't phone once.

It was getting on for four o'clock when Liz ushered in the last family. 'Mr and Mrs Wordsworth,' she announced, 'and a boy and girl.'

'William and Dorothy?' Brian said, smiling archly to show it was a joke.

'Ha ha,' I contributed, wishing he would stop these opening salvos. (He had said 'Never say Dai' to some Welsh parents once, and that had gone down like a lead balloon too.)

'Clint and Marilyn,' said Mr Wordsworth, one of those unsavoury middle-aged men who wear denim shirts unbuttoned to the foothills of the belly. 'You got the reservation, didn't you?'

'Reservation?' echoed Brian, who had now spotted the various items of hoof and horn depending from leather thongs around the neck of Wordsworth senior.

'Booking form,' I said, trying to allay confusion. 'Clint and Marilyn Wordsworth. Remember?'

Products of the one and nines, Brian, the ones we made up that Ron and Eth sketch about when we had the booking, remember?

He remembered.

'Clint and Marilyn, how nice.'

Then Mum Wordsworth, the most corrosive member of this charmless family, took control and launched into a boring soliloquy about the achievements of 'my Clint', the least of whose accomplishments appeared to be an ability to generate solar energy from his backside.

Clint waited until Mum ran out of steam, then prompted, 'You didn't tell them about my judo.'

'Sorry, son, I was just comin' to that. My Clint, he goes to judo four nights a week and he's got his belt...'

'What colour, Clint?' I interrupted.

'What?' said Clint.

'Your judo belt. What colour are you up to?'

Clint fixed me with a look – he had cold blue eyes – and said nothing. Brian lit his fourth cigarette and said pleasantly, 'Faith's hobby is judo. She's got a green belt. What colour are you up to?'

'Clint's is red,' said Mum proudly. 'That's nearly black Clint says.'

'Yes, nearly,' I agreed heartily. 'He's only got six to go before he gets to black.'

'Six?' said Mum. 'No, that's all wrong, you tell 'em, Clint.'

'Six,' I said firmly. 'The colour sequence is first red (for novice), then white, yellow, orange, green, blue, brown and black.'

I felt childishly pleased to have scored off the revolting boy. He was thirteen and big for his age, and he would have been handsome if it hadn't been for that give-away mouth, which reminded me of the unfortunate Scott's. He *couldn't* have been going to judo four nights a week: if he had, he should have gained at least a white belt by now.

Common courtesy dictated that we should go through the motions of welcoming all our guests impartially, but our instincts told us to return this family's deposit and show them to the door.

'And the girl won't be no trouble, will you, Marilyn?'

Poor, apathetic Marilyn, programmed from birth to accept the family religion of Clint worship, shook her head. At last the parents rose to go.

'One last thing, Mrs Wordsworth – the children's pocket money.'

'Clint's got it in his wallet. £35 each we've given them.'

'£35! Mrs Wordsworth, that's *far* too much. A pound or two will be plenty.'

Mum pursed her lips stubbornly. 'It's their money. I've give it to them now, so it's theirs. And Clint'll mind it so as Marilyn don't lose it.'

'No, Mrs Wordsworth,' said Brian, 'I will *not* have a thirteen-year-old carrying £70 around with him. I take charge of all the pocket money and dole it out when we go to the shops.'

'You'll have to sort it out with Clint, Mr Addis, but I'm telling you for your own good that you'd better let him have his own way.'

'Clint and Marilyn will be treated exactly the same as all the other children,' said Brian coldly, postponing the question of the pocket money until we got rid of the parents. Mr and Wordsworth were going on a touring holiday, so they couldn't leave any forwarding address of their own. Instead, they gave us Auntie Beryl's neighbour's number, which they assured us would reach Auntie Beryl in case there was an emergency.

After the senior Wordsworths had gone, I took Marilyn to her room, leaving Brian to relieve Clint of the £70. I called Jos upstairs and introduced her to Marilyn.

'Marilyn, this is Jos. She's been staying with us for quite some time, so she can help you to unpack and then show you round.'

Jos loved helping the new girls unpack. She would examine each garment separately and compliment its owner on the style or colour, before carefully folding it and putting it into a drawer. Marilyn sat silently on her bed while Jos organized her clothes, as I left them to get acquainted in peace and went down to see how everybody else was getting on.

Garry and Craig turned out to be delightful boys, full of fun, quick-witted and friendly.

'Wotcha,' they greeted me cheerily. 'Ain't it smashing – all them animals – we're gonna be on the telly tomorrer.'

'Hello boys. How do you know about the telly?'

'Jeremy told us. Are they gonna take pictures of that poor calf – it's all shitty?'

'I expect they'll just photograph the head end,' I said, wondering at the unfailing attraction of John's diarrhoea.

Liz, Sue and Vicky came over and we sat on the grass for

a moment while the old children introduced the new children to all the animals. We compared notes on the new arrivals, and I was dismayed to learn that the girls thought we had at least two misfits among the kids they had welcomed in: they weren't talking but Clint and Marilyn, who were still indoors with Brian and Jos.

'Show me the two you mean,' I asked. Liz indicated a tall girl sitting under the oak tree, and Rudi, who I already knew slightly.

'Rudi?' I was surprised. 'But his parents brought him for a visit some time ago.'

'Have you spoken to him?' Sue asked.

'Not really. Jos took him off on a conducted tour and the parents didn't stay long.'

'I think he's a bit backward,' said Sue. 'He talks like a three-year-old, but you wouldn't notice if Jos was there talking nineteen to the dozen.'

'Oh crikey, what a fool I am not to have noticed. Tell me about the tall girl now – might as well get all the bad news over quickly.'

Liz said, 'She's called Cordelia and she's done nothing but criticize since she arrived. That chubby girl next to her is her friend – they came down by train together – and she's very nice. She's been trying to get Cordelia interested in exploring, but Cordelia's in a bit of a sulk.'

'Oh well, that doesn't sound too bad,' I said hopefully, 'sulks can't last a whole week.'

Then I told them about Clint, and asked them to keep a sharp look-out for any signs of bullying.

'Thank goodness we've got Mark for another week,' said Vicky, 'he can keep Clint in order, I should think. Have you noticed the way he creates diversions if the kids start to bicker? He's a born diplomat.'

'Two of the girls have brought riding hats and grooming kits,' said Liz.

'Hooray. And Garry and Craig are sweet – not right bleeders at all – so all things considered, this group should get on all right.'

Soon it was time to see to animal feeds and have supper. Jeremy, Garry and Craig volunteered to lay the tables for me, and I tried to include Rudi with them to make him feel at home. Poor little kid. I realized that Sue was quite right about his being backward; he leaned against the wall and sucked his thumb, while the other three boys skidded cutlery across the tables. Soon he started to cry and I had to ask Sue to come indoors and comfort him while I got on with the supper.

'Want my mummy,' he sobbed, but his mummy – and his daddy for that matter – had flown off to Italy for two weeks, leaving no kindly granny for us to telephone. Sue was marvellous with him and in the next two weeks developed a very close bond with him; it was always Sue he ran to in times of stress, and she normally managed to cheer him up quite quickly.

During supper, Brian told the children about the BBC coming to film them tomorrow. They reacted in various ways, from wild excitement to 'What a bloody bore' (from Cordelia). Mark wanted to know if he could show his ferret, and Jo was determined that Precious Pup should outshine Lassie with his cleverness. Jos planned to resurrect her Spanish dress for the occasion, but, in the event, changed her mind and appeared in gumboots, anorak and umbrella to show how English she was. Anne and Alexandra, who were pony mad, decided to get up early and brush all the ponies before breakfast.

Supper was interrupted four times by phone calls from parents who had sent their children by train. The phone was situated in a cubby-hole behind the dining-room door, and all conversations were audible in the dining-room. Each child wanted to speak to its parent, and we overheard three almost identical conversations, the gist of which was that the farm was smashing, super and great, the animals ever so friendly, gorgeous and great and the children's supper smashing, delicious and great. Craig added that he was going to be on the telly tomorrer, and wasn't that smashing?

Then Cordelia was summoned to the phone to speak to her mother.

'Yes, or course I've arrived safely, you stupid bitch...no, it's bloody horrible, so I hope you're satisfied...'

We were surprised to hear that the farm was 'bloody horrible', 'a sort of hostel for babies', and that there was nowhere to wash. Cordelia's poor mother must have wished she hadn't bothered to phone, especially as Cordelia hung up on her in mid-conversation before flouncing out of the back door. Her little friend Hannah looked embarrassed, and to cover up, started asking Alexandra and Anne how to brush a pony.

It would seem that Liz's estimation of Cordelia's plight was correct; she hadn't wanted to come and was going to sulk for as long as possible. The children sitting at Cordelia's table cashed in on the situation and polished off her peaches and ice cream, sharing out each spoonful with meticulous fairness.

Each child was expected to put his empty plate and cutlery on the trolley when the meals ended. Clint, fortified by his supper and Cordelia's attitude, decided that a show of strength was required. He refused to carry his plate to the trolley and sat in his place tipping his chair back insolently as all the other children jostled round the trolley. Marilyn ran to collect his plate but was forestalled by Brian.

'Off you go, dear. I'll help Clint with his plate.'

'No, I don't mind, honest.'

Liz, Sue and Vicky tactfully sent the children to fetch sponge bags and towels from their rooms ready for the evening wash in the river. Marilyn was carried along in the general rush, and soon the dining-room was empty, except for Clint still tipping his chair, and Brian, who prepared to sit with him until the plate was put on the trolley.

I withdrew to the kitchen and put the milk on a low heat so that it would be ready for the bedtime cocoa when we all got back from the river. Jeremy came in after a while, leading Rudi by the hand.

'I've had a wonderful idea, Faith,' he whispered, poking his finger into the creamy milk and sucking it with relish.

'What's the whispering for, you toothless monster?' I whispered back.

He gave me a bear hug and pulled me down to his level so that he could whisper properly.

'Let's you and me and Rudi have a secret together.'

'Okay. What is it?'

'Let's go down to one of the other bridges tonight, just the three of us. A secret expedition.'

'That *is* a lovely idea, Jeremy. I'd enjoy a break from the herd. I must tell the girls where we're going, though, but it'll still be our secret.'

Liz was appalled. 'This shameless favouritism has got to stop, Faith. You and your Jeremy. What happened to scrupulous fairness and treating him just like all the others?'

'I'm taking Rudi too,' I said defensively, but the girls were not fooled. Still, they started off for the river first and we waited until they were out of sight then started off ourselves.

'Faith?'

'You don't need to whisper now, Jeremy, they've gone.'

'You know you said Rocky is getting a wee bit fat?'

'Yes,' I said, guessing what was coming.

A short time later the two boys were sitting on Rocky's fat, bare back, Jeremy in front holding on to Rocky's mane and Rudi holding on to Jeremy's waist. Rocky's tiny new shoes clopped importantly through the lanes and I told the boys that the fairies had made the shoes as no human could make them small enough. This gave Jeremy an opportunity to bring up to date on the latest fairy news from Ireland, and we discussed leprechauns, rainbows, crocks of gold and the exchange rate for a front tooth.

The elves and pixies who had accompanied us on our walk down to the river didn't want to go in the water. Jeremy said that land fairies didn't like getting their feet wet and would prefer to sit with me on the river bank. Some cousins of theirs – wood nymphs and water sprites – were already playing in the river and invited the little boys to join them.

I helped Rudi to undress, then both boys waded into the cool water. Jeremy instructed Rudi in the art of catching sprites – you have to creep up behind them and grab – but the sprites were too quick for them and slithered through their fingers.

The evening air was so charged with magic that even Rocky forgot his stomach for a while and stood beside me on the bank, ears pricked, watching the water intently. The boys tired of catching fairies and made up a sort of underwater clog dance.

When they'd had enough, and before they turned blue, I fished them out and enveloped them in bath towels. One at a time I sat them on my lap and rubbed their hair dry.

'I wish I could stay here for ever,' Jeremy said suddenly. Rudi nodded agreement. He felt safe and happy.

Idly, I shared out a big bar of Cadbury's fruit and nut; I was miles away, remembering how one of my own kids had said he wanted to stay forever playing in a little river in a valley. I reflected that the Chinese proverb 'Be careful what you set your heart on for you will certainly attain it' was dead right for once...

'Faith, what are you thinking?'

'Sorry, Jeremy, I was dreaming. What did you say?'

'I said Rocky was going to eat your chocolate, but it's too late now – he has.'

'Rocky, get your great hairy face out of that bag,' I said, trying to sound stern. The boys giggled and Jeremy started to compose a couplet rhyming 'Rocky' with 'chocky', but it was not his day for artistic endeavour and the poem was as clumsy as the dance.

I dressed the boys and tried to teach Rudi how to buckle his sandals. He was as wooden as Pinnochio and had about as much brain. Poor little blighter, I thought, as I swung him up on to Rocky's back. I wondered why nature had endowed one boy with looks, intelligence, physique and charm and the other with so little.

On the way home, walking slowly this time, as it was all uphill, Jeremy told me about his family. He was looking forward to seeing Mummy tomorrow, and not at all apprehensive about the filming. We talked about Ireland and school and Jeremy's small sister, who was as brave as a lion. Daddy came across as someone possessing the wit of Clive James and the looks of Dave Allen. I was quite sorry it was Mummy we were to meet and not Daddy.

Chapter Thirteen

Brian and I overslept on Sunday morning, despite putting the alarm to go off at 6 a.m. Clint had kept us awake until nearly 2 a.m. by crashing along the landing and opening all the bedroom doors after all the other children had gone to sleep. He started this at about ten o'clock and woke half the younger children, who then had to be settled down again. Then he locked himself in the lavatory so that everyone he had woken up was compelled to use the downstairs one.

At about midnight, and with murder in his heart, Brian told Clint that if he got out of bed once more he would be locked in the van for the rest of the night, though we hoped we wouldn't have to carry out this threat as we feared for the safety of the van if we did so. We stayed awake for a further hour listening for signs of trouble, and by one o'clock were too tired to go to sleep, so went downstairs to make a pot of tea.

By breakfast time, we were thoroughly bad-tempered and inclined to snap at anyone who said good morning. Clint we ignored totally, not trusting ourselves to go near him. And Cordelia was already being a pain in the neck.

'What's that filthy muck?' she cried, as a 3-pint jug of fresh milk was placed on each table. She had put on some black nail varnish and was feeling quite the *grande dame*.

'Milk,' said Vicky shortly. 'And it's not filthy muck.'

'Charming,' said Cordelia, who was always saying 'charming' or 'bloody'. 'You don't seriously expect us to put unpasteurized milk on our cereal, do you? You can catch all sorts of things from milk.'

'You'll be catching the 10.30 back to London if you don't behave yourself. Get on with your breakfast.' Vicky was furious.

'Vic's got 'er knickers in a twist,' sniggered Clint from the other side of the room.

'I simply shan't bother with cereal if I can't have proper milk,' said Cordelia. 'Just give me toast and marmalade.'

Then there was a knock at the back door and it was David, together with Jeremy's mother, Diane.

'What marvellous timing, good morning,' I said, showing them in.

'Marvellous timing?'

'Yes. Things were getting to flash point in the diningroom.'

'Nothing trivial, I hope?' said David, with an eye to a newsworthy sensation.

We invited them in to our own sitting-room, so seldom used nowadays that it looked unnatural. Jeremy hugged Diane and started to tell her all about Bill and Billy, the ponies, the puppy and Lee. She was just as nice as we expected the mother of Jeremy to be and listened enthusiastically and without interruption to all his news.

'I think he's enjoyed himself,' she laughed, during a brief lull while Jeremy drew breath.

'And we've loved having him,' I said. 'If only all our kids could be like Jeremy, we'd be in clover.'

We told David and Diane about Clint and Cordelia and how sorry we were that they should be filming this week instead of last. David was intrigued to see what all the fuss was about, and we invited him to go and see for himself. He did so and joined us again, grinning broadly.

'She's amazing, isn't she?'

'In what way?' we asked.

'She's so *typical*, isn't she? – saying she lives in Highgate when she lives in Muswell Hill, and being so patronizing about everything. And those fingernails!'

'Like Dracula?'

'Yes. Amazing really, poor child. She's very pretty though. She should look well on film.'

'Are you going to interview her?' I asked apprehensively. I didn't fancy the idea of Cordelia being portrayed as a typical guest.

'Oh, we can edit the tape and lose a few swear words.'

I begged David to edit Clint clean out of the whole project.

In fact, I got into such a stew about him that I said I'd rather call the whole thing off than have him included in the film. David must have thought this odd, but then Clint hadn't kept him awake half the night.

Diane now produced a white T-shirt for Jeremy to wear. It had NATIONWIDE printed across the chest and the plan was for Jeremy to walk alone up the drive with perhaps one or two co-operative small animals alongside. The camera would be positioned at the top of the drive and would shoot Jeremy coming up and meeting his mother as she arrived by car. She would get out of the car and ask him how he had enjoyed his holiday. Then the two of them would walk away from the camera down to the house, and their conversation would be recorded as they walked.

After this, the day would be spent filming the children and interviewing some of them. Diane was the reporter and would do the interviewing, two cameramen would see to the filming and a sound recordist would capture the words – selectively we hoped.

The girls had been asked to keep the children together in the yard while Jeremy's opening scene was shot so that their heads wouldn't appear suddenly in the film and detract from the business in hand.

When all this was settled, Jeremy collected Bill and Billy and plodded sturdily up the drive. I positioned myself behind a tree to the left of the drive so that I shouldn't be seen either and waited for the action to start. Then, with great panache, Diane swung her car through the gate, stopped smartly at the allotted position on the drive, and leapt out.

'Hello, Jeremy,' she cried gaily. 'What darling baby lambs.'

Jeremy got the giggles. '*Goats*, Mummy,' he corrected, only he said 'goots', 'they're wee baby goats.'

'Gosh, so they are.' Diane was unconcerned at this small zoological error and knelt down to embrace Jeremy, Bill and Billy. Then they started to walk down the drive away from the camera and I couldn't hear what they were saying. The cameraman, his assistant and the soundman pelted down after them, filming and recording as they went, and I was filled with admiration at this feat; the equipment looked as though it weighed a ton and the temperature was by now in the nineties.

Then David called 'cut' and they all crowded round him for further instructions. He wanted the scene shot again, so up the drive they toiled and the whole thing was redone. Even then, he didn't seem satisfied and asked them to do it yet again. By now I was getting hot and bored, so David asked me to go down and tell the others that they wouldn't be long.

In the yard there was a scene of near mutiny. The children, who would usually be perfectly happy playing in the yard, had objected to the element of coercion and were all trying to escape. Liz, Sue and Vicky had so far managed to outwit them, but were exhausted with the effort and very relieved to see me. The children gathered round me like angry bees.

'What's the big idea making us stay here?'

'I'm too hot.'

'I want to climb the tree.'

'We want to take Parsley for a walk and pick flowers.'

'I want my mummy.'

'Thought you said we was gonna be on telly.'

'It's more like a bloody concentration camp than a holiday. Why don't you give the girls machine-guns?'

Cordelia was absolutely right, and I collapsed on to a bale of straw helpless with laughter. I pictured David and the film crew and their carefully laid plan to chance upon our little yard full of the laughter of merry children at play. The more I thought about it, the more my sides ached and tears gushed down my cheeks. That started the girls off, and the children, with one disgusted look at their elders and betters, climbed over the gate and were off up the field.

'Shall we stop them?' asked Vicky, wiping her eyes.

Then Marcus appeared at the gate; he had been tidying up the tree house so that things such as fossilized doughnuts shouldn't be seen on the film and mar our image.

'The kids are out, did you know?'

This started us off in fresh paroxysms of laughter and we fantasized a procession of local farmers calling to tell us that the kids were out. ('I don't mind ponies or pigs, Mr Addis, but

I must ask you to keep your children under control.') Our imaginations ran riot and we were still at it when Diane hurried into the yard looking troubled.

'I'm awfully sorry but there's been a slight delay. The film crew has gone on strike.'

'On *strike?*' we chorused, and Marcus added, 'I'll kill those kids.'

'Oh no, it's not your kids,' Diane said. 'It's just that your drive has proved the last straw. You see they've been filming for five weeks without a single day off and they're exhausted. They're saying that they're going to phone their union and complain.'

Privately, I thought that it had been rather silly of David to insist on the men carrying all that equipment up and down our steep drive, but I was tactful for once and didn't say anything.

'What shall we do now?' Liz asked Diane. Diane said that David was waiting for tempers to cool before recommencing work. He was going to take them to a pub at lunchtime and hoped to persuade them back afterwards.

'So could you keep the children on the premises today?' asked Diane. 'Then as soon as the crew are ready, we can ask you to start the riding and swimming. It may be some time before they start, though, and we are truly sorry to muck up your day like this.'

She went away to help David talk his merry men into a frame of mind where they would feel privileged to carry heavy burdens around in tropical sunshine.

The day passed slowly. All the children were on edge waiting for something to happen, and when it didn't, they understandably annoyed. We tried to amuse them but they knew we were all just killing time and wouldn't co-operate at all. Gavin went indoors to watch television on his own – a hitherto unheard of activity on a sunny afternoon, and which shows how boring he found our attempts at diversions. After a while, he came out again, saying the TV was broken.

'Broken!' we shrieked. 'But it was only fixed yesterday. What did you do?'

It transpired that he had removed the Sellotape from the

channel buttons and pressed something he shouldn't. He claimed not to have read the DON'T TOUCH notice that we had stuck over the buttons, and we could believe him. Next to Rudi, he was the dullest-witted child imaginable.

Poor Gavin, poor us. In the course of his first full day he broke not only the television, but also the best cricket bat and the dining-room window.

By suppertime we were all so cheesed off at the non-appearance of the film crew that we told Diane (who had been popping in from time to time to keep us informed about the strikers) that we were going to take the children riding and wouldn't be available for filming. Diane agreed – in any case the light was failing by now – and said she hoped that filming could start again first thing in the morning.

I looked in the diary to make sure that the filming wouldn't clash with anything important, and discovered that Parsley was booked in to be mated the next day. Dog mating is a caper that has to be timed pretty accurately. A few hours either side of the red-letter day is all right but anything longer than that and the bitch may go off the boil.

Parsley's forthcoming wedding was to take place at Cullompton, some 30 miles away. I phoned the stud owner and explained the situation, and she kindly altered the appointment from 12 noon to 6 p.m., by which time we hoped the filming would be finished and Parsley raring to go.

Marcus, who had a day off work, decided to forsake his beloved river for the day in order to be in the film. He made a useful additional income for himself from the trout he caught almost daily. His office colleagues bought them for 50 pence each, and as he was saving up for a bigger motorbike, this came in very handy.

Even through the terrible drought conditions of 1976, the River Otter must have been one of the very few not to be too drastically affected. True, the level of the water went down, but there was always plenty of flow and plenty of trout. The children had to use soap instead of shampoo when they washed their hair in the river and the fish seemed to thrive on it.

Diane arrived before breakfast with the good news that everyone had kissed and made up and that filming would commence as soon as we liked.

The children hurried through breakfast and shot outside to rehearse the scenes they had planned with the animals. These scenes had little relevance in a film about unaccompanied children's holidays, comprising as they did such games as Craig lying helpless with a broken leg while Garry galloped over the distant horizon to fetch help. Garry had overlooked the fact that he couldn't ride, couldn't even get on to a pony unaided, and if the event had really taken place, Craig would have died from surgical shock or boredom before his buddy had even departed.

I had impressed upon Jo the importance of sleep in the life of a growing lad like Precious Pup. I need not have bothered to, since PP from choice slept for about twenty-three hours a day. Jo would wake him up, feed him and then show him the place he was to use as a lavatory. PP was always anxious to return to his bed as soon as possible after his outings, and Jo would have to plead with him to come and play. Now that the two kittens no longer disturbed him, PP was able to indulge his slothfulness in peace.

'Can I bring Precious Pup on to the lawn to be filmed, please?' Jo asked.

'Yes, provided Mark keeps his ferret on the lead. We don't want Precious Pup bitten, do we?'

Bill and Billy, Toggles, Melly, Charles and Adam were captured and led to the garden, where they all promptly evaded their captors and skipped around grabbing mouthfuls of roses.

Brian intervened and tethered Toggles and Melly, driving the posts into the ground with a 15-lb sledgehammer. It was difficult to remember that this arid desert had once been our lawn. The lambs were shooed back to the ponies' field, but Bill and Billy were allowed to stay as they were still too small to do any damage.

Filming started and the men made up for their lost day by swiftly filming everything from every conceivable angle. I don't think they overlooked anything that had entertainment potential, from the ducklings and chicks to the pigs and ponies. Naturally, Bill and Billy stole the show; they were friendly and so nosey that they included themselves in all the scenes. They even dared to go as far as the pigs' enclosure, but the electric fence deterred them from a direct confrontation with Phyll and Rosie.

Rosie's Gloucester Old Spot foster piglets were a great hit with David and his crew. All piglets are as playful as puppies, but the Spots are an especially friendly breed and let the children stroke them and roll them over on their backs to be tickled.

By the time every furred and feathered creature had been immortalized by the BBC, it was one o'clock and we all stopped for lunch. David said the programme for the afternoon would include riding, swimming, a battle in the hay, a picnic supper under the oak tree, interviews with individual children and an interview with Brian and me in the hay-barn.

'Why in the hay?' we asked weakly. The thought of the afternoon's itinerary was daunting enough, without having to finish up being questioned in the hay. We would probably fall asleep.

'To show the parents how you involve yourselves with the children. We shall film the battle in the hay with you sitting on a bale watching them. Then we cut and turn the camera on to you with that glorious view of the valley behind you.'

'There's that glorious view from any vantage point on this place,' we objected, but David was adamant.

Marcus and Liz took fifteen of the children down to the river, Sue and Vicky saddled six ponies, and Brian and I went indoors to wash up and start preparing the picnic supper.

David and the film crew drove down to the village. They were going to set up the camera in the village and film the ponies as they passed through. The locals were quite used to us clattering by each day, but must have wondered why on this occasion we had a BBC unit in attendance.

At half past four we heard the ponies' hooves on the drive and rushed out to meet them. The ponies were black with sweat and the children wanted to rub them down.

'Sorry kids, you've got to go and have a battle in the hay now, it's getting late.'

151

'It's only half past four,' objected Hannah.

'Yes, but we've got to take Parsley to be m…married at five o'clock, so hurry up and start your fight or we'll never get finished.'

How we were to regret that pitched battle in the hay! It seemed a harmless enough idea at the time, but the repercussions were not to be felt until the following year when all our little guests who had 'seen it on the telly' seemed to think it a sort of compulsory initiation ceremony to ruin £200 worth of good meadow hay.

Mercifully, we are not gifted with second sight, and there we sat, smiling benignly as the hay flew and the children shrieked at each other ferociously.

Five o'clock came and the filming was not finished. There was nothing for it but for Brian to take Parsley to the stud while I stayed to see to supper.

Six of the children begged to be allowed to go with Brian for the ride.

'It's sixty miles, you'll be bored stiff,' Brian objected. He was quite looking forward to having a quiet drive with just Parsley to talk to.

Perhaps I ought to have shed a maternal tear or two as my youngest dog was driven away, but I felt too dehydrated to bother. Brian had given in to the six kids, who sat in the van singing 'Here Comes the Bride' off key.

David was still finding us amazing and sensational. He found the bale of hay that we had sat on and repositioned me on it so that it would look as though I had been there all the time. Then Diane asked me how we liked having all the kids to look after and I waxed eloquent about the joys of having Jeremy. This was somewhat embarrassing as Diane was his mother; she might have thought I was putting it on to please her, but I wasn't.

It is a fairly unpleasant sensation to have a camera looking down your tonsils as you talk; I felt ridiculous and hoped the glorious view was in sharp focus to distract attention from me gibbering on in the foreground.

A million years later they switched off the machinery and

thankfully I escaped to the relative normality of supervising the picnic supper.

It was going to be apparent even to the most myopic viewer that our children dined off cold sausages and ice-cream cornets. Every child brandished a fistful of sausages in one hand and an ice cream in the other. What had happened to the lettuce and tomato rolls, the bananas and the apples? There was no opportunity to re-equip the children with balanced rations before the blasted camera was in action again, zooming hither and thither and, it seemed, *delighting* in taking dozens of close-up shots of sausages...

Then it came to rest on Gavin and the soundman angled a microphone so that the noise of the other children receded. Diane stepped in front of the camera.

'Hello, what's your name?'

'Gavin.'

'Are you enjoying your holiday, Gavin?'

'Not much.'

'Oh dear, why's that?'

'The telly's broken and so's the cricket bat.'

I was too outraged to listen to the rest of the interview. The *effrontery* of the child – when *he* had broken them! I felt it only needed in-depth interviews with Clint and Cordelia to clinch it – the last nail in the coffin. Thank goodness the aphasic Rudi had gone with Brian and would not be available to record *his* contribution.

But David kept his word about not including Clint in the film. Although he shoved himself in front of the camera as often as he could, it didn't get him anywhere, as the cameraman merely switched off and waited for him to go away.

When, eventually, the light faded and the recording gear was packed away, I felt safe enough to approach David without fear of the microphones eavesdropping. I pointed out that the last two days had hardly been typical ones at Phillishayes and that not too much attention should be given to the criticisms voiced by the new children. Some of them had said they were bored: of *course* they were bored being asked to perform the same actions again and again. Craig and Garry had been the

153

only children to enjoy the filming – Jeremy didn't count as he was semi-professional – the others had soon tired of throwing grain for the chickens and giving the baby goats six bottles in half an hour (pretend ones that is) and were justifiably cheesed off. David got the point and promised to edit carefully.

'But I think you're worrying unnecessarily. Surely Jeremy's insisting on staying on another week is going to outweigh by far the remarks by Gavin.'

'Staying on another week? Who says?'

'Jeremy. He's been on at Diane ever since he saw her. She says she'll think about it. By the way, we should like to take you and Brian out to dinner tonight to round things off.'

'Cor,' I said inelegantly. 'Thanks.'

Diane and Jeremy were sitting on Jeremy's bed chatting.

'I've been conned by this horrible son of mine,' said Diane. 'He says he wants to stay here. Would it be too much trouble for you to have him until the end of the week?'

It was a bit like asking a magnet if it would mind looking after a pin.

Brian was delighted to hear about the dinner invitation and recklessly ran water into our bedroom basin to have a shave. While we washed and changed into posh – well, clean – clothes, he recounted his traumatic experiences of the afternoon.

The drive to Cullompton hadn't been too bad; nobody was sick and nobody wanted to stop for a pee. When they got to the kennels, the owner was out, but had left instructions with her kennel-maid that Parsley was to be mated to Joey at six o'clock.

Blithely Brian disappeared into the house.

'Shan't be a tick, kids,' he said, expecting to hand Parsley over to the kennel-maid at the door. To his horror, he was told to bring Parsley in and hold her head while the kennel-maid supervised Joey's activities at the other end.

'It was terrible,' he said, cutting himself with the razor at the memory. 'Really terrible. There I was, eyeball to eyeball with this dolly bird, both kneeling on the floor, both holding these blasted dogs…'

'Why did you have to hold them?' I interrupted. 'I thought dogs just *did* it – like rabbits.'

'Not like rabbits, like…like…' he gestured imprudently for an analogy and drew yet more blood from his chin. 'They *stick together* for hours.'

'Stick together? You're pulling my leg. For hours?'

'Not quite hours. It was twenty minutes and it seemed like years. I couldn't think of anything to say to this girl so we just knelt there. Then I said, "That's a nice-looking dog."'

'What did she say?'

'She said, "Yes".'

'Riveting conversation.'

'*Don't* say riveting, please, it's too near the knuckle. Then the kids started chanting "Why are we waiting?" That wasn't too bad, just irritating, then they cottoned on to what was going on inside and they started shouting "Get her knickers off" and much worse.'

'Go on,' I said, giggling at the conjured-up picture and immensely relieved that I hadn't been there.

'My mind's a blank after that,' Brian surveyed his mutilated face and dabbed the blood with a clean towel. 'She gave Parsley a drink. Not me, just Parsley. Then I just got out as quickly as possible.'

'Did you tell the kids off for chanting?'

'No. There didn't seem much point by then. Don't forget, they'd been cooped up in the van all that time and they were very good not to get out – they were roasting hot.'

'Poor you,' I sympathized, struggling with a safety pin. I had lost a stone since the heatwave began and all my clothes had to be pinned in.

The evening out was a great success; the food was delicious, although I rather suspect that to anyone who has been cooking non-stop for weeks, anything – even boiled rattlesnake – would taste delicious, provided someone else had boiled it.

Vicky's fears about the film crew were quite unfounded; they didn't drink beer or tell dirty jokes, but regaled us with hilarious accounts of practical jokes they got up to when staying in hotels. David and Diane were very witty and impressed us no end with the sheer speed of their repartee. We had not realized until then that sophistication and wit didn't appear very often in our new lifestyle; conversations with other adults tended to be confined to topics such as the safety of the drinking water and Samantha's incipient verruca.

'Isn't this fun?' Brian whispered, as we moved into another room to drink coffee. 'Just like old times.'

Nostalgically, we recalled supper parties with our old friends. Tonight's mildly theatrical atmosphere and acid humour reminded us that all life wasn't bland and everything would be different in September when we would be free to see our friends again. Phillishayes, I assured Brian, would once again reverberate with Wildean humour, and *bons mots* would be served up with the cornflakes.

The prospect appealed to him enormously.

'Have another Grand Marnier,' he urged.

Chapter Fourteen

Jo danced around the dining-room waving a letter which had arrived by the morning post.

'Mum says I can buy Precious Pup! My very own dog at last – I must go and tell him he's mine.'

'That's marvellous, Jo. I'm really pleased he'll be getting such a good home. Did you tell your mother that he's a crossbred?'

'Yes. But I shan't want to show him so it doesn't matter. Mum says she's always liked spaniel crosses.' She raced out to the chalet to tell PP the good news.

Jeremy reminded me that we needed more kittens. He made it sound as though we were out of bread, and I remembered him saying something about more kittens last week.

'Jeremy, did you know you were going to stay two weeks?'

'No, I didn't *know*, I just wished and wished. I'm a good wisher.'

'You're a con man.'

He giggled. 'That's exactly what Mummy calls me. Do you like my Kickers?' He climbed on my lap and stuck out his feet to have his new shoes admired.

'You're a snappy dresser. I've never seen such lovely shoes. Did they come from Colts?'

'No, Paris. That's in France.'

'Really? Who are you going to kick?'

'If I was bigger I could kick Clint. Do you know he's really horrible?'

'I had noticed.'

'If Clint twisted Craig's arm until it broke, would you send him home?'

'Don't imagine silly things like that, Jeremy,' and I tickled him until he wriggled off my lap to escape.

Craig and Garry offered to carry the picnic things out to

157

the van. There was a lot of stuff as we were going to make a long day of it and take them all fishing at Lyme Regis before lunch, then spend the afternoon on the beach.

Craig looked preoccupied and kept finding reasons to return to the kitchen and hang around us. He was unusually quiet. Normally he and Garry kept up a non-stop patter of jokes – Croydon's answer to Morecambe and Wise, Brian called them – and his subdued manner worried me. I wondered if in fact Clint had threatened him.

Brian and I managed to have a quick word in private during the time that the children were all safely battened in the van prior to moving off. It had to be a quick word because experience had taught us that if lift-off was delayed even for a few minutes, someone would want to go to the lavatory and then an epidemic of full bladders would sweep through the van. This could cause a delay of up to half an hour and was very tedious.

I told Brian what Jeremy had said about Clint. Brian had an instant brainwave – 'Let Craig and Garry sleep in the tent tonight.'

'Amazingly good idea.'

(Ever since the advent of David we kept saying things were amazing or sensational. It doesn't sound funny now, but it seemed hilarious at the time.)

As the Transit kangarooed up the drive – it didn't like extremes of temperature any more than we did, and was apt to stick in first gear – I made the usual threats about anyone who was sick forfeiting his boat trip. Actually, the genuine sufferers had been equipped with squares of brown paper shoved up their T-shirts; a preventive measure that I heard about on *Woman's Hour* and which really does work. The threats about the boat trip were merely to discourage malingerers and were moderately effective.

'Ten Green Bottles' proved to be the song of the day. We always liked to hear a busload of children singing for the simple reason that if they were singing they weren't vomiting, but 'Ten Green Bottles' sung non-stop for ten green miles made Brian beg for a change. He was even hotter than the passengers as the Transit's heater was stuck in the ON position, and he asked them to sing cool songs. 'Not "Frère Jacques" please, I can't stand that "ding dang dong" bit. What about "White Christmas"?'

Nobody knew 'White Christmas', so we finished up crawling down the hill into Lyme Regis to the accompaniment of 'Rudolf the Red-Nosed Reindeer'. They were still singing bits of it as we counted them into two fishing boats that were plying for hire on the quayside.

Jos wore her anorak and carried her umbrella and Jeremy had chosen to wear a rather dashing Fair Isle sweater and jeans. The temperature at Lyme Regis was 110°F.

The fisherman baited one line between each two children and instructed them how to reel in when they thought they might have a bite. The children bickered happily over turns and soon had the boat festooned with tangled lines and flapping mackerel. Patiently the fisherman untangled their lines and rebaited their hooks. For a while they fished quietly, then suddenly, just as I was snapping Jeremy standing like a little Viking by the mast, there was an outraged bellow from the fisherman.

'That little girl has hooked me, she's *hooked* me!'

'Oh, crikey!' Brian and I jumped forward to help him. Jos stared in horror at her hook firmly embedded in the man's thumb and tugged at her fishing line which meant that the fisherman was being reeled in like a mackerel, only no mackerel ever had such an extensive vocabulary. Then Jos made matters even worse by trying to run away, but tripped over her own lines and *still* failed to let go.

Meanwhile, the other children fished on, each trying to catch the record number of fish. The poor fisherman stared disbelievingly at the mounting heap of fish waiting to be unhooked, each one attached to about 30 feet of line. The lines were everywhere, round the children's legs, criss-crossed all over the floor of the boat.

I rummaged through my bag and offered the fisherman a choice of Dettol, Savlon, TCP and flea powder (which I had brought by mistake, thinking it was antibiotic powder). He refused all these and rolled his eyes up to the sky as though he wished a thunderbolt might just happen along and put him out of his misery. But it didn't, and the saintly man set to and untangled the children's lines for them.

'Just keep *that* one out of my way,' he pleaded, nodding at Jos who had been sent to sit at the furthest end of the boat. 'I don't mind the others. I like kids, really, I do. I like kids.' The way he said it gave us the impression that he was reassuring himself and not us.

The other boat trip had gone without incident and we counted up the mackerel when we met again on the quay.

'Sixty-two!' The children shrieked, waving bunches of mackerel at unwary holidaymakers.

'That's nice, dear,' said an old lady to Craig. She was sitting on a bench and was a captive audience for Craig, Garry and Jeremy, who were dying to show off their catches. 'You going to have a nice herring for your tea?' she asked.

'No, they're for Phyll and Rosie,' said Garry.

'That's nice. Pussy cats, are they?'

'Small is the cat,' said Jeremy.

'Funny way of putting it but I know what you mean. He'll grow if you give him a nice herring, won't he?'

'No, Small is the cat. Phyll and Rosie are pigs.'

'Oh, they all are, dear, when it comes to fish. You make sure to take all the bones out. You their mother, dear?' she said to me.

'No, they're on holiday with us.'

'Wonderful the way you girls take in foreigners these days. I shouldn't have a moment's peace with a foreigner in the house.' I looked round for Jos, but she was in the other group. She must mean Jeremy I thought, shepherding the boys back to the others.

'Why do people think I'm foreign?' asked Jeremy.

'It's because you talk garlic,' said Garry.

Liz and Sue offered to stay on the beach and count heads while Brian and I went back to the van to deposit the mackerel and fetch the picnic things. It was Vicky's day off and we envied her as we toiled up the hot streets with sixty-two mackerel dangling from our hands. We had become quite thick-skinned about funny looks we got whenever we returned from a fishing trip. I suppose people must have wondered how two people could catch so many fish in an hour and, indeed, *why* we should want so many. The way we looked at it was that with the fishing costing us 50 pence a head and pig nuts costing £112 a ton we needed every fish we could catch.

'Shall we have a cup of tea from the flask before we go back?' Brian suggested.

'Seems a bit mean leaving Sue and Liz coping on their own,' I said half-heartedly.

'Just a quick cup; it'll save carrying it.'

We wiped our hands on a wet flannel and sat in the shade of the van sipping the tea.

Lyme Regis stretched below us, the beaches teeming with holidaymakers and the sea sparkling so brightly that it hurt your eyes to look at it for too long.

'I wish we liked the sea,' I said, dunking biscuits in my tea. 'Some people would enjoy being us, being paid to stay on a beach all day.'

'Do stop doing that to those biscuits, they're meant to be crisp. What is it about the sea that puts us off?'

'It's wet and noisy for a start.'

'And full of people.'

'Did you bring your swimming trunks?'

'Good God, I wouldn't set foot in it if you paid me. Tell you what, let's buy a paper and do the crossword while we count heads.'

The girls had staked a claim on a small area of pebbly beach near a breakwater. Quite soon we had a much bigger area as people moved their deck-chairs and towels out of range of our group. We issued arm-bands to our non swimmers and pocket money all round and the children rushed off to the kiosks or the water as their fancies took them.

Liz and Sue had a swim while we took first guard duty, then they watched while we rested. The afternoon passed eventually and nobody drowned or got lost, so I suppose it counted as a good day. But we were thankful to start prising sandals on to clammy little feet in preparation for the homeward journey.

Inevitably, there were too few sandals for the proffered feet; a tearful Rudi had managed to lose his shorts as well, and one of the smaller girls found that she had acquired a large bath towel.

'What do you mean you found it? Isn't it yours?'

'No, mine's orange. I found it with my things when I came out of the water. I don't know where it came from.'

'Perhaps it belongs to Pat Jennings,' said Gavin.

'Or the Duke of Edinburgh,' I snapped in exasperation. What had the Spurs goalkeeper to do with anything? Then more kindly: 'Why should you think the towel is Pat Jennings', Gavin?'

'Because it says P. Jennings on the name tape.'

It did and inwardly I blushed.

'Sorry, Gavin, I thought you were being facetious.'

'The fishes will be smelling very much I think,' said Jos suddenly.

We had never caught sixty-two before and Jos's prognosis was correct. As we opened the back doors of the bus a wave of fishy odour hit us like a force nine gale.

'Cor, dunnit stink!'

'Worse than Mark's ferret.'

'Charming.'

'I'd sooner walk.'

All the children made a rush to sit in the front of the bus away from the bag full of fish. Brian removed the bag to the space in front of the passenger seat and the children surged to the back seats.

'SIT DOWN please, I've got to count you.' Brian started counting. 'Sit down please, Clint, so that I can see everybody.'

Clint remained standing. Brian changed tactics. 'Stand there, Clint, just where you are, nineteen, twenty, twenty-one, thank you.' He started the engine. Clint, aware that he had been made to look foolish but unable to work out how, sat down.

I squeezed in between Garry and Craig and endured fifteen miles of knock knock jokes.

'Knock knock.'

'Who's there?'

'Segovia.'

162

'Segovia who?'

'Segovia new carpet!'

That was the best one.

'We've got a book of jokes,' confided Garry. 'We read them to one another in bed.'

'That reminds me, you two. Would you like to sleep in the tent tonight?'

'Not 'alf.'

'Smashing. Just us?' said Craig meaningfully.

'If you like, you can have Jeremy and Rudi, but you don't have to if you'd rather be on your own.'

They conferred. Then Craig said, 'We'd prefer to have Jeremy and Rudi too, but *not* Clint.'

'Not Clint,' I promised. We had plans for him.

As soon as we got home, all the kids disappeared, leaving us to cope with the urgent task of freezing the mackerel. Phyll and Rosie could eat only 5 lb a day each, so all the rest had to be parcelled into 5-lb packs and frozen quickly before the miasma attracted the attention of the local health inspector. We were half-way through this chore when there was a horrendous crash from the yard, followed by the noise of breaking glass, followed by the patter of tiny footsteps across the concrete drive.

We rushed outside to see what was up. Or rather, down. Where there had been a glazed door leading to an old dairy was now a gaping hole. It was not just a broken door; the entire wooden framework had been pushed outwards and had smashed to splinters on the concrete outside.

Grimly, Brian went off to look for Clint, while the girls cleared up the broken glass and I finished the mackerel.

A sullen and uncommunicative Clint was sent to sit in the dining-room alone, while the other children who had been in the yard, told us what had actually happened.

'He locked himself in the dairy by mistake.'

'Then what happened?' we demanded.

'Then Clint said, "Sod that".'

'Never mind what he *said*. What did he *do*?'

'He kicked the wooden bit round the door.'

'He's ever so strong.'

'He goes to karate.'

'Then he pushed his back against the wooden bit.'

'Then the glass broke.'

'Then he pushed the whole door out and climbed over.'

'Then he ran away.'

Brian looked as though he'd like to run away too. He hates mending broken frames with all the fuss and mess of spirit levels and cement. He strode into the dining-room and banged his fist on the table. 'What have you got to say about this, Clint?'

'Get stuffed.'

'I don't propose even to attempt a conversation with you, Clint. Your parents will have to pay for the damage, which will cost something over £40. And if you cause any more trouble, you will be put on the next train home.'

That night we rearranged the bedrooms. There were four vacant beds, as Craig, Garry, Jeremy and Rudi were sleeping in the tent, so we moved Mark and Gavin into Jeremy's room. This left Clint the sole occupant of the big boys' room and we hoped everyone would get a bit of peace with the new arrangement. All the boys in Clint's room had complained that he kept them awake at night, so they were delighted at the prospect of a good sleep.

We should have known better. Clint was seething at the way he had lost face in every single encounter he had had with Brian; the pocket money, the crockery trolley, the filming and now this. To give him his due, he had the sense not to bully the little ones – he merely threatened them – but confined his activities to breaking things up and boasting.

That night, while the girls were getting ready for bed, Clint burst into their room and, vandal fashion, broke just about everything breakable in sight. He was only in there a few moments – as soon as we heard the girls shrieking, we were upstairs in a flash – but in that time he had reduced the room to a shambles.

It was Sara's room that we were using as the girls' dormitory and we had left her trinkets, posters and ornaments for the enjoyment of the little girls. Sara had put away her most treasured things – china horses and so forth – but had left ceramic tiles, shells, dried-flower arrangements and posters in the room. All were ruined.

Oblivious of the presence of the small girls, I grabbed Clint by his pyjama jacket and dragged him out on to the landing. Before Brian could intervene, I gave the boy what was probably the only hiding he had ever had in his life. Montessori training, common sense and A.S. Neill were forgotten as I hit him until my arm ached. Then Brian marched along the landing and put him back in his room.

'If you leave this room again tonight, Clint, you'll get another hiding.'

As I went downstairs, I heard Jos say primly, 'In Spain we do not allow the capital punishment.'

I phoned Auntie Beryl's neighbour. She fetched Auntie Beryl.

'Hello Mrs er...um, I'm sorry to trouble you but your sister gave me this number...'

'It's Clint, isn't it? You'll be sending him home. Little sod.'

I warmed to Auntie Beryl.

'Yes, but...how did you know?'

'How did I know? I ought to know by now. Clint and Marilyn get sent home from every holiday place they've been to. I'm surprised you've kept him until Tuesday, that's all I can say. He's usually home by Sunday night. Didn't he tell you?'

'No. He doesn't say much to us. He's caused quite a lot of trouble though.'

'Don't tell me, I can imagine. Thieving?'

'No, just damage.'

'Don't bank on it. Have a look in his case before you send him. That boy'll end up in Borstal. Needs a damn good hiding, that's what he needs.'

'Yes,' I agreed fervently. 'We'll put him on the 10.40 tomorrow and perhaps you'd be kind enough to meet him?'

'Him? What about Marilyn?'

'She's no trouble; there's no need for her to leave.'

'Well, I don't know,' said Auntie Beryl doubtfully. 'They generally get sent back together, but of course it's not fair on the girl. Tell you what, May and Ted will be phoning me later tonight, so I'll get May to phone you to tell you what she wants done about Marilyn.'

About ten o'clock the phone rang. I had been looking forward to telling Clint's mother some home truths about her son, but in the event I didn't get a chance. From the moment I lifted the receiver she didn't let up for a second.

'My Clint!' she shrieked. 'Everyone's against him; you're all the same, toffee-nosed tarts all of you. He's a good boy, he is. I don't care what those teachers say or that pansy headmaster ...'

There was quite a lot more in this vein and, as she was paying for the call, I held the receiver away from my ear and let her rant on. Brian and the girls crowded round the phone to listen, and we all got a bit giggly by the time the fourth lot of pips went.

'Pity David's not here,' Liz chuckled. 'This really is amazing and sensational.'

Eventually Mrs Wordsworth ran out of steam; the flood of epithets became a trickle and I felt a sense of Zen oneness with all 'them other holiday places' who had not appreciated the company of the boy wonder. I brought her back to the matter in hand.

'We shall put Clint on the 10.40 tomorrow, but Marilyn will stay. She is enjoying her holiday and I see no reason to involve her in Clint's troubles.'

Before Mrs Wordsworth could get wound up again, I replaced the receiver. We waited a few minutes to see whether she would ring again, but the phone stayed silent.

'Phew, what an old dragon. Put the kettle on someone, I'm parched.'

'I don't know why *you're* parched,' said Liz, filling the kettle. 'You hardly got a word in edgeways.'

We had a quick cup of tea, then the girls went upstairs to check that all was well and Brian and I strolled down to see how the boys were getting on in the tent. There was much scuffling and giggling coming from the tent, whose sides bulged first here, then there like someone in the last weeks of pregnancy.

We squatted down and put our heads through the tent flap. There was a lovely smell of bruised grass and canvas. The boys were pleased to see us and invited us in.

'Innit *smashing*?' squeaked Craig. 'We've never been in a tent before.'

They were all zipped into Terylene sleeping bags with the zips done up as far as their waists. They looked so sweet, as if they were emerging from a chrysalis state. None of them looked a bit sleepy.

'You all right, Rudi?' Rudi was wedged between Jeremy and Garry and was sucking his thumb happily.

'Course he's all right,' said Jeremy indignantly. 'We're looking after him. Garry's reading jokes from his joke book.'

'Not *more* knock knock jokes,' we groaned.

'I'll tell you a real joke, then,' said Garry kindly. 'Get off my feet, Brian, you're paralysing me.'

'Is that the joke?' asked Brian. 'It's not very funny.'

Garry punched him and moved his feet to a more comfortable position.

'There was this Martian. He came down to Earth and landed in a garage. So he goes up to this petrol pump and he says, "Take me to your leader". Well, of course the petrol pump doesn't do anything, does it? So this Martian, he shouts, "TAKE ME TO YOUR LEADER" and this petrol pump doesn't do anything. So this Martian, he says, "Listen, mate, if you'd take your cock out of your ear you could hear me".'

All four boys screeched with laughter and kicked their feet in the air. Brian, fighting to keep a straight face said, 'Did you tell that one to the film people, Garry?'

'Course not, silly.'

'Well, I just wondered.'

'How could I? I only heard it myself today.'

Not having Clint was a great relief, like not having toothache. The rest of the week passed fairly smoothly and we felt reasonably sure that all the children, bar Cordelia and Gavin, were having a good time. For all we knew, these two might have enjoyed themselves, but they would have died rather than admit it.

On Thursday we took them all to a local gymkhana, the sort where every other family has a Land Rover, a yellow labrador and two children with prep school accents and beautiful manners.

'Mothah,' mimicked Garry.

'Yes, deah,' said Craig.

'Mothah, you're standin' in horse shit.'

'Dung, deah, not shit. I shall hev to get the butlah to wash it awf.' The boys writhed on the grass choking with laughter. I pretended I wasn't with them and hurried away to buy an ice cream for Rudi.

Mark was already in the queue for ice cream. He waved cheerily.

'Hello, Faith, don't bother to queue up – I'll get something for Rudi. And by the way, I've discovered something really interesting.'

'Have you, Mark?'

'Do you know rabbit droppings are insoluble?'

I should have been quite happy to remain ignorant about the solubility of rabbit droppings and wondered why Mark had to enlighten me in such a public place.

'Are they?' I said lamely.

'Rabbits mark out their territories with them, and the territories last a long time because they're insoluble. Two choc-ices, please – and the reason they keep in territories is to stop the spread of disease.' He handed a choc-ice to Rudi and looked slightly hurt as I took Rudi's hand and walked away.

It's always heartening to come across kids who still read Konrad Lorenz and Henry Williamson, but I wish they would be a bit more selective about the facts they assimilate, and not dwell so lovingly on the alimentary processes.

Rudi and I ran Brian to earth in the bus. He was alone, happily reading, and not overjoyed to see us.

'Go away,' he said, all subtlety and charm.

'You can't monopolize the bus,' I said, climbing in. 'Anyway, I only want a wet flannel for Rudi.'

Brian looked at Rudi's face, hastily passed me the flannel and went back to his book.

'Aren't you going to watch the gymkhana?' I asked, excavating field-flavoured choc-ice from Rudi's ear.

'Can't you train that child to find his mouth – draw a diagram or something? No, I am not going to watch the gymkhana. I find it too embarrassing to stand next to our kids. They cheer whenever the ponies fart, and I can't stand it. I'm quite happy to have a quiet read.'

As he was re-reading a book about bee-keeping, I thought it prudent to let him get on with it. I am extravagant with honey, and was looking forward to having our own bees in due course.

I fended off complaints from our kids that it wasn't fair: everyone else had brought ponies to ride and why hadn't we brought ours? As only Jos and Jeremy were good enough riders to enter in a competition, we were not prepared to get involved in long arguments with the eighteen remaining children who were not. Nonetheless, the kids enjoyed the gymkhana and some even managed to cadge rides from earnest Thelwell-type little girls.

It made a nice change to have the bus reeking of horse instead of mackerel, and not even Cordelia complained. Anne and Alexandra sat in a trance-like state of ecstasy and begged to be allowed to remain unwashed so that the smell could linger until tomorrow.

'Had I been riding in those competitions,' said Jos, whose use of English always astounded us, 'had I been riding, I should have won all the games.'

This remark might have impressed Fowler, but it cut no ice with our busload of hooligans; they jeered and catcalled at Jos, who was not put out in the least and told them they were all stupid. The abject Marilyn linked arms with Jos and murmured words of sympathy. She had transferred her allegiance to Jos once Clint had gone, and used to act as her doormat whenever Jos felt the need to remind everyone how a Spanish aristocrat behaved.

During his stay with us, Mark had cleverly organized the refilling of the garden pond. It had dried up soon after the drought started in spring and, as it was only cement-lined, it was pointless to refill it; to cart gallons of water from the stream only to see it evaporate overnight was nobody's idea of fun, so the pond remained empty.

But Mark wanted to see the conclusion of an experiment before he went home, so he refilled it. He put a polythene liner in the pond, weighted it down with rocks all round and directed a succession of children to carry water to fill it. If we had formed a child slave-gang like that, I'm sure we should have had the NSPCC round in no time, but Mark's volunteers seemed quite happy, so we left them to it.

Way back in May, Sara had set up an experiment with newt tadpoles. She had learned that iodine is a growth inhibitor and had added a few drops to a tankful of tadpoles to see whether the iodine would delay their metamorphosis into newts. All except two had grown into normal newts, despite the presence of the iodine, but the remaining two were still big fat tadpoles. Now, twelve weeks later, Mark wanted to see whether he could effect a delayed metamorphosis by transferring them to iodine-free water and extending their space. He thought that psychologically the tadpoles might feel that it was worth the effort of growing up if they had a bigger world to play in. As he said, nobody would want to grow up if they couldn't see any advantage to be gained. We awaited the outcome of the experiment with bated breath.

The tadpoles, who were called Perry Mason and Princess Margaret, had been transferred to their new home in a delicate, fluted bone china sugar bowl – the children, being forbidden to carry glass jam jars outside, had made do with Royal Doulton – and had spent three days hiding under some water-weed.

'Why don't they *do* something? the smaller children asked impatiently. They wanted to stir things up a bit with a stick but Mark was stern.

'You leave them alone. They're shy and frightened, like the first day at school. They'll soon start coming out if we stay quiet.'

In due course, Perry Mason explored the perimeter of the pond but Princess Margaret stayed in hiding. Even Mark's patience was wearing thin, so he introduced more life into the pond with water-boatmen, trout fry and daphnia. He asked me to buy a goldfish from the pet shop, so on my next trip to Taunton I purchased Tarzan, a broad-shouldered, pugnacious-looking chap with lovely peachy-coloured scales.

Mark was delighted with Tarzan and carefully took the polythene container from me. I went indoors to put the kettle on and Mark carried Tarzan down to the pond. Before the kettle had boiled, there came a collective howl from the garden and all the kids poured in through the back door. I decided to make the tea very strong.

'He's *swallowed* Princess Margaret!'

'Just *hoovered* her up – she didn't even struggle.'

'Too bloody ghastly for words, the absolute limit.'

'A cannibal.'

Vicky and Sue, fighting a losing battle to smother their laughter, tugged pieces of kitchen roll from the holder and issued them to the tender-hearted.

'Poor P...Princess M...Margaret,' the little ones sobbed. Tears gushed down their faces and Sue, with practised skill, wiped noses and shoved biscuits into mouths as fast as she could.

Brian put his head round the door to see what the noise was about.

'What on earth has happened?'

'Tarzan ate Princess Margaret,' I said.

'Oh, I am sorry. Is Perry Mason all right?' This benign attitude was so out of character for Brian that I suspected he had had a major breakthrough on the horticultural front.

'Has something gone right in the garden?' I asked. He leered mysteriously and went down to help Mark rescue Perry Mason.

Tarzan was fished out of the pond and sentenced to solitary confinement in the aquarium. Perry Mason, though appearing to maintain a stiff upper lip, must have been affected by his sister's murder because for the rest of his life he remained a tadpole.

Brian's happy state of mind was due to the fact that he had successfully harvested a bucketful of melons – the Ogen variety – which he had grown outdoors. The flavour was ambrosial and was one of the few advantages that we had from the drought year.

Chapter Fifteen

Jeremy's mother wanted him home on Friday so as to avoid the holiday crush on Saturday. She had booked a seat for him on the 3.30 from Taunton to London, and as it was only a two-hour journey, had asked him if he would like to travel alone. This appealed to Jeremy's sense of adventure and he jumped at the chance of finishing his holiday in style; he saw himself arriving at Paddington like a world-weary traveller.

'Just imagine,' he said, 'some people might see me and think I've come all the way from Penzance alone.'

On Friday morning I wished him 'top o' the milk' as cheerfully as I could in view of the fact that I was feeling a bit leaden at the prospect of losing him, and he responded as usual – 'It's top o' the *mornin'* and we don't say it at home.'

Jeremy's imminent departure reminded some of the others that they would be going home tomorrow, so they did the farewell rounds with Jeremy – a masochistic activity if ever there was one. The routine was always the same every week. First they would seek out and kiss the larger animals; this was easy because the ponies and Bambi could he held by their head-collars while wet kisses were plonked on their faces. Then they worked their way down the animal population in order of size; the whole operation became more difficult and more unhygienic, until in the end there might be four or five children crawling round the guinea-piggery trying to catch the elusive guinea-pigs for the obligatory kiss. By the time they got to the ducklings and chicks, they tended to make do with blowing kisses into the runs. The whole thing could keep them occupied for hours, by which time they might be weeping from a combination of sentiment and exhaustion.

However, Jeremy started his stint briskly enough, and not tear was shed until he got to Bill and Billy. These were his special favourites and he squeezed the breath out of them as he kissed their soft little faces.

'Goodbye, lads,' he whispered, and blinked hard as they nuzzled his bare knees, hoping it was time for a bottle.

'Hurry up, Jeremy, or we'll be late for your train.'

Reluctantly he came indoors for a wash. The girls had set up a treasure hunt for the kids, but Garry and Craig wanted to come with us and see Jeremy off on the train.

There was a kiosk on the platform selling sweets and papers. Jeremy didn't say a word, but looked so wistful that I bought him an assortment of sweets and a few comics.

Brian said, 'Do you know, Jeremy, in ten years' time you'll have them eating out of your hand?'

Jeremy giggled modestly and said he hoped they wouldn't bite like the wee ducklings. He gave Garry and Craig half his sweets, then followed Brian to the guard's van. The guard looked hot and cross, but when Jeremy grinned at him, the cross look vanished.

'Come on, Sunshine,' he said, 'let's find you a seat, shall we? My word, that's a nice fishing rod. You been on your holidays, have you?' Jeremy gave us a quick hug and a kiss and climbed on to the train. He sat down by the window and mouthed something through the glass as the train moved forward.

'What's he saying?' I asked Brian.

'Goodbye, I think. And something about the top of the milk.'

Suddenly there seemed to be quite a bit of dust in my eyes...

Later in the van Craig said, 'What's it called when everybody likes you?'

Brian grinned at him. 'A miracle?' he suggested.

'Don't be rotten, Brian, I didn't mean me – I meant Jeremy. There's a word for it, isn't there?'

'Popularity,' said Brian.

'Well how do you get popularity?' persisted Craig. 'I mean, take that rotten old guard, if that'd been me, I'd have probably got a clout, but that guard will sit with Jeremy and talk to him all the way to London. I want to populate like that,' Craig was

173

very earnest, but we couldn't help him much beyond advising him to wash more often.

Garry said, 'Shall I cheer you up a bit?' He knew Jeremy had been our favourite and was generous enough not to mind.

'No more jokes, *please*,' we begged.

'Oh, go on, just one? It's about these two bishops in bed together.'

'Garry,' said Brian firmly, '*no more* smutty jokes if you please.'

'It's *clean*, it's in our book. These two bishops was in bed together...'

'*Were*,' said Brian.

'Were what?' said Garry.

'*Were* in bed together. And it's obviously not clean, so shut up.'

Garry was offended and looked out of the window of the van. Craig took up the tale, muffed the punch line and looked gratified when we laughed at his discomfiture.

'I think I'm getting popularity,' he said gleefully. I handed him a box of tissues and suggested he removed the worst of the debris from round his mouth before he got typhoid.

They were a chirpy pair and we were pleased they were staying for two weeks. The average age of the children who were coming the following week was eight, so Garry (who was eleven) would be an elder statesman, which should boost his ego.

In addition to Garry and Craig, there were only two – Jos and Rudi – who were not going home tomorrow. Nobody was looking forward to coping with a tearful Rudi as he saw the arrival of everyone's mummy but his own, but Garry and Craig promised to divert him if they could. They had thought out a programme of activities that included a game of spider-racing in the tent, and I made a mental note to avoid that particular race-course tomorrow. I can't stand spiders; next to estate agents, they are my most unfavourite creatures.

Only two more full weeks, we thought that evening, as we supervised the consumption of sausages round the Friday night bonfire. The schools were re-opening on 3 September and we had only four children booked for the last week in August. Tonight's children were being astoundingly greedy with the sausages and we looked forward longingly to the time where there would be only four mouths to feed.

'Do you think they've got tapeworms?' Brian asked, watching Jos polish off five chipolatas without pause.

'Shouldn't have. I cooked the sausages right through.' (We never let the children cook the sausages over the fire in case they were too impatient to wait.)

'Must have taken ages to cook all those.'

'Yes, I put both grills on and did them in four batches.'

'Four batches? How many did you cook for heaven's sake?'

'Six each – two hundred and forty-four.'

'Christ Almighty, that's over twelve each! No wonder it looks like a Roman orgy.'

It was a bit much. In addition to nearly two gross of chipolatas, the kids were happily getting through a 5-gallon drum of orange and three tins of assorted biscuits to the accompaniment of the 'The Carnival Is Over'.

The absolute bloody limit, as Cordelia would say.

There was the usual panic on Saturday morning to get all the children ready in time to catch various trains, but by now we were getting used to the routine; we didn't allow ourselves to get side-tracked nearly so often, and the whole business, though still exhausting, was less nerve-racking.

So when Marcus came in and said there were two homicidal maniacs walking down the drive, we didn't immediately rush out with pitchforks but continued tying anoraks on to suitcases with bits of baler twine.

'They've got staring eyes and shiny shoes. I'm sure they're not parents,' said Marcus.

'Jehovah's Witnesses,' Brian and I chorused. We had suffered from them in London and had never worked out the best way to get rid of them. We were just beginning the 'You go', 'No, *you* go' routine when six of the piglets rushed up to the visitors and welcomed them piggy-fashion. It is not everyone's cup of tea to have six powerful little rubber noses exploring their polished brogues and before we had time to prepare our defences – (sorry we're atheists/Buddhists/Scientologists) the Witnesses had fled.

'Miss Kerr said Gloucester Old Spots are very intelligent,' I said, scratching Rose Hip where she liked it, just between the shoulder blades. 'Who's a clever girl then?'

Brian, wondering why the all-embracing love of God didn't extend to piglets, drove off to Honiton with all the train departures and the laundry. He looked very cheerful because there was only one trip necessary today: nobody had to be met in the afternoon as they were all coming by car.

When he had gone, Jo's mother arrived and calmly announced that she had changed her mind about letting Jo have a dog just yet as they were not quite settled in the new house. It is still painful to recall Jo's misery but worse was to come. The dealer wanted the pup back if we hadn't sold it, as he had a prospective buyer coming to look at it that day. I put Precious Pup in a box and delivered him back to the dealer together with a pound of mincemeat and a diet sheet. Mr C took the pup into his house and I drove away after arranging to call back later if the pup wasn't sold. As soon as I had driven off, Mr C had turned the puppy loose in his yard, where within ten minutes it had been run over and killed. It was small consolation to remember that we had given Precious Pup two happy weeks; I reproached myself guiltily as one does on these occasions. If only I had bought PP myself, if only Jo's mother had not changed her mind, if only I'd taken him back an hour later...

It was lovely having such a young group at last. There were three six-year-olds, six eight-year-olds and the rest were all around nine or ten, with the exception of Garry and Mick, who were eleven. Mick was a neat, reliable boy who liked to carry a row of pens in his shirt pocket under a prefect's badge. He was the sort of child who, when sent to the village shop to buy beef cubes, would come back with beef cubes. No moody teenagers at all, and what a difference it made.

The new children flitted round the yard like butterflies, if you can imagine butterflies in denim shorts and with sturdy brown thighs. They shrilled with excitement as they discovered the kittens, baby guinea-pigs and rabbits. The ducklings and chicks were too quick for them to stroke, but they watched in delight as the ducklings splashed in and out of their water bowl.

'Are they cynics?' asked seven-year-old Scarlett. She and her twin sister Dawn had tried to catch a duckling between cupped hands.

'*Cygnets*, silly,' said Melanie, who was six.

'Duckth don't have thignets, they have ducklingth.' Richard made up in brains what he lacked in teeth, and the others regarded him with respect, as he had already recognized that Bill and Billy were not lambs.

'Aren't they sweet?' I enthused to Brian, as we watched the children exploring. He looked like the cat that swallowed the cream, but it was probably the near-topless young mothers who had had that effect and not the children at all.

Perhaps I'm being unfair. We had always planned for *young* children at the farm; our advertising had been directed at first-time-away-from-home kids – a sort of nursery slopes to prepare them for the tougher holiday centres – and here they were.

Craig, Garry and Jos soon made them feel at home with tales of 'what we did last week', as they conducted them round and showed them the likeliest places to find outlaid eggs. (Most of the chickens scorned the purpose-built nest boxes and chose to lay in the hedges.)

It was all too much for Dawn, Scarlett's twin sister.

'I want to live here for ever and ever,' she said. And then taking Brian's hand, 'I like you, Brian. Our daddy's called Brian.'

'Well, he's not our real daddy,' Scarlett said. 'Our real daddy's called Alan. But Brian is a good friend of Mummy's.'

Brian walked along holding hands with both little girls and trying to stifle his amusement as they explained how Daddy was always away on his ship, so Brian lived in their house to keep Mummy company. It seemed that when Daddy came home on leave, Brian hopped it; hardly surprising, I thought, conjuring up a picture of a brawny sailor bursting into the house brandishing his kit bag.

And that was not all. As the week progressed, Brian's two-member fan club, as we nicknamed the twins, revealed more and more of Mummy's peccadilloes, sometimes in quite embarrassing detail. It seemed hardly credible that Mummy had really thrown her nightie over the banisters one day and cried dramatically, 'I need a *man*.' I mean, it doesn't sound a very *English* thing to do. But apparently she had, and then rushed out of the house and slammed the door.

'What, naked?' I asked incredulously. (Brian had been bringing me the latest instalment.)

'I don't know,' he said. 'I never ask questions. I just let them babble on. That Scarlett is a marvellous mimic, though. She has me in stitches.'

'Go on about the nightie.'

'It was her best nightie – Daddy had bought it in New York – and she peeled it off and threw it over the banisters. Then she went out.'

'She must have dressed first,' I objected. 'It's too cold in Essex to rush out in the evening with nothing on.'

'This was in the morning. The kids were having their breakfast – Shredded Wheat and a boiled egg – and the cat had been sick in the night.'

'Sounds familiar,' I giggled. 'Then what happened?'

'She came back in again.'

'Oh, *what* an anti-climax. No man?'

'Not immediately. The twins had to go to school after breakfast, but when they came home, there was a Christmassy smell in the house.'

'What sort of smell – mince pies and turkey?'

'*Cigars*, idiot. You don't get lovers smelling of mince pies.'

'Could have been the village baker, couldn't it? Does Mummy tell the kids what she wants a man for?'

'Yes. She says she can't move the heavy furniture to hoover round, so she needs a man. She's not very strong.'

'She sounds pretty robust if she can entertain the cigar-smoking baker after breakfast.'

All that week's kids were delightful in their various ways, but Melanie was the most unforgettable. She was six, very pretty and very feminine. When we first saw her, she was wearing a Laura Ashley dress – not really appropriate for the rigours of the farmyard but carried off with such panache that it didn't seem incongruous.

'What a lovely dress,' I said. 'Is it a Laura Ashley?'

'Yes, it is. I love all her clothes. And do you know, my brother is called Ashley too? Isn't that a coincidence?'

Eight-year-old Ashley, tall and handsome with thick hair framing his face like a Roman god, was proud of Melanie.

'She's devastatingly intelligent,' he confided, 'and inclined to be a bore about clothes. Daddy said you mustn't let her rabbit on like she does at home or she'll drive you mad.'

By suppertime on Saturday, everyone had more or less got to know each other and were nattering away like old friends. That's another good thing about younger children – they form instant friendships and waste no time in baring their souls.

'I like you. Can I sit next to you?'

'No, sorry, Johnny's sitting here. You can sit opposite, then you can see me.'

'What's your name? I've forgotten.'

'Dirk.'

'What a funny name. Mine's Paul, I'm in Mixed Infants.'

'I'm in Juniors. I can go on a bus by myself.'

'I have to go by car,' lamented Paul.

There was one child still to come. He was booked in for Saturday and was being brought by car, but it was not until after the smaller children were in bed that his mother telephoned. Brian lifted the receiver and gave the number. He winced and held the phone about a foot from his ear as a voice screeched, 'I'VE HAD A BREAKDOWN!'

'Nervous or mechanical?' he enquired politely.

'WHAT?'

'I said nerv – oh, never mind it wasn't very funny the first time. Is that Mrs Robertson?'

'I'M WAITING FOR THE AA. SAM'S WET HIMSELF.'

'I'm hearing things,' muttered Brian. 'Where are you Mrs Robertston?'

'WINCHESTER. I'VE BEEN HERE THREE HOURS.'

The pips went and the line was dead.

'Perhaps she'll phone again.'

'She hardly needs a phone with those lungs.'

Half an hour later Mrs Robertson phoned again. The AA had arrived and were repairing the car. She would be on the road again shortly and would we please wait up for Sam?

'Couldn't you find a bed and breakfast for tonight?' Brian asked hopefully. It was nine o'clock and Winchester was a long way away. No, she couldn't; she was booked in for a course of lectures at Dartington as part of her Open University studies, which started at 10 a.m. tomorrow.

The girls went to bed at eleven, but Marcus offered to stay up and keep us company. We played Bismarck, a three-handed solo, and as usual Brian won.

It wasn't until 1 a.m. that we heard the car coming down the drive. Marcus switched on the outside light and we waited for the car to stop.

Mrs Robertson parked the car and got out.

'Crikey,' breathed Marcus, 'no wonder the car broke down.'

Mrs Robertson must have weighed about 20 stone. She was dressed in a multi-coloured kaftan which did nothing for her.

'HELLO, I'VE MADE IT THEN,' she bellowed, probably imagining herself still in Winchester. We made shushing noises and pointed up at the children's bedroom windows. She came down a few decibels and offered the information that Sam could sleep through anything.

Brian carried Sam indoors; Marcus picked up the suitcase and followed and Mrs Robertson started to go back into her car.

'Aren't you coming in to see Sam to bed?' I asked.

'Oh, no need for that,' she said. 'Sam will kip down anywhere. Ever since my husband walked out on us, Sam's had to pig it in all sorts of places. You can't trust men,' she added.

I didn't agree, but it seemed pointless to start a discussion at that time of night. If she had said engines or sums or teenage daughters I should have had a fellow feeling, since in my world these things behave rather unpredictably. But not men.

She drove off and I waited until the red tail lights had disappeared before I turned off the outside light and went indoors. Sam was too tired to want a snack, so I took him straight up to bed, where he fell asleep as soon as I had tucked him in. He looked rather pale and thin, so I imagined he must take after his father.

After Brian and I had checked that all the landing lights were on and the bedroom doors ajar, we staggered into bed. It had been a very, very long day.

'What did you think of Sam's mum, then?' I asked.

'I should think she'd yield a good 4 gallons,' Brian said, switching off the light. 'But I prefer Bambi any day.'

Chapter Sixteen

Charles and Adam had got to the stage where they were too big and too rough for the smaller children to play with. Although neither of them had horns, they could give a hefty butt with their hard heads, and anyone on the receiving end of one of these butts knew all about it.

They'll have to go to the butcher's soon, Brian and I told each other almost daily, but did nothing about it because we were rather cowardly in those days; we called it tender-heartedness, but it was cowardice.

Then, on the Saturday that the smaller children arrived, the sheep decided their own destiny by (a) getting into the vegetable garden and (b) butting the new children and frightening them.

'I thought only goats butted,' sobbed a newcomer, who had been sent flying by Charles.

'He didn't mean to be rough – he doesn't know how strong he is,' we comforted.

We considered tethering the sheep, but it seemed cruel to tether them at such a late stage, so we just had to face the fact that they had both reached meat weight ages ago and were living on borrowed time.

'We *must* phone the butcher.' Brian sounded firm.

'You phone.'

'No, it's your turn.'

We took turns at unpleasant jobs, such as blocked lavatories or anxious mothers; obviously, signing a lamb's death warrant was going to rate pretty high on the list of unpleasant jobs and put the party concerned well in credit for a while. We failed to agree whose turn it was this time and tossed a coin.

'Tails,' I called. I always do and it hardly ever is.

'Hard luck,' said Brian, then magnanimously, 'I'll drive them there when you've booked it.'

I phoned the butcher.

'Nine a.m. Monday 16th,' I wrote on the notice-board above the telephone, but didn't put what in case the children saw it.

At 8 a.m. on Monday Brian swung open the back doors of the Transit and the two lambs trustingly jumped in. Both the dogs and Bill and Billy jumped in too. Brian shouted at the dogs to get out and the noise brought the children running out to see what was happening.

Rather than get involved in explanations about who was going where, Brian took one look at the advancing tide of children, hopped into the driver's seat and drove away with all six animals in the back.

'Where's he going?'

'Bill and Billy are thtanding on the theats.'

'Can we go for a ride too?'

I took a deep breath. 'Go back indoors and finish your breakfast please, kids. Brian won't be long.'

'But *where's* he going?'

'He's taking Charles and Adam to a new home. We haven't got enough grass here, so they're going to a new home where there's plenty of grass.' I thought I sounded quite convincing. I had forgotten Jos.

'Since all Europe is in the grip of drought...' Jos began, but I cut her short.

'Mars bars?' I said loudly.

'For *breakfast*?' said Jos in delight She led the surge of children to the larder door, all Europe forgotten in anticipation of chocolate for breakfast. Liz had made toast and was cross when she saw the Mars bars.

'You must be mad giving them those, they'll never eat their toast.'

'Sorry,' I said meekly, wondering what had become of the good old days of forelock-pulling serfs. Actually, some of the toast did get eaten. Ashley demonstrated how you can melt a Mars bar on top of a piece of hot toast and then eat the lot together.

'Hurry up and clear your plates, chaps,' Mick ordered. 'I've heard a rumour that there's going to be some sort of a game outside.'

Each week Marcus and the girls set up a treasure hunt for the children. They wrote the clues in very bad verse: for example, 'If the prize you want to win, look for the clue in the old blue bin.' And so forth. The treasure hunts had provided hours of fun for the kids (and the compilers) and the prizes cherished as though they were diamonds.

For these smaller children it had seemed sensible to concoct simple clues and to shorten the actual length of the route they had to follow. We had all underestimated the intelligence of our tiny tots, and the hunt, which should have taken a couple of hours to complete, was over in about fifteen minutes.

'You should have written some of the words in code or in French to mislead us,' said eight-year-old Johnny who, partnered by a six-year-old, had won first prize.

Oddly enough, quite a number of that week's children came from so-called 'broken' homes. The poor unfortunates who had two parents apiece were made to feel rather inferior. Indeed, on one occasion, when we were all driving along in the bus, young Lucy dissolved into sobs and refused to be comforted.

'My parents are only married to each other,' she wailed piteously.

'But Lucy, most parents are only married to each other.'

'Mine aren't.'

'Nor mine.'

'My daddy has custody of me.'

'My daddy has reasonable access. Mummy got care and custody.'

'I've got eight grandparents.'

Poor little Lucy, no wonder she was crying. Up to now she had probably thought custody was something to put on stewed fruit. Mick gave her the loan of his yoyo and tried to cheer her up.

'Never mind, Lucy. I expect your parents are very nice as they are. Mine used to shout at each other a lot before the divorce.'

This struck a familiar chord with some of the other kids, and they contributed to the cheering-up process.

'Yes, in many ways you're lucky with just two parents, especially if they don't quarrel.'

'Not so good at Christmas, of course.'

'Or Easter or birthdays.'

'Mummy has to work full time now; she gets really tired.'

'Our mummy gets tired and she's not divorced.'

Brian and I grinned at each other. We knew why the twins' mummy got tired!

Lucy stopped sniffing and remembered a time when Mummy had phoned Daddy at the office and called him a fool. He had left the car lights on all night and Mummy couldn't start the car to take her to school.

'A fool? Is that all she called him? They're nowhere *near* a divorce yet.'

'Why didn't she use the jump leads and start the car from someone else's battery?' Dirk said.

This proved a tactful conversation stopper and the discussion on divorce petered out. It had been quite an eye-opener, though, to see how casually the children regarded their parents' dramas. It seemed they felt far more aggrieved if their mothers chose to stay indoors when there was snow around; *that* was truly abnormal behaviour if you like.

The long, hot summer made the blackberries ripen early, so we introduced a new pastime into the programme – blackberrying. Each child was equipped with a 1-gallon ice-cream container and sent off to fill it to the brim. For every full container we awarded a small prize, and soon the freezer contained 60 lb of blackberries. Then the children cottoned on to the fact that they were being exploited and went on strike. Garry, as the eldest, was appointed their spokesman.

'They want more than a quarter of sweets for the black-berries,' he explained rather shamefacedly. He had enjoyed doing the picking just for fun.

'What do they want?' we asked.

'Later bedtimes for a start, *and* bigger bags of sweets.'

'Out of the question, Garry. Anyway, we've got enough blackberries to be going on with, so they can stop if they're getting tired of picking.'

The workforce did not mind being laid off. They seemed to

pick just as many as before, only now they ate most of them instead of selling them to us. This meant that they got stomach-aches in addition to stings and scratches, but they didn't complain much about this either. They were very agreeable kids. Bill and Billy and the ponies loved blackberrying with the children, and we took some lovely photographs of various child/animal combinations with purple-stained mouths all round. Melanie was the only one who always stayed clean and tidy no matter what she did. She used to change her clothes about three times a day, much to Jos's annoyance. Jos would have liked an extensive wardrobe like Melanie's, but as *we* were doing her laundry, she had to make do with one T-shirt and one pair of shorts a day.

'It is unfair,' she stormed. 'Why can I not have some beautiful linen blouses like Melanie? My papa is richer than Melanie's.' It was the first time for ages that Jos had had one of her Spanish tantrums; she had so enjoyed the company of these articulate and intelligent children that she had forgotten her silly airs and graces.

'They're not linen, they're cotton,' I said. 'And I'm *not* ironing cotton tops in this weather so shut up.'

'They are LINEN,' shouted Jos. 'Melanie said they are linen cotton.'

'Lawn cotton, actually,' said Melanie helpfully. 'Linen is coarser and heavier, not really suitable for small children.'

Jos liked that phrase and adopted it for the next few days. She managed to find quite a lot of things that were 'not suitable for small children', from chicken drumsticks to TV advertise-ments. Sometimes, when she became really obsessive about something, we realized why her parents wanted to send her away for over three months at a time. On the whole, though she had improved enormously during her stay at Phillishayes and often ran errands or performed small acts of kindness without expecting a round of applause each time.

She also loved reading aloud, and was always delighted to find a fresh victim who would let her read a story at bedtime. Her renderings were usually hilarious, as she was too proud to seek advice over difficult words and would bravely tackle them head-on. Once we heard her read dramatically, 'Come out with your hands up – the house is surrounded by *uninformed* men!'

We had struck lucky again with that week's group; only a few wanted outings, and they were out-voted by the majority, who wanted to stay on the farm. So apart from the mackerelfishing expedition, they stayed on the premises and our blood pressures levelled out.

Although they were mostly children who were used to lots of stimulation in the form of outings to museums, libraries, theatres and so forth, none had had the opportunity before now to involve themselves with livestock. They loved every aspect of farm life and were blissfully happy to be given real work to do; even chores such as cleaning out the poultry houses didn't daunt them. Tentatively, we suggested that the cobbled yard could do with a sweep, and were amazed when they organized themselves into two teams and got on with it. It was rather a pity that they discovered that dry horse droppings make effective substitutes for snowballs, since the ensuing battle reduced the yard to its pre-swept state.

'We're all shitty,' said Ashley happily. It was impossible to be cross with them.

'Would you like to de-louse the pigs for us?' I asked brightly. Brian was horrified.

'You can't expect them to de-louse the pigs, Faith. Their parents...'

'Aren't here,' I said firmly. 'Look, they can't possibly get any dirtier, so it's a good opportunity to get another messy job done.'

De-lousing pigs *is* a messy job. You get a canister of louse powder and sprinkle some along each pig's back, then brush the powder into their hair with a stiff brush. The powder gets up your nose and into your hair and clothing.

The children clamoured to be allowed to do it.

'I bags first.'

'I'll do little Rose Hip.'

'I'll do Blue Bum.'

Garry went first, clutching a dandy brush in one hand and

187

the tin of powder in the other. He chose to do Phyll, who knew all about de-lousing and grunted with pleasure when she saw the stiff brush. Pigs love being brushed – next to eating their favourite pastime – and Phyll wriggled estatically as Garry brushed the powder along her spine. She sank down on to her knees then kneeled over on to her side so that he could do her armpits. When he had finished one side, she obligingly turned over so that he could do the other.

The children couldn't wait to take it in turns; they hopped over the electric fence and started brushing, handing round the tin of powder as though it was the sugar bowl at a tea party.

'Have you had enough? Take some more for the other side.'

Soon the pig enclosure was thick with dust and louse powder and it looked as though the kids were going to be as louse-free as the piglets. The had managed to cover themselves with powder from head to foot.

'Isn't this *fun*?'

'Super.'

'I've never touched a pig before.'

'I mutht write my pothcard home tonight.' (I made a mental note to censor *that* one.)

'Come on kids, that's enough powder now. *Straight* down to the river for a wash. I'll clear up the brushes.'

There was a note by the phone 'Brown Ale – rabbits – CCHA?' I went to look for Brian in the vegetable garden. He was hacking his way through a big patch of sunflowers, which he had grown as a crop for feeding to the chickens.

'You look like an explorer in the jungle. What are you doing?'

'I lost my knife again,' Brian said, peering through the undergrowth. He was always losing his knife; his jeans were so old that even the patches had patches and nothing stayed in the pockets.

'What does this note mean? Are we having a party?' showed him the note.

'Oh, that. It was some woman on the phone. Have you brought me a cup of tea?'

'No. *What* was some woman?'

'Brown Ale. She said her name was Brown Ale, she wants to talk to you about rabbits.'

The penny dropped. 'Brown *Owl*, cretin. She wants to do some Girl Guide rabbit tests.'

'I thought they used toads.'

'Don't be disgusting. What does CCHA mean?'

'City Children's Holiday Association. They're sending an inspector down to inspect us.'

The CCHA is an agency that arranges holidays for parties of schoolchildren accompanied by their own teachers. The holidays are usually taken in term-time, and the hotels or field-centres that cater for the groups are able to offer reduced, out-of-season terms.

We had been trying to think of ways to earn money during term-time. We toyed with the idea of having adult guests, but then decided that if we did, we should probably end up with an establishment that would make Fawlty Towers seem like the Savoy. So we had written to several children's organizations, including the CCHA, to see if they would be interested in out-of-season holidays with us.

'When is he coming, this inspector?' I asked.

'He just said some time this week. He and his wife are on holiday in the West Country and will just drop in.'

'Oh.'

The last time officialdom had dropped in was when the Public Health inspector had appeared on the day that the vacuum cleaner had ground to a halt. This apart, it had been one of our good days: none of the lavatories was blocked up and there was not a single dead pig in the kitchen. Addy had been in charge then (was it really only Easter? It seemed a million years ago), so of course the place had been spotlessly clean.

'Don't say "oh" like that,' said Brian. 'We have nothing to hide. Have we?' he added anxiously.

'Only Craig's fingernails.'

'Well, cut them. Cut his fingers off while you're at it – that'll stop him picking his nose.'

That evening after supper we asked the children if they would mind being a bit quieter if they saw that we had visitors later in the week.

'Quieter than what?' Ashley asked.

'Quieter than you usually are. You all shout at each other as if you're deaf.'

Garry grinned. 'Pardon?' he said, cupping his hand behind his ear.

'He's pretending he's deaf,' Craig explained.

'Oh, Craig,' groaned Mick. 'You don't have to spell it out; we got it the first time.'

'That Sara's a rat,' I said, scanning a pencilled postcard.

'Who?' said Brian.

'Sara. Our daughter, Marcus's sister.'

'Oh, *Sara*. Sorry, I'm so used to other people's kids now. Why is she a rat?'

The fortnightly trips we made to the Cash and Carry at Budleigh Salterton were practically the only times Brian and I could have a private chat. We would have an early breakfast, grab the post and get in the van before any of the children could waylay us.

We had driven through Honiton and turned off on the Budleigh road before I got to Sara's postcard.

'Look,' I said, waving the missive in front of the steering wheel.

'Don't do that in this narrow lane,' Brian said. 'What am I supposed to look at?'

'Sara's postcard. Look, she's too mean to buy a picture one: she's sent just a plain one.'

'What does she say?'

'Not much. "Got bored with Gower Coast, so have moved on with Terry. Perfectly safe, don't worry, love Sara."'

'Does she say where they've moved to?'

'No, that's all there is.'

'What's the postmark?'

I turned the card over. 'Biarritz,' I said, and fell forward as Brian stood on the brakes.

'BIARRITZ!' he yelled. 'That's in France!'

'I didn't suppose it was in Herne Bay,' I shrieked, furious at nearly breaking my nose.

Brian grabbed the postcard. 'Who,' he said grimly, 'is Terry?'

'One of the gang she went camping with, I imagine.'

'I'll *kill* her. I'll kill him, then I'll kill her,' Brian vowed, lighting a cigarette from the stub of the old one.

'Oh, marvellous. My life *will* be complete. Thirty-seven year-old, dark-haired mother of delinquent teenager tells our reporter "I didn't know my husband was a mass murderer". No, seriously,' I went on, 'there's no point in getting hysterical. She's in France, we're in Devon, so what the hell can we do about it except chew our fingernails and wait?'

Brian started the engine. 'She must have planned this all along.'

'Mmm,' I said thoughtfully, 'I remember now she asked me how long passports last. I said I didn't know.'

'Five years.'

'So hers was still valid? She had it for that school trip a couple of years ago.'

An ulcer-making knot of anxiety settled uncomfortably in my stomach. The one that was already there – the one that had arrived the same day as Marcus's motorbike – moved over a little to make room.

'In any civilized society,' Brian said, 'you'd be able to put your kids in the deep freeze as twelve-year-olds and get them back when they're twenty. Read me the rest of the post, I'm immunized now. No, let me guess, the building society wants to foreclose, the bank rate's gone up and my mother has broken her leg.'

'Nearly right. A bill for pig nuts, they've gone up again; an enquiry for a missing T-shirt – red with Liverpool FC on it – and a letter from your mother. She hasn't broken her leg, but she says the heat's getting her down and her annuals have died.'

'Short letter – hardly worth the stamp.'

'I'm picking out the salient points.'

We drove on, noting with interest how other people were

coping with the drought. There were standpipes in most villages and posters telling us not to waste water. There was so little grass that many farmers had started to feed hay to the grazing cows. One or two pick-your-own fruit farms were managing relatively well, and the green foliage of the fruit bushes was a welcome sight in the Devon desert.

Shopping at the Cash and Carry was still fairly enjoyable as shopping goes. We bought cheese in 2-foot-long slabs, 20 lb of butter, half a gallon of margarine for those children whose parents had brainwashed them into worrying about cholesterol; catering-sized tins of sardines with fifty or so in each tin, 14 gallons of ice cream, 10 gallons of orange squash, 56 lb of biscuits, enough Elastoplast to equip a casualty ward and the inevitable sack of cornflakes.

We stacked the shopping in the coolest part of the van, sent up a small prayer to the patron saint of raspberry ripple and headed home, our brush with the bright lights over for another fortnight. We didn't speak of Sara. Brian smoked even more heavily than usual and I hoped that Terry was 6 foot 3 inches and sensible.

On Thursday we decided to give the kids a cooked lunch as we were going to have a picnic supper for a change. The butcher had phoned to say that the meat was ready for collection, so while Brian went to fetch it, I busied myself in the kitchen. We were going to have roast lamb with mint sauce, potatoes and peas followed by the inevitable blackberries and ice cream.

It was one of those mornings that life sometimes dishes out to kid you all is going well. The kitchen was cool with all the doors and windows open; the telephone was silent. Small's kittens played tidily in their basket under the table (they had not yet reached the mountaineering stage), and the dogs, excused guard/circus/tracker duties lay in the shade of a bush and dozed. Sue was having a day off, and Liz and Vicky flopped in what remained of the grass keeping an eye on the children at play.

Someone had found a shuttlecock and a variation of

badminton was being played. Bill and Billy acted as a mobile net, while the children tried to keep the shuttlecock airborne. The goats scored a point every time the shuttlecock fell to the ground.

From the kitchen window I could see Melanie, armed with a pair of blunt-nosed scissors, snipping away at the mint patch. She had already filled a large bucket with mint as though anticipating a siege or a banquet.

Brian put his head round the door.

'Ooh, you made me jump,' I said.

'Ssh,' said Brian. 'Help me get the meat into the freezer before the kids see it.'

The meat.

We had carefully called it the meat since Monday morning, but now, confronted with the reality of Charles and Adam parcelled into polythene bags, words were not going to help. I stared in horror at the neat little labels – stewing, leg, shoulder – and burst into tears. Brian looked stricken.

'It's done, now, please don't cry...I thought we'd decided...John Seymour...'

'Festering skunk!'

'Oh, come on, you agreed to sending them. You can't blame me.'

'Not *you*, John Seymour. He...he didn't say it made you feel like murderers.'

Sadly, I helped carry the joints to the freezer. I thought about cockerels and drakes, bulls, boars and billy goats; everything unlucky enough to be born male had to have its life telescoped into weeks rather than years.

Brian delved down inside the freezer and brought out two catering packs of fish fingers.

'I'll finish putting the lam – meat away, you see to some lunch, eh?'

Melanie was sitting at the kitchen table chopping mint leaves into small pieces.

'It's terrible being born a boy,' I informed her unthinkingly.

'Oh, it *is*, it is. My brother has to start Latin next term, they say it's even worse than French, not that I know any

French yet, except easy things like 'merci', *and* he can't wear nice things, unless you count his best shirt...'

I put the potatoes on to boil and set the fish fingers under the grill.

'Your eyes are all red, have you been peeling onions?' Melanie asked.

Grateful for the idea, I peeled and chopped a largish onion.

'What a funny lunch – mint sauce, onions and fish fingers. I thought we were having lamb.'

'Er, it's not unfrozen enough. I made a mistake,' I said.

'You don't have to pretend,' said Melanie. 'It's because it's Charles and Adam, isn't it?'

'Don't you mind?' I asked weakly. Was Melanie really only six years old?

'I don't mind much; after all, they weren't really my friends, were they? I only met them on Sunday and on Monday they went to their new home.'

Hurriedly I said, 'Have you tried mint sauce with fish fingers, Melanie?'

'No, have you?'

'No,' I confessed, giggling rather wildly.

The children had finished their lunch – 'mint sauce with fish fingers' – and were helping to clear the tables when a car appeared in the drive.

'It'th your vithitorths,' said Richard importantly. Mick took command. 'Right men,' he said, 'you know what we arranged? Well, starting *now* – the sponsored silence. OK?'

Jos said, 'Scarlett, Dawn, Melanie and I are not men.'

'I'm warning you, Jos,' said Mick, 'shut up or it'll be Sellotape for you.'

'Kids,' Brian reasoned, 'please, just be your usual selves, eh? No long silences, just play normally.'

I always picture inspectors to be tall, thin and gimlet-eyed. This one was small, fat and jolly.

'How do you do. This is my wife, Dorothy.'

'How do you do, Mrs Bishop.' We shake hands all round and I stifle the urge to tell them Garry's joke about the two

194

bishops. Mrs Bishop had nice, friendly brown eyes, not the sort to notice newts in the washbasins I hoped.

'What a beautiful view,' she said. 'I'm sure I should never get any work done if I lived here – I should spend all day looking at it.'

I sensed that Brian was going to make one of his corny remarks about the fact that *his* wife never did any housework, so I ushered them in through the seldom-used front door and aimed them towards the sitting-room. They looked around with interest and peeped into the playroom as they passed.

Brian made a soft moaning sound and rolled his eyes towards the ceiling. In the playroom were the children, all of them. They were sitting in neat rows on the floor, their jaws clenched shut, their eyes staring with the effect of remaining silent. Jos, to all intents and purposes was bound and gagged; her mouth was covered in strips of $1/4$-inch Sellotape and her wrists were tied together with baler cord.

Vicky and Liz were clattering around in the kitchen preparing a tray of coffee for our visitors. We sat Mr and Mrs Bishop in the two armchairs that still had their springs intact and made inane remarks about the drought.

'Mallards,' said Mr Bishop suddenly.

Our ducks were muscovies, but we were quite happy to let Mr Bishop tell us about mallards if he wanted to.

'Yes?' I encouraged.

'You really shouldn't take mallards you know, lovely place like this – they'll ruin it.'

'They're muscovies actually,' I said.

'What are?'

'The ducks. And we keep them penned.' Perhaps he thought they were a health hazard?

'I'm not talking about the ducks, Mrs Addis. I mean those children. Mallards.'

'He means maladjusted,' said Mrs Bishop. 'We refer to them as "mallads" – mal-ad, you see?'

'I think I see. But those children aren't maladjusted. They're perfectly normal children, well, all except Rudi, and he's just a bit backward...'

Mr Bishop beamed and shook his head. 'Catatonic,' he said firmly.

Brian said, 'Excuse me a moment, I'll just go and see how the coffee is coming along,' and headed purposefully towards the playroom.

The Bishops were very encouraging about the idea of us having school journey parties. They told us that we must insist that the schools send at least two members of staff, and preferably three, to accompany each group of twenty children. The CCHA would organize the itinerary each week and all we should have to do would be to provide sleeping accommodation, breakfast, packed lunches and an evening meal.

'You'll have no trouble at all,' Mr Bishop said. 'The teachers will be responsible for their behaviour and will settle up for any breakages before they leave. As long as you steer clear of the Social Services, you'll be all right.'

We were agog to hear all about the goings on in the Social Services, and the Bishops needed little encouragement to enlighten us. The villains of the piece appeared to be the case-workers, part of whose duties was to arrange holidays for children – usually the dreaded mallads – in order to give the parents a break. This was called parent relief, and because, not surprisingly, it was difficult to find hosts who were willing to take mallads, the caseworkers resorted to low cunning in their efforts to help their clients.

'You get them phoning up,' said Mr Bishop, 'and telling you a plausible tale about this family living below the poverty line – you know the sort of thing, father's in prison, mother's on the game – and could you take, say, four of the children and a social worker to look after them. So you agree because it sounds a manageable group. Then, when they turn up, you find they've lumbered you with a couple of extra kids and as often as not an alcoholic mother or two. You have to lock all your cupboards because the social worker can't be alert for twenty four hours a day, and by the end of the week you'll be reaching for the bottle yourselves.' He laughed at the looks on our faces and fortified himself with a sip of coffee.

I allowed myself a brief reverie in which a group of mallads mugged their way through the village, their bottle-wielding mums reeling after them. Dimly I heard Mrs Bishop listing some of the other categories of needy children – spastic, autistic, blind, deaf, in care, incontinent, pregnant and poor.

'Don't forget delicate,' reminded Mr B. 'They'd better avoid delicates – remember what happened to young Parkin...?'

'More coffee, Faith?' Brian was glaring at me under the artificial smile and telepathically telling me to stop daydreaming.

'Do help yourselves to biscuits,' I said, pushing the plate nearer to Mrs Bishop. 'Now, do I take it that you think we shouldn't accept any handicapped children?'

'No, no you misunderstand. You'll be perfectly all right with most types of handicapped children, but *not* maladjusted and *not* delicate. But in fact this place is so very suitable for junior school parties that I should think you will be booked up with those in no time...'

Mr Bishop was interrupted by Jos, who charged into the sitting-room without knocking. She stared haughtily at our guests and announced that there was a frog in the washing-up water.

'Jos is Spanish,' I apologized.

'Half Spanish,' Jos corrected. 'And the water is not too hot, but I do not think the frog will change into a prince at all.'

Mrs Bishop hooted with laughter and we all rose to go and investigate the frog in question. He turned out to be a rather amiable toad and seemed none the worse for his swim in the sink.

'I picked him up before Small got at him,' said Johnny, 'but he went all black, so I gave him a bath.'

'That was kind of you, dear,' said Mrs Bishop. 'Now when he turns back into a prince, he'll be lovely and clean, won't he?'

Jos gaped at her. 'You mean you *believe* he will turn into a prince? I thought Johnny was teasing me.'

'You never know with frogs,' said Mrs B.

'Or pumpkins,' contributed Brian who had grown three giant ones that were so big you could almost ride on them without waving a magic wand.

Johnny fished the toad out of the sink and dried him on a

197

clean tea towel. 'There you are, Froggy,' he said. 'All nice and dry. Shall I take you down to the pond, then?'

We followed the procession down to the pond and watched the toad hop away into the rockery. Mr Bishop beamed at the children as they flopped on their towels round the pond. Jos and Melanie squatted uncomfortably under Jos's small umbrella.

'I suppose this is a Caribbean beach?' suggested Mr B, then after a quick look round the outside of the farm, he and his wife drove away, promising to recommend us to the CCHA as being eminently suitable for school parties. As soon as they had gone, the children surged round us clamouring for acknowledgement of their collective goodness, quietness and saintliness.

'Weren't we *quiet*? I bet you never knew we could be so quiet.'

'It was Mick's idea. He said you'd give us a penny for every quiet half-hour.'

'Brian was horrible to stop us being quiet in the playroom.'

'Yes, he said we looked gormless. Why did you say that? It was really hard work not talking.'

Brian said, 'Well, you haven't had much practice, have you?' and was immediately grabbed and sat on by the indignant mob.

Craig, triumphantly sitting on Brian's head said, 'Blimey! *Us* gormless? What about that man going on about the pond being a Caribbean beach? Or that lady thinking the frog was going to turn into a blinking prince? They were dimwits, wasn't they?'

'Or mallads,' said Brian indistinctly.

Chapter Seventeen

Saturday morning. Another scorcher. Armed with soapy flannels, the girls attacked the dirt on the faces of the home-bound children, while I stripped the beds and Brian dismantled the Hoover, which had been complaining of overwork for some time.

'Don't *want* to be washed,' someone whined. 'I'm all hot and sticky.'

'Sticky as shit in a blanket?' asked Garry innocently.

'GARRY!' Brian exploded. 'Where did you get that revolting expression from?'

'Tony. He said his old dad used to say sticky as sh –'

'That will *do*, Garry. I might have guessed it was Tony's old dad again,' said Brian grimly.

Tony had a pied piper attraction for the children, combining as he did the dual talents of a master farrier and born raconteur. His tales of his upbringing by a strict Victorian-type father – a horse dealer by trade and a sadist by inclination – were often hair-raising, and we sometimes had to ask him to tone it down when he was entertaining the children in case the little ones were nervous. Not that they actually *seemed* nervous; indeed, they seemed to love hearing about the good (?) leatherings that Tony and his brothers had received at the hands of their late parent. In addition to his barbaric treatment of his family, the old reprobate seemed to have had a *mot juste* for every occasion, and it was these to which we objected. Not to put too fine a point on it, the language of Tony's old dad was *not* the sort of stuff we wanted our kids to take home as souvenirs.

Then Craig, with unconscious good timing, got Garry off the hook by bursting into tears. Tears, like blood, are something Brian prefers to leave the women to deal with, so he dived back inside the Hoover.

'I want a baby rabbit to take home,' Craig wailed.

'Of course you can have a baby rabbit, you nit, you can have two if you like. Provided your mother says it's all right,' I added hastily, remembering Precious Pup.

'I want that small one – the one you said is going to die.'

He would. Trust tender-hearted Craig to want Munchie. Munchie was the runt of a large litter, ignored by his mother and bullied by his bigger siblings. Craig had taken it upon himself to give Munchie the will to live, and to this end he plied the little creature with all manner of snacks. Munchie remained glassy-eyed in the corner of the rabbit pen, making occasional sorties to suck water from a drip-feeder. At six weeks old he weighed only 1½ lb, and it seemed only a matter of time before he hopped it for good.

We all pleaded with Craig to take a healthy rabbit, but his mind was made up. 'I'll take a bigger one as well,' he said generously, 'to keep Munchie company when he gets better.' His mother's permission having been obtained ('As long as it's not a rat, it's welcome'), Craig climbed on to the London-bound train clutching Munchie in what I thought of as his coffin, and a big New Zealand white in another box.

(Surprisingly, the story had a happy ending. Both rabbits not only lived happily ever after, but produced – incestuously – several healthy litters. We are reluctantly forced to conclude that smoky bacon crisps are indeed a panacea for the terminally ill.)

When Jos and I had waved goodbye to the departing train, we returned to the launderette to wait for a couple of machines to become vacant. Each Saturday the queue of customers got longer and longer, and everyone became quite pally, drawn together by the drought. Jos wanted to have her hair washed at the hairdresser's; the poor kid was getting tired of being dunked in the river water and her hair looked dull and lifeless, so we treated ourselves to proper hairdos while the laundry was getting done.

Feeling refreshed and almost human again, we humped the bags of laundry into the van and drove back to the farm, hoping that the others had managed to see to the departing children nice and early. No such luck. The place was teeming with parents as we freewheeled down the drive.

Vicky and Sue opened the van doors and carried the laundry bags indoors.

'Why is everyone still here?' I asked. 'Haven't they got homes to go to?'

'It's Brian: he's in great form today and everyone's getting a conducted tour. Brian's trying to get Monty to do his impersonation of the Ming horse.'

Monty was too hot to do his Ming horse or his Lloyds Bank act, and stood in the shade swishing his tail.

'Go on, Mummy, stroke his nose, he won't hurt you.' Mummy backed away. 'No, thank you, I'm scared of horses.'

'He's not a horse, he's a pony, and he's been gilded, so he's lovely and friendly.'

'*Gelded*, stupid – gilded means covered in gold paint,' said Ashley scornfully.

'What does gelded mean then, clever dick?'

Brian and I, fearful lest Tony's old dad complete with two hot bricks should suddenly pop up in the conversation, moved as one.

'Shall I fetch some water for your radiator?'

'Have you lot remembered your swimming things hanging on the line?'

Eventually the last stragglers were shoe-horned into their parents' cars and we adjourned to the house for a reviving brew-up. Liz had made some cheese and tomato rolls. 'I didn't cut this one up,' she said holding out a huge tomato, 'I've never seen such a whopper, so I weighed it – 8 ounces!'

Brian looked modest. 'Outdoor Girl,' he said. 'A poor thing but mine own.'

Jos converted the ounces swiftly. 'It is only 200 grams,' she said disparagingly. 'In Spain that would be considered average.'

'But you have better weather in Spain for growing vegetables, Jos.'

'Better everything,' said Jos feelingly. 'In Spain we have running water for taps and...'

'Hey, Brian!' Marcus erupted into the kitchen. 'Sara's back – she's coming down the drive with Terry!'

'*Terry?*' Brian stood up. I collared the bread knife before he got ideas.

'I'm going to get a clean shirt,' Marcus said, pelting upstairs.

'What's the matter with him? A clean *shirt* for Sara's lout? It's Terry who'll need a clean shirt. And some new teeth.' Brian strode out.

'He's going to kill him,' I wailed.

'No, he's not,' said Liz. 'You can't infer murder just because he said that about broken teeth.' I had forgotten Liz was studying law.

Sara entered, sunburned and unraped. 'Hello everybody.'

'*Sara*! Are you all right?'

'Fine thanks. Come in, Teri, they've killed the fatted cheese roll for us.'

Teri.

She was a petite, dark-haired girl with fine bone structure; next to her Sara looked like a Hereford heifer. Teri smiled shyly.

'Teeth intact,' murmured Liz.

'Oh, Sara,' Weakly I sat down; Brian slid on to the bench beside me. 'Your spelling will be the death of us. We've been so *worried*.'

Brian turned to Teri. 'We thought you were a man,' he explained.

'Marcus didn't.' Liz grinned.

Jos stared at Teri. 'Brian said he will make you a dirty shirt and break your teeth.' Then looked at Sara questioningly and Sara shrugged. 'I told you they're rather conventional.'

Brian said, 'Now girls, let's have the story, only make it snappy because there are trains to be met and a million things to do.'

'There's not much to tell really,' said Sara. 'Didn't you get my postcards?'

'One postcard, and that wasn't exactly a mine of information. Why did you leave Wales? And where are the tents?'

'Still in Wales – we left the others there. Teri and I met these two boys – Damian and Jeff – and they had this terrific idea of us joining forces and going to Bordeaux for the grape harvest. They knew the ropes, you see; they'd became grape-picking last year.'

'With their long arms, I suppose?' Brian said witheringly. 'It's a mighty long pick from Biarritz to Bordeaux.'

'Oh, yes, well Biarritz was a bit of a mistake actually. We split up at Le Havre and arranged to meet the boys at Bordeaux, but we kept getting the wrong sort of lifts and we ended up at Biarritz. It's your fault really,' Sara went on blithely. 'If you'd let me hitch-hike before now, I'd have been more experienced and we wouldn't have got lost. Anyway, our money ran out at Biarritz, so we thought we'd better head for home.'

'We tried to phone from Le Havre,' put in Teri, 'but they didn't understand about reversing the charges.'

'How old are you, Teri?' I asked.

'Seventeen.'

'And do your parents let you hitch-hike?'

'Not alone. Well, not at all really,' she flushed.

'You must phone home straight away and let them know where you are. Where do you live?'

'London, Blackheath. I phoned Mummy from Southampton and told her that I was coming here. Sara said it was OK – I hope you don't mind. I need to borrow the fare back to London.'

'You'd better stay the night – the trains will be packed today. Tell your mother we'll put you on the morning train tomorrow. Sara will show you where the phone is.'

A gust of Brut heralded Marcus's reappearance. Sara said, 'Marcus, this is Teri, she's staying until tomorrow.'

'Oh good,' said Marcus, dazzling in a white T-shirt which affirmed that its wearer was not averse to chicks. 'Can I get you a drink, Teri?'

Teri looked surprised. Sara looked amazed.

'There's milk,' Marcus said, rummaging in the fridge, 'or squash, but I don't recommend that – we have to use horrible boiled water – or Coke, or how about a cup of tea?'

'Milk would be lovely, thanks. Sara said you had your own cow, Bambi isn't it?'

Marcus plonked a 2-pint jug on the table. 'There you are, my flower,' he said in a grotesque Devon accent, then in his normal voice, 'You don't mind a mug, do you?'

'I've got to go', Brian said, getting up. 'Where's my train list?'

I went out to see him off, and when we were alone we giggled at Marcus's hamfisted wooing technique.

'Not exactly suave and sophisticated, is he?' said Brian.

'I know. I could hardly keep a straight face when he put that great jug on the table in front of her. Mind you, I don't suppose you'd have done any better at seventeen.'

'Girls hadn't been invented when I was seventeen, there was a war on. What are we going to do about Sara?'

'Short of putting her under lock and key, nothing. We can't have a big scene with everybody here – can you imagine Jos's letter home if we did? – and I'm jolly thankful she's home in one piece.'

'I knew you'd say that. She's *impossible*. Tomorrow when I take Teri to the station I'll make Sara come too – on her own – then I can read the riot act on the way home.'

And so it was. The riot act was read and Sara settled down to home rule again, but I had an uneasy feeling that, like a volcano, she was merely dormant.

On Monday Sid, the TV man, was summoned again.

'This is the seventh time in four weeks, you know,' he said, unscrewing the back of the TV set and opening his tool box.

'Have some tea,' I propitiated.

'Thanks, cor, chocolate biscuits today too. How's it going then?'

'Not bad. The kids are a bit older this week.'

'Only a week older surely?'

I laughed immediately to please him, but he still chucked me out of the room. We were always hoping that we might learn how to get the TV going without having to call him in so often, but he wasn't having any.

'You can give me a refill,' he said, handing me his empty tea-cup, 'but you're not watching, and you can keep those ruddy kids out until I've finished too.'

The ruddy kids had gone to Widecombe Bird Gardens with the girls and the house was peaceful. Smallest and Humphrey padded through the empty rooms, pouncing at the particles of dust in the sunbeams; they had turned up their noses at the half-chewed mouse their devoted mother had presented to them, and it lay gruesomely under the kitchen table.

'Very hygienic,' Sid commented when he came into the kitchen to wash his hands. 'What are you having for dinner, ha ha?'

'You'd never guess, Sid. I'm cooking some lamb at last.'

'Go on? You going all brave then and having another bash at those lambs?'

Two legs of Charles (or possibly Adam) were sizzling away in the oven. I wished my early imprinting had not been via Beatrix Potter.

Later, when we dished up, Sara looked at the meat and asked cheerfully: 'Anyone we know?'

Marcus went really pale and left the table, his meal untouched. I raced upstairs after him and found him sitting on the edge of his bed looking out of the window at Mr Bartlett's Friesians grazing in the paddock next to ours.

'You're not really going to eat Charlie, are you?' He was close to tears. 'It's so...so *unethical*.'

Oh, crumbs, I thought, it's going to be a long session if he starts on ethics. For, truth to tell, Brian and I had not yet come to terms with the ethics of meat-eating.

In London one purchased anonymous joints and salved one's conscience by not buying veal or any other meat that had been produced by inhumane methods. Here in Devon we were choosing to rear animals of which a proportion would inevitably be male and – since we couldn't afford to run an animal sanctuary – would inevitably end up on somebody's table. Economically, it was better that the table should be ours. Ethically, who is to say?

I sat down next to Marcus and for the next half-hour we thrashed out the problem. At last he said with a watery grin: 'You should have been a biology teacher – I've never heard the carbon cycle explained so clearly before'.

'What I don't understand,' I said, 'is your enthusiasm for fishing if you think killing animals is wrong.'

'I don't understand it either. You don't think of the killing part when you're fishing and anyway, I throw back more fish than I kill. Perhaps after this I'll throw them all back unless they're foul-hooked.'

'Come on, let's go downstairs, I'll make us an omelette.'

'I'm going to be a vegetarian from now on,' Marcus said.

'Fine. I'll get a vegetarian cookery book from the library,' I said, thinking this would be a nine days' wonder. But it wasn't and from that day to this Marcus hasn't touched meat, not even sausages.

There was a rodeo advertised in the local paper and all the kids begged us to take them. We were rather dubious as it was going to be one of those shows that continue all evening, and we didn't fancy searching for strays by moonlight. But we weakened when Vicky said she would like to go in for the rodeo as a competitor, and made all the children promise to stay together at least in twos so that it would be easier to keep track of them.

The competition was divided into two groups – male and female – and the winner in each group would be the rider who managed to stay on an unbroken pony the longest. In the men's group the first few were going to have to ride a steer after the pony riding to decide the ultimate champion but the ladies were excused this on the grounds that it was too dangerous.

The children were wildly excited as our van trundled into the showground, and disappeared into the crowd as soon as we let them out.

'Meet back here at six o'clock for a picnic supper please, kids,' Brian instructed. 'Then you can sit on top of the van to watch the show.' This was a good ruse to get them all in one place before it got dark.

The show was a good one, well organized with lots of side-shows, craft stalls, snack bars and lavatories. We wandered about, keeping half an eye open for the kids and encouraging Vicky, who was feeling nervous now that the time had come. 'It seemed a good idea when I read about it in the paper,' she said apprehensively. She was a good rider but realized that she'd have to be a *very* good rider to sit a wild moorland pony for long.

The wild ponies were penned in a small enclosure next to

the ring and looked a lively bunch. The would-be competitors had to queue up and give their names and ages before getting a ticket to ride; this was a great relief to us, as we had been afraid that Jos would want to have a go, but we needn't have worried – the competition was strictly for the over-eighteens.

At six o'clock half the children appeared at the van and started to make inroads into the picnic supper.

'Where are the others?' asked Liz.

'Eating pancakes.'

'But the pancakes are 20 pence each. How on earth can they afford them?'

'The lady is giving them the spoiled pancakes for nothing,' volunteered Eric, then in the manner of ten-year-olds being grilled, suddenly remembered an urgent appointment elsewhere. Plainly, there was no more information to be had, so Liz hurried off to fetch the pancake-eaters before their share of the picnic was demolished. They returned looking slightly sick and declined cold chicken and sausage rolls. 'Just a cold drink, please,' they requested.

'How did you manage to cadge enough pancakes to fill you up?' I asked suspiciously. The children looked at their ring-leader, Kevin, and Kevin looked sheepish.

'Because she was very kind,' he explained.

'Who was?'

'The pancake lady. She said why were we so hungry, were we from an institution?'

'Oh, *Kevin*, you surely didn't say you were from an institution, did you?'

'No, I didn't say we were exactly.'

Jill, sister of clammed-up Eric, came to Kevin's rescue. 'The lady did all the talking. She said we must be orphans, didn't she, Kevin?' Kevin nodded.

'But why? Why on earth should she think you're orphans?'

'Well, she said were we with our parents and Kevin said no, we were just on an outing. For a special treat,' she added.

'So the lady thought we didn't have any parents, so she gave us pancakes. Some spoiled ones at first then she made us some good ones.'

Just then the announcer's voice came over the Tannoy.

'There's a little boy in the office who says his name is Julian. Would his parent please collect him straight away. Thank you.' Click.

Julian was one of ours, needless to say, and Sue offered to go and collect him. He returned grinning from ear to ear. 'I was lost,' he said proudly. 'And I heard them say my name on the *air*!' We were so pleased, because Julian was partially deaf and it must have been a big moment for him to hear his name announced loud and clear over the Tannoy.

Brian lifted the kids up on top of the van and made them all sit down facing the same way. There was a bit of pushing and shoving, but nothing serious, and they were very pleased with their bird's-eye view.

'We can see Marcus,' they yelled. Marcus had said he would come to the show straight from work, and sure enough, there he was, weaving his way across the showground on his motorbike.

'Am I too late?' he asked. 'Has Vicky been yet?'

'No, you're in plenty of time. They're having all the men first. Do you want to have a go?'

'Only if they've got brakes, thanks.'

Vicky didn't really enjoy the men's competition; she was feeling too shaky to watch properly. The ponies were put one at a time into a cattle crush, each rider gingerly lowered himself on to the pony's back, then the gate was raised and the pony shot forward into the ring. How they bucked! The riders weren't allowed a strap to hang on to and had to clutch at the mane for support. There was no cruelty involved (unlike at American rodeos): the ponies merely bucked to rid themselves of their unaccustomed burdens, and the average numbers of bucks taken to achieve this objective seemed to be about six. After this, the rider would find himself sprawling on the hard ground.

The sun was setting as the men's event finished, and Vicky, with Sue for moral support, prepared to meet her doom. She buckled her chin-strap firmly and walked steadily to the competitors' enclosure.

'Isn't she *brave*?' shrieked the children. We didn't need a Tannoy system.

The first lady rider shot into the ring. Buck, buck, buck, buck, buck...crash!

'Six seconds,' said the judge calmly.

Number two entered. Buck...shiver...crash!

'Three seconds.'

Now Vicky's turn. Our hearts thumped. The children clutched each other silently.

Vicky lowered herself on to her pony's back, took a thick twist of mane in one hand and nodded to the attendant to raise the gate.

The pony thundered into the ring, twisting and bucking. Vicky sat well back, her legs gripping tightly round the pony's shoulders, her right hand firmly embedded in the mane. Round and round they went, the pony trying every trick in the book to dislodge Vicky. The children counted the bucks aloud, their voices growing to a crescendo, six...seven...EIGHT! And then she fell.

'Twelve seconds,' said the judge.

'TWELVE SECONDS! She's leading! Well done, Vicky! Three cheers for Vicky!'

Two of the children fell off the van in their excitement, but were unhurt as they landed on some people standing below. The people were not unhurt and swore imaginatively as they picked themselves up.

We hurried round to meet Vicky and showered her with congratulations as we conducted her back to the van.

'It was the longest twelve seconds of my life,' she grinned, and hopped up on to the bonnet to watch the rest of the competition, a sausage roll in each hand and a mug of coffee balanced on the headlamp.

There was one nasty moment for all of us when another lady rider managed a ten-second ride, and might have managed a few seconds more if we hadn't all been willing her so hard to fall off.

Vicky was announced the winner and was invited to come to the judges' tent to collect her winnings.

'£10!' She showed us the two fivers in an envelope.

'Thanks Vicky, I'll have a gin and tonic,' said Brian jokingly, but Vicky took him at his word and bought us all a drink. The children took advantage of our inattention and had a second picnic on top of the van while they watched the Grand Finale – the men's steer-riding competition. This was the big time and sorted out the men from the boys.

Each steer had a leather neck-strap and the riders hung on grimly with both hands as the great beasts plunged round the ring. Each ride lasted less than five seconds – it was evidently much more difficult to sit on a steer than on a pony – and the champion was eventually declared as the rider who stayed on for five and a half seconds. He staggered out of the ring and straight into the beer tent!

It was quite dark when the show finished, but the children were not a bit tired. Sue counted them into the van – 'No, of course you can't ride home on the roof, stupid' – while Brian cleaned melted ice cream off the windscreen.

'All in, Brian,' called Sue.

'Thanks, Sue,' said Brian. 'Fourteen?'

'*Fourteen?* I made it fifteen.'

'Oh, Christ, they've started breeding,' said Brian.

'Perhaps I shouldn't have had that drink,' said Sue. 'I've never had spirits before.'

We unlocked the back doors and climbed into the van. I struck a match and Sue counted again.

'It is dangerous to play with matches,' said Jos.

'Faith, there *are* fifteen' said Sue. 'You count again.' I counted while Sue struck matches. There was no mistake, we had fifteen.

'Is there anybody here who shouldn't be here?' I called.

'You sound like a medium,' said Sue and we both got the giggles.

'What on earth's going on in there?' Brian and Marcus peered in through the back.

'We've got one too many.'

'It's probably a rucksack. Get them all out again and we'll start from scratch.'

Kevin said, 'Who's that next to Julian?'

'He's my friend,' said Julian defensively. 'His name's Polo.'

'Paulo,' said a small sleepy voice.

Brian found the torch and shone the light on to the stow-away, who was a cherubic-looking six-year-old.

'Can I keep him?' asked Julian hopefully. Paulo was hauled off to the lost property office amid a chorus of 'shame' and 'how mean' from our kids.

Eventually, we were ready to start for home; we had the right number of children and each child confirmed that it had a sandal on each foot.

'Right then,' said Brian brightly. 'No more surprises? Then let's go,' and the van lurched and bumped across the field to the exit gate. Marcus led the way on his motorbike, his crash helmet muffling the shouts of the children as they poked their heads out of the windows.

'You look like a police escort!'

'An armed guard.'

'Yoohoo, Marcus, can you hear us?'

'SHUT UP,' Brian yelled. 'For goodness sake talk quietly or sing a nice song instead of leaning out of the windows.'

The kids sat down obediently and Eric said, 'I've got fleas.'

Brian didn't crash the van, just swerved a bit as he digested this intelligence.

'Fleas?' he said hollowly.

Fleas, it seemed, were a status symbol these days; everybody who was anybody had them. The children chatted about their school flea inspections as calmly as they would about spelling tests. Flea ladies came round twice a term and issued special shampoos to any louse-ridden child.

'And sometimes you get a note for your mother telling her how to catch them.'

'Our flea lady says it's central heating and cats.'

'We haven't got a cat, but I still got fleas last term.'

'Same here.'

'My sister broke her arm,' said Eva, who hadn't fleas and was obviously feeling left out of the conversation. Eva's mother was a friend of ours and we felt proud to have a flealess friend and, moreover, one who had both cats *and* central heating.

'In Spain we do not have the fleas,' Jos admitted, 'but we

are not allowed to go near strange dogs because we catch the rabies.'

Eric said, 'I've got an idea. Let's go down to the river tomorrow and get right under the water like foxes do to get rid of *their* fleas.'

'Ooh yes, good idea. We can put cottonwool in our mouths and float on our backs, then the fleas will all go on to the cottonwool.'

'I've got an even better idea,' said Vicky. 'Why don't you all put cottonwool in your mouths right now and shut up?'

'Vicky! How can you be so mean? You only won tonight because we all *willed* you to.'

Vicky grinned. 'Gosh, and I thought it was because I was a good bronco-buster.'

The van rolled down the drive and ground thankfully to a halt. It was getting more like a steam-engine every day, and would hiss and bubble for some minutes after being switched off.

The dogs bounded out of the back door and greeted us as though we had left them for a month. Sara, who had been out baby-sitting, came out to see how Vicky had got on.

'She won, she won!' the kids yelled. 'She won £10 and they all got drunk!'

'We didn't,' I said indignantly. 'We had one drink.'

Parsley stopped jumping up for a moment, sat down, and gave herself a good scratch.

'I think she's got a flea,' said Sara.

'Join the club,' said Vicky.

Chapter Eighteen

Despite the heat, the older children wanted to go on an outing nearly every day, and as this was the last fully booked week, we somehow found the energy to indulge them. In addition to the rodeo, we also took them to a gymkhana, shopping in Honiton, mackerel-fishing twice, Bird Gardens, also twice, and to the river every day.

Toggles and Melly got so accustomed to river expeditions that they were able to accompany the children without having to be put on their leads; they would prance on and off the road-side banks all the way down to the river, where we usually tethered them if we could catch them. The grass along the river bank was still green and juicy, and the goats took full advantage of this to fill their bellies before they had to return to the dustbowl conditions in our own fields. Parsley and Honey always enjoyed going to the river; Honey, being old and arthritic, just lay in the shade, but Parsley, who had only recently been a puppy, swam and fetched sticks thrown by the children. Then she would clamber up the bank and shower everybody with icy water as she shook herself.

Sara took Rocky right into the water one day. He and Noah were sometimes allowed to join the evening washing party, but not often; they were a bit of a tie and someone always had to hold their reins so that they didn't wander off. Sara led Rocky into the water until it came up to his shoulders then he took a couple of steps forward and found himself swimming! He paddled around for a few minutes looking so anxious that we all burst out laughing, then he heaved his fat little body up the bank and rushed over to Noah, who didn't like water very much and, even in those heatwave days, would only ever venture up to his knees. Rocky rolled in a soft patch of clover right where Noah was standing, and Noah looked as disgusted as anyone would who has just seen their bacon and eggs squashed flat.

'Oh, *Rocky*,' the children laughed. 'Noah was saving that bit.'

'Look at Toggles,' someone shouted. 'She's being Billy Goat Gruff.'

Toggles stood on the wooden bridge gazing at her reflection in the water. She and Melly were always ready to co-operate in any of the children's games, except those involving water; nothing would induce them to get even their feet wet, so it was quite adventurous of Toggles to stand on the bridge. Some of the children had brought cameras and snapped away at the animals and at each other, punctuating their photography with cries of 'I'm up to number seven already' and 'Wait till I've got my pants on!'

Like Ratty, I never tired of the river. After an enervating session at the seaside, there was nothing like it to recharge your batteries: in fact, its effect was precisely the same as a battery charger – you stuck your terminals (feet) into the sparkling river and straight away you began to feel the energy returning.

'My sandals are floating!'

'They'll be carried out to sea.'

'To see what? Ha ha.'

Serenely, I wade in and retrieve the bobbing sandals. Every mum should be issued with a river along with the vitamins and orange juice.

Phyll and Rosie were due to come into season again very soon. Sows are normally re-mated about a week after their piglets are weaned, so we figured that if we took the piglets away on Sunday, the sows would be ready for the boar by the following Sunday. At that point the large group of older children would have gone home.

It wasn't that we objected to the children watching piggy nuptials – after all, a farm holiday is a farm holiday – but we didn't know what the parents' reaction might be when the children gave them a blow by blow account.

There was a local farmer called Mr Woollacot who hired out his stud boar by the week. (We had decided on the real thing for Phyll and Rosie after the meagre results with the AI service.) The boar – Bartholomew – was booked to be delivered to us on Sunday of the next week, but Phyll and Rosie put a spanner in the works by coming on heat on Friday morning. Rosie was the first one to make her needs apparent. She broke out of her enclosure, lumbered down the drive and into the kitchen. The kids were overjoyed.

'Rosie's in the kitchen – she won't move!'

'She's staring into space!'

'She hasn't even eaten Small's food.'

Small was aghast to see Rosie, and spat at her, tail fluffed up like a bottlebrush. She was probably afraid that Rosie was after Smallest and Humphrey, but nothing was further from Rosie's mind. There she stood, solid pink pig, blocking the kitchen door. Our fire regulations stated that all exits must be kept clear at all times, but I don't think the person who drew up the rules realized just how difficult it is to move a randy pig.

'I can't budge her an inch,' Brian gasped, leaning his whole weight against her. Someone went to fetch some pig nuts, but Rosie politely declined these and stood firm, her trusting blue eyes gazing up at us. Brian unbuckled his leather belt and one of the kids screamed, 'Don't hit her!'

'Of course I'm not going to hit her, you stupid child,' said Brian. 'But we can't leave her here.'

'I'll go and phone Mr Woollacott,' I said.

Brian and Sara each took an end of the belt and placed it across Rosie's chest. Inch by inch they backed her out of the kitchen until she was in the yard, then we closed the kitchen door. Rosie continued to stand patiently.

'Never mind, Rosie,' Brian said. 'One day your prince will come.'

Mr Woollacott stopped his van at the top of the drive and opened the door at the back. Bartholomew hopped out nimbly – he was a graceful pig, despite his size – and followed his master down the drive. Mr Woollacott asked where we would like him to put the boar.

'Would you mind just bringing him down to the house for a moment, Mr Woollacott?' I asked. Mr Woollacott gave me an odd look, pushed his cap back and scratched his head. Then whistling to Bartholomew as though he was calling a dog to heel, he walked down to the house.

'Keep your sows here then?' he asked politely.

'No, not *here* exactly, but Rosie got out – she always comes to the kitchen door when she gets out – and we wondered if Barty could persuade her to move.'

Mr Woollacott scratched his head again and regarded the scene round the kitchen door. Julian and Jos, being small and light, were sitting on Rosie's back, while the other twelve children sat on the concrete watching.

Suddenly, Rosie got a whiff of Bartholomew, and raised her head expectantly. 'My hero!' she grunted (in pig) and charged over to Barty leaving Jos and Julian sprawled on the ground.

Barty introduced himself by sniffling in Rosie's nostrils, then he hurried over to where she had been standing and finished off her pig nuts. Rosie pursued him, and brazenly rubbed herself against him as he ate. He ignored her, finished all the nuts and started exploring the yard.

'He's not very enthusiastic,' I complained.

'Barty is a gentleman,' said Mr Woollacott in his lovely chocolatey Devon accent, 'But 'ee won't fail 'ee, will 'ee, my son?'

''Ee' didn't, and on Christmas Day Rosie gave birth to thirteen piglets; Phyll was not long after her – she produced ten piglets on Boxing Day. The funny thing was that nobody actually witnessed either of the two unions. Barty was indeed a gentleman.

One day, shortly after Sara's return from her hitch-hiking holiday, I found some white tablets lying on the floor just outside her bedroom door. I knelt down and collected them together in the palm of my hand, counting them as I did so. There were twelve of them, each about half an inch long and sausage-shaped. Oh, my God, I thought, she's on drugs...whatever shall I do? Must look at her for symptoms...take her to a doctor...

Brian had gone to help a friend dismantle and transport a large poultry house and wouldn't be home until suppertime. I couldn't tell Liz or Sue or Vicky that my daughter was a junkie; there was nothing for it but to wait for Marcus to get home from work. The problem gnawed away at me all the afternoon as I worked in the kitchen. I told Small to make the most of her kittens while they were still babies – 'They'll be nothing but trouble when they're teenagers,' I told her, but she ignored me.

At last, I heard the motorbike purring down the drive and I rushed outside to meet it.

Marcus is a solid, dependable sort of person. It had been a great disappointment to me when he joined the Civil Service straight from school, as I would have preferred the sort of son who buys an old Land Rover and travels overland to India. But dependability has its virtues too, and I gibbered impatiently as Marcus parked the bike and slowly unbuckled his helmet.

'What are you going on about?' he said. 'I couldn't hear you with my helmet on.'

'Come with me, I've got something awful to show you.' I dragged him in through the front door.

'*Front* door? I wish you'd let go of my hand. I won't run away, you know,' he said. He followed me upstairs, along the passage and into our bedroom. I locked the door.

'For goodness sake, have you got heatstroke or something?'

'Sit down,' I said. He sat on the edge of the bed and I unwrapped the hanky containing the drugs.

'Look,' I said.

He looked.

'Marcus,' I squawked. '*Say* something.'

He looked mystified. 'What do you want me to say?'

'Do you know what these are?'

'Yes.'

'Yes?' I yelled.

'*Please* stop yelling,' Marcus said, 'and tell me what's going on.'

'*How* do you know what these are?' I asked suspiciously. 'Have you be en experimenting too?'

'Experimenting with what?' asked Marcus.

'Drugs,' I moaned.

'Drugs?'

'Drugs. I found them outside Sara's room. I think she must have got them off those boys she went to France with.'

'These,' said Marcus patiently, 'at Tic Tacs.'

217

'Is that what you call them? Are they LSD?'

'They're *Tic Tacs* – sweets to you.'

'Sweets?'

'Yes, sweets…S-W-E-E-T-S. Not drugs, not contraceptive pills, just non-addictive common or garden sweets.'

'Oh,' I said lamely. 'Are you sure?'

'Of course I'm sure, you demented old trout. Honestly, you really are losing your marbles. Do you realize that you've had Sara kidnapped, abducted, alcoholic and pregnant, and now, to crown it all, a drug addict. Wait till I tell her.' He lay back on the bed and rolled around laughing.

I said with what dignity I could muster, 'Don't be insolent. It's very difficult having a teenage daughter. I thought I could rely on you for some support.'

'Tic Tacs,' he hooted.

'Purely as a matter of interest, what *are* Tic Tacs?'

'Peppermints. You get them from vending machines.'

'What a relief. Do you have to tell Sara?'

'Naturally. You don't think I'm going to let this one go to waste, do you? Divided we fall, and all that.'

'You signed the Official Secrets Act at work,' I said hopefully.

'When I'm convinced that Sara's Tic Tacs are a threat to national security, my lips will be sealed. Where *is* Sara by the way?'

'I don't know. She's gone off for the day with a friend and they're going to some Young Farmers' disco this evening.'

'Young Farmers? Coo, aren't you afraid she'll come back with foot and mouth or blight or something?' Still chuckling, and with a mouthful of Tic Tacs, Marcus unlocked the door.

As always, Saturday morning was hell. Vicky, Sue and Liz were leaving for a well-earned rest before returning to their studies, and we faced the prospect of seeing to trains and parents without the support of our trusty staff.

Jos, Julian and Julian's brother Dean were staying on for one more weekend and half the following week – the schools were going back early this year. So, I decided to forget the laundry and make do with spare clean sheets for the children and last week's sheets for the rest of us.

Sara volunteered to give the three kids a riding lesson, but unfortunately chose to do so in full view of the departing children, who were furious.

'You said the ponies always rested on Saturdays – it's not fair.'

'I don't want to go home.'

'No, nor do I. I shall ask Mummy if I can stay on too.'

Various Mummies arrived to collect their offspring, only to find them in a state of mutiny.

'*Please*, Mummy, just another week?'

'No, dear, you've got to go back to school on Wednesday.'

'*Thursday*, Mummy, not Wednesday.'

'Oh, dear, is it? I shall have to cancel my hair appointment on Wednesday then.'

Brian got back from Honiton at eleven o'clock, having put three London-bound children on a train. He expected to find that I had got rid of all the other departing kids and was looking forward to a peaceful few hours.

'But they're still here,' he complained.

'Sorry,' I said and, as the morning wore on, dispensed gallons of tea while some children grizzled, other children hid and nobody showed the slightest sign of actually going. Sara and the three stayers-on finished their ride and came indoors to cool off.

'There's a man in the yard talking motorbikes with Marcus,' Sara said, running her face under the cold tap.

'Turn that water *off*, Sara. Who is the man?'

'Someone's father. He can't find his own kid, so he's talking to Marcus.'

Someone's father had arrived on a motorbike, and to my dismay, I saw it was an English make. I knew Marcus would want a nice long chat about Japanese versus English bikes, so I went outside to see if I could abort the conversation before it turned into a week-long conference. I couldn't, and as the kitchen was still bulging with mothers, I gave up hope of seeing them off, and took the opportunity to have a nice quiet walk around the farm on my own. It was idyllic with only Bill and Billy for company, and I was savouring every second when:

'Faith!' yelled Jos. 'They have all gone home now.'

And: 'Where have you been?' from Brian. 'The kids are hungry.' That meant he was.

'I've had such a lovely quiet walk,' I said, and tried to describe how peaceful it was in the fields and how lovely the animals looked in the sunshine. I opened a tin of baked beans and thought of being married to someone like H. E. Bates – someone who would enjoy just standing and watching two baby goats dancing in the sun...

'I wish I had married H. E. Bates,' I said. Brian looked at the baked beans.

'*I* wish you'd married H. E. Bates,' he said mournfully. 'Then I could have married Mrs Beeton.'

After lunch, we decided to break the news to Jos that her father was coming tomorrow to take her home. He had made the arrangement a week ago, but had been insistent that we left it until the last possible moment to tell her. He had said she would be difficult to manage if she had too long to wait, and naturally we thought he meant she would be impatient to go. How wrong we were!

'Go home!' she yelled. 'You mean Papa is coming *tomorrow*? Oh, no, not so soon. *I will not go*!'

'But Jos, you've been here for fourteen weeks, that's much longer than any of the other children. Don't you want to go home?'

Jos pulled off one of her sandals and flung it at the wall. 'I will hide. I will not go, I will jump off the moving train!'

'Don't be daft, Jos, all I the others are going home soon too.'

Bam! The other sandal hurled through the air.

'Fetch it, Parsley,' said Dean.

'It is not a *game*!' Jos's fury was making her red in the face. 'Always when I enjoy myself I have to stop.'

Brian suggested that I took her to Honiton to buy some presents. Her father had sent some money for her to get a thank-you present for Ursula, who had so patiently tutored her earlier in the year, and she had some pocket money saved to buy her mother a present too.

She simmered down a bit at the prospect of a shopping spree, and we went to a glass and china shop in Honiton, where she chose a rather dreary thimble for her mother and two beautiful china dogs for Ursula. One was a Cairn terrier like Cinnamon, and the other a Cavalier like Parsley.

Ursula was touched. She was moving shortly to a smaller cottage and had bought a stripped-pine dresser for the new kitchen.

'I'll put them on my new dresser, she said, 'then everyone will see them when they come in.'

Jos said, 'And you will tell them they came from Jos.' It was more of a command than a question.

'Of course I will.'

'Then I will see them next year.'

There was a meaningful silence. Ursula and I looked at each other and Ursula raised her eyebrows and mouthed 'next year?' questioningly.

'Yes, next year,' said Jos firmly. 'I will tell Papa I wish to come again.' Even after fourteen weeks, Jos was still telling and not asking.

As Ursula showed us to the door, she whispered, 'You tell Papa I'm emigrating – I'm not going through that tutoring lark again.'

Next day we found Jos hiding in a tea chest in the garage, so we prised her out and dusted bits of silver paper out of her hair. She had grown quite a bit during the summer and her jeans were at half-mast.

Her father, stepping off the train at Honiton, regarded her with mixed feelings.

'She must have new clothes,' he said.

Jos was thrilled. 'Ooh, yes Papa. Brutus jeans and a red T-shirt.' But Papa had other ideas. He wanted her to go home in a white dress with gloves and a hat.

'It will be Sunday when we go home,' he explained to me, 'and her mama will wish her to have the white clothes.'

I should hate to have to try and get an eight-year-old into gloves and a hat in summer – but Papa had the situation under control. He strode into a clothing shop and announced firmly that he wished for the jeans of Brutus. The thunderstruck assistant didn't have the jeans of Brutus in Jos's size, but was able to offer Levis. Jos tried them on; they were a bit big but she said she preferred them big and could easily get some safety pins in

Boots. Then her father pointed to a white polo-necked jumper.

'I want red,' said Jos.

'White,' said Papa.

We left the shop with the jeans, a red and a white T-shirt, a red and a white jumper, a white skirt and some white gloves.

They didn't sell white hats. Then Papa led us into Boots for the safety pins.

'You don't say "pins of safety", Papa, you say "safety pins",' Jos informed him condescendingly. Papa beamed.

'Her English is good?'

'Very good indeed, Mr D,' I said truthfully.

'I know poetry, Papa,' said Jos.

As far as I knew the only poetry Jos knew was a tongue-twister about a pheasant plucker, so I was greatly relieved to hear her father suggest going for some coffee before it was time for their train.

We sat down and ordered coffee for two and an ice cream for Jos. I gave Mr D his bill and the receipts from Marks and Spencer, which I had kept since our first shopping expedition. He added the whole lot together in his head and paid me in fivers, which made it look a fortune. Then he reached down into his briefcase and presented me with a huge bottle of Napoleon brandy!

'For you and Brian – will keep you warm! Ho ho!'

'Thank you,' I gasped. I had never seen such a big bottle of brandy. 'Thank you very much indeed.'

The waitress brought the coffees and ice cream. 'Oh my,' she said, eyeing my litre of brandy. 'That *will* make a nice table lamp.'

So here we were, nearly at the end of the last week with just Julian and Dean to look after. Dean said with a cheeky grin that it was a good idea to save the best bit till last. We were very fond of these two brothers, and were inclined to spoil them, especially Julian, whom we admired for the good-natured way he coped with his hearing disability.

On the last day of the boys' holiday, Julian, for some unaccountable reason, decided to paint the pigs red. Perhaps it was a sort of infant equivalent of painting the town red. At any rate, red they were and red they had to remain, since the colouring stick Julian had used was indelible.

'Bloody hell,' said Tony, who had dropped in to repair some bridles for us. 'Your pigs have got erysipelas.'

'Felt pen!' Julian yelled, triumphant at the success of his trick. 'April fool, Tony!'

Tony looked closely at the red spots on Rosie's body. 'I really was taken in by that,' he admitted. 'But you'll have to wash it off before someone reports you. Erysipelas is a notifiable disease, you know.'

'It won't come off,' said Julian giggling. 'It looks like measles, doesn't it?'

Then Dean suggested confusing the issue by adding green and blue spots to the red ones, which they did, and it was a very glamorous pair of pigs that lumbered out for their evening feed. Dean, breaking raw eggs into their feeding bowls said – 'You're going to miss us, Phyll and Rosie, aren't you? No one to play with you tomorrow, no one to paint you or tickle you or...'

'Steady on, Dean,' I interrupted. 'Brian and I will still be here, you know.'

'It's not the same though, is it? said Dean. 'I mean you won't play with them like we do, will you?'

'Not quite like you do,' I admired, thinking somewhat longingly that tomorrow I should not be called upon to tie Rosie's sun bonnet on for the umpteenth time. Pigs are not too well endowed with chins, and I regretted ever agreeing to letting the kids have hats for Phyll and Rosie.

'What will you *do* without us?' Julian asked earnestly. 'Will you be bored and lonely until we come next year?'

'I'll be counting the days,' I assured him gravely, and Dean laughed because at twelve years old he could appreciate a hint of irony.

But next morning, after the boys had been collected by their parents, Brian and I *did* feel a slight sense of loss. Not that we had envisaged flying around like two-year-olds – we were physically very tired after expending so much energy for so long – but we had imagined that our new-found freedom from responsibility would give us some sort of a kick. Freedom is supposed to be heady stuff, but there must have been something wrong with our chemistry because it didn't affect us like that at all. We wandered round the deserted house, mechanically picking up stray wellingtons and T-shirts and chucking them into the lost property box. Brian picked up a postcard – unstamped and so unposted – and, smiling broadly, showed it to me. 'Dear Mum, Can you loose your way wen you fech me so I hav to stay her. Ther is pigs and kitens not much washing the water drid up.' At this point the space on the postcard ran out, so we never learned who it was that wanted to stay on.

'Could have been anyone,' Brian said, gazing out of the bedroom window at the brown fields on the other side of the valley. Some of the farmers were already having to take hay out to their sheep and cattle, as there had been no regrowth of grass since haymaking in June.

'Yes,' I agreed. 'They all seemed to enjoy it, didn't they? Have you seen the post today?'

'No. More rebookings?'

'Four more rebookings and a couple of fresh ones,' I reported with relish. For surely with bookings coming in by post we could pronounce our project a success? And this was *before* the promised Nationwide transmission later in the year, when, we had been assured, six million viewers would see Phyllishayes at play.

'You know,' said Brian, 'if it doesn't rain soon, we have to try and rent a bit more land somewhere to give our paddocks a rest. The price of hay is going to be astronomical this winter, and it'll even affect us with our few animals. Shall we put an ad in the local paper and see if we can send the ponies away for some grazing?'

'Mmm.' I agreed, only half listening. I was thinking of those six million viewers and wondering how many of them would want to send their children. One per cent?

'How much is one per cent of six million?' I asked.

'Sixty thousand,' replied Brian promptly. (Wonderful the way he never has to use his fingers.)

'Sixty *thousand*?' My poor, tired brain tried to translate this figure into pairs of wellingtons.

Gosh, I thought, sixty thousand. We'll have to buy some more sheets.